JACOB A. RIIS

and the American City

Kennikat Press
National University Publications
Interdisciplinary Urban Studies

General Editor

Raymond A. Mohl
Florida Atlantic University

JACOB A. RIIS

and the American City

James B. Lane

National University Publications
KENNIKAT PRESS • 1974
Port Washington, N. Y. • London

Library of Congress Catalog Card No. 74-77650
ISBN: 0-8046-9058-8

Manufactured in the United States of America

Published by
Kennikat Press Corp.
Port Washington, N.Y./London

to Toni

CONTENTS

PREFACE

Most students of American history know just a little bit about Jacob A. Riis. A Danish immigrant who became a successful New York police reporter, he wrote a hard-hitting exposé of East Side tenement house conditions, *How the Other Half Lives* (1890), which won him enduring fame as a leading publicist for progressive programs. A muckraker more than a decade before his good friend Theodore Roosevelt derisively coined the term, he spearheaded a generation of examination into the nether world of the city slums. Source books on turn-of-the-century reformers commonly contain excerpts from one of his books, e.g., *The Children of the Poor* or *The Battle with the Slum*. And textbook writers have reproduced his realistic photographs of Mulberry Bend, especially the interior shots of the ramshackle buildings which were the first of their kind in America. His quaint autobiography *The Making of an American* has furnished insights into the assimilation process of immigrants. Beyond that, studies on Riis have been meager. The only published biography has long been out of print. Because he was at odds with the leading exponents of scientific philanthropy and professional altruism near the end of his life, scholars have tended to characterize him misleadingly as a well-intentioned but backward-looking amateur whose techniques were obsolete in the twentieth century.

In an age when there is widespread disenchantment with the spiritual ancestors of those city managers whom Riis distrusted, it behooves us to take another look at a humanitarian reformer who thought in terms of the person rather than the mass, whose concept of community rehabilitation began with emphasizing the local bonds of family, school, church, and neighborhood rather than with centralized planning by distant experts. While Riis was most important as a publicist, his lesser-known activities deserve scrutiny as well, such as his settlement work, his role on tenement house and parks committees, his coordination of good government clubs in New York, and his close relationship with Theodore Roosevelt on the municipal, state, and national level.

This study has been conceived as both a biography and an examination of Riis's philosophy of urban reconstruction. He lived in an age when reason, progress, and morality were articles of faith, and he hoped that the "two Americas" that he knew so intimately—one rich and the other poor—could evolve into an organic unity. The world has lost its innocence and illusions in the last two generations, but Riis and his contemporaries, who grappled with problems similar to ours, can help us better understand from whence we have come and how much further we have to go. As historian Otis A. Pease has stated in an essay entitled "Urban Reformers in the Progressive Era," which appeared in *Pacific Northwest Quarterly* (April 1971): "In our search for an acceptable vision of community, it is wise to recall how many of our own dreams were once in the possession of men who were much like us in what they asked of their society and of themselves."

I wish to acknowledge my debt to Professor Horace Samuel Merrill for his expert advice and kindness in supervising my doctoral dissertation, out of which this project grew. Other teachers who taught me to appreciate the complexity of history are H. Martin Jones, William H. Harbaugh, Charles H. Hunter, and Louis R. Harlan. Several friends provided useful suggestions and offered good fellowship in graduate school, including Ray Smock, Pete Daniel, Daniel Weinberg, Walker Rumble, Dennis Burton, and David Goldfield. Critical comments by Raymond A. Mohl and John Parke facilitated revision of the manuscript. For their help I thank Mrs. Rosalie Zak and Miss Betty Shaw of Indiana University Northwest, and the staffs of the Library of Congress (Manuscript Division), the New York Public Library, the American Jewish Archives, Columbia University Library and Oral History Project, the Russell Sage Library of the City College of New York, the Cornell University Library, the Museum of the City of New York, the Ethical Culture Society Archives, the New York Municipal Archives and Records Center, the National Archives, the Swarthmore Peace Collection, the Harvard University Library, the New York State Chamber of Commerce Archives, and the Southern Historical Collection of the University of North Carolina. A summer fellowship from Indiana University Northwest facilitated the revision of this manuscript. Various portions of this manuscript have appeared in a different form in *Maryland Historian, Social Service Review,* and *Societas—A Review of Social History.*

My parents, Victor C. and Mary V. Lane, gave me their love and guidance and helped prepare me for the rigors of the academic world. My sons Philip and David offered delightful diversion when the words stopped coming. Finally, I would like to dedicate this book to my wife Toni, who endured with good humor and understanding the many times when my mind was consumed with "Jake." Editor, typist, and, most importantly, loving companion, she deserves more thanks than words can impart.

JACOB A. RIIS

and the American City

Jacob A. Riis, taken in later years (From the J. Riis Owre Collection, Miami, Florida.)

1

CHILDHOOD IN DENMARK

In the winter of 1864 in Ribe, Denmark, a fifteen-year-old youth decided to run away from home to help the Danish army defend his homeland against the Prussians. Days later, however, before he could act upon his plan, the powerful military machine of Otto von Bismarck routed the poorly equipped forces of the Danish king. The only service Jacob Riis performed in the war was to dump twenty-five ancient flintlock muskets from the Ribe Latin School into the North Sea so that the Germans would not capture them. Once Vikings had traveled forth from the spot where the muskets sank, and Denmark's monarchs had resided nearby. The only tangible traces from those lustrous years were an empty castle and a moat filled with large reeds where children searched for imaginary pirates and wild animals. At the end of the war, Denmark ceded Holstein and Schleswig to Prussia; the new boundary line was within sight of Jacob Riis's home. Denmark's humiliating defeat at the hands of Europe's newest industrial power angered the nationalistic youth. It did not stifle his romantic spirit but made him more dissatisfied with the languid pace of life in Ribe, where the world seemed to be passing him by.[1]

Repellent and destructive as Bismarck's victory seemed to

Riis, he realized that it represented the triumph of a new industrial order of technology and organization, which was the wave of the future. Six years later he emigrated to the United States, the most dynamic and expanding country in the world. Thereafter he moved in the milieu of the urban metropolis, the primary symbol of industrialization. New York City, he discovered with mixed feelings, was the environment which best suited his talents and energetic personality.

Throughout his adult life Riis sought to apply to his urban surroundings the values which he had acquired in a traditional rural environment. As a police reporter he satisfied his aspirations for personal security and status and also became involved in a diverse variety of humanitarian reform movements that were natural outlets for his idealism, restlessness, and combativeness. In 1890 he wrote a book concerning tenement house conditions in New York City, entitled *How the Other Half Lives,* which established him as the foremost American publicist of life in urban slums. He crusaded for public measures to eradicate the harmful effects of industrialization, such as fair housing codes, child labor laws, the abolition of sweatshops, and the creation of parks, playgrounds, and humane institutions for the sick and the homeless. He worked to reconstruct city life in a manner which would preserve human dignity and strengthen the bonds of family and community by the creation of institutions such as neighborhood social centers, settlement houses, and better public schools.

In spirit Riis represented the mood of the progressive movement, a movement which his proselytizing did much to create. Energetic, moralistic, sentimental, nationalistic, and above all optimistic, Riis was confident that the rational and scientific control of the environment could set the conditions for a world of harmony by allowing the spirit of goodness that was in all men to flower. An enthusiastic supporter and frequent adviser of Theodore Roosevelt, Riis looked upon his famous friend as the truest embodiment of his beliefs. Limited by his imperfect understanding of the new economic order, he nevertheless perceived the disastrous consequences in chaining millions of people to a life without promise. The practical, humanitarian programs which he inaugurated in order to ameliorate this suffering established him as one of the most useful allies of the poor.

Growing up in Ribe

Ribe, Denmark, Jacob Riis's birthplace, was an ancient, tradition-bound town of three thousand residents. No railroad or steamboat connected Ribe with the outside world, and only one factory despoiled its preindustrial environment, a cotton mill which Riis later described as "grotesque in its medieval setting, and discredited by public opinion as a kind of flying in the face of tradition. . . ." The residents of Ribe lived in an elegant collection of gabled houses packed together next to cobblestone roads. At night a watchman cried the hours as he walked along gloomy streets which received their only light from iron-chained whale-oil lanterns. The center of community life was an ornate cathedral, the Domkirke, whose history spanned eight centuries. Most people distrusted change and clung to their old habits; they used goose-quill pens and sealing wax for writing letters and tinderboxes for starting fires. The constant patterns of life produced an intimacy which bound together families and neighbors. People in the community held common values and were often kinsmen. "Neighbor knew neighbor," Riis wrote later, "and shared his grief and his joys."[2]

Ribe's many farmers and sailors and its few businessmen and professionals were all very dependent on the whims of nature. The beauty of the surrounding meadows, marshlands, heath, woodland, and seacoast made the people adventurous, romantic, individualistic, and rich in pride. On the other hand, frequent natural disasters forced men to be practical, cautious, and frugal. The picturesque Nibs River wound through colorful fields of wild flowers, grass, and rye. But inland from Ribe, which rested on a large plain, was barren ground where no foliage broke the impact of the strong west wind. Sand dunes and fertile meadows lay between the town and the coast, but floods engulfed it two or three times a year. In his autobiography *The Making of an American* Riis later remembered how on these occasions "we boys caught fish in the streets of the town, while red tiles flew from the roofs all about us, and we enjoyed ourselves hugely" (p. 28).

Ribe was once a feudal town, and the vestiges of a class system remained. Even though divisions of wealth were minimal and leadership resulted more from talent and tightfistedness than from birth, still people were conscious of their rank and place in society. At Christmas the townspeople participated in a ceremonial ball at the Domkirke. During this formal occasion the town officials, clergy, and masters of the church-run Latin school held the highest places of honor. Under them were the middle class tradesmen and burghers, and finally came the lower rank of laborers.

Niels Edward Riis, a senior master at Ribe Latin School, was a stern and ascetic man who possessed a wide breadth of interests. The son of a prosperous farmer and distiller, Niels had studied Latin, Greek, and other classical subjects at the University of Copenhagen. In 1846 after a brief tenure at a rural village school near Copenhagen, he accepted a teaching position in Ribe. He had a wry sense of humor, and named two of his sons, Sextus and Nonus, for Latin numerals. Deeply religious, Niels wrote poetry that celebrated a pantheistic unification of God and nature. His habits were traditional and wedded to the past, but he welcomed some change and believed that decay began when growth ceased. The path to progress, Niels taught his sons, was through religion and education. His intellectual horizons transcended the narrow confines of Ribe and its Latin school. He followed with fascination contemporary political affairs in Europe, and his primary pleasure and hobby was the study of modern languages.

Carolina Riis, Jacob's mother, was a romantic and sentimental woman. She was born at Kronborg Castle in Elsinore, the ancient home of Prince Hamlet. Her father served there as a warden before becoming first a farmer and then a baker. For a short time Carolina attended the Queen's School in Copenhagen until financial difficulties forced her to work as a governess. In October 1844 she married Niels Riis and bore him a son six months after their marriage. Jacob August, her third of fourteen children was born on 3 May 1849. A gentle and emotional woman, Carolina Riis cried unashamedly at church festivals and during moving sermons. She dedicated her life to her family and often opened her home to guests and relatives.[3]

When Jacob Riis was one month old, his mother took him north of Ribe to escape an expected attack by the Prussian army which was supporting the German residents of Schleswig in their dispute with the Danish monarchy. The citizens of Ribe had first prepared to defend their town with muskets, battle axes, spears, and a hundred-year-old cannon. But when a royal staff officer told them that the logical defense included the costly operation of flooding their fertile meadows, the mundane townsmen decided to offer no resistance. Diplomatic pressure from Great Britain and Russia eventually enabled Denmark to retain her territory, but in June 1849 King Frederick VII succumbed to pressures to liberalize the Danish constitution in order to gain support and funds for the war. The Constitution of 1849 abolished the nobility and restructured the ministry to give more power to the spokesmen of the middle classes. It established universal suffrage in selecting members of the lower legislative body while large taxpayers gained control of most seats in the upper house. The constitution upheld the Lutheran religion as the state church but guaranteed freedom of speech and religion and the writ of habeas corpus. Niels Riis supported the National Liberal Party which held power against the reactionary landowning classes until the military debacle of the 1860s, and he greatly admired King Frederick VII for sanctioning the liberalization of the Danish constitution.[4]

Niels had to struggle constantly to support his growing

family. He enjoyed the prestige but not the wealth of the gentry class. The Riis family lived first in a century-old annex of the Domkirke, then moved in 1856 to a sparsely furnished rented house. Jacob later wrote about his father, "How bitter was the fight he waged those forty years and to what straits he was put." Nevertheless, when his sister died Niels took into his household an orphaned niece named Emma. The young girl in time became closer to Jacob than any of the other children in the family, and he always referred to her as his sister. As befitted their social status, the Riis family employed a maid. Niels wrote editorials for the town's weekly newspaper to earn extra money. Yet one winter the financial situation was so bleak that the children went without overcoats. Ashamed of his predicament, Jacob formed a Spartan Club which required its members to go without coats.[5]

Worries deepened Niels Riis's austerity of character and made him seem somewhat distant to Jacob. In addition to his financial problems, six of his sons died from tuberculosis, another drowned, and of all of his fourteen offspring only Jacob and two sisters survived past their adolescent years. Closer in affection and temperament to his mother, Jacob nevertheless respected his father's singularity of purpose and persistence. Describing him in *The Making of an American* in terms not unlike the way he himself wished to be remembered, he stated: "I rather think he was the one link between the upper and lower strata in our town . . . enjoying the most hearty respect of both . . ." (p. 22). As a boy he grudgingly accepted the justice of his father's discipline, even if he did not always heed his advice.

Jacob was a precocious child who loved the outdoors much more than school. At the age of six he protested against going to kindergarten and refused to cooperate until the teacher put him into a barrel and then threatened to slit his ears like a hog if he continued to misbehave. From then on formal education for him was barely endurable. He preferred the excitement of catching silver fish and red-finned perch, chasing snakes, and gathering blackberries. Along the banks of the Nibs River, Jacob and his friends often built fires to cook fish and roast potatoes. In a twenty-acre patch of woodland two miles from the school, they collected nuts from hazel-bushes and pretended to hunt for wild animals. For sport in winter they skated on the frozen river and hunted for black-headed ducks.[6]

During his childhood Jacob made a bird feeder. Inside it he wrote this inscription: "This box is damn well not for sparrows but for starlings only." He raised some pigeons for food but could not bring himself to eat them. He had a better appetite for sparrows. "We used to borrow the cook's long stocking," he later wrote, "and go out to the straw-thatched barn by night and dig into the nests in the thatch which we knew of. When the stocking was full we had enough for a good meal."[7]

When Jacob was nine years old, he began to attend the Latin school. Founded in 1137, the institution still retained its emphasis on medieval ways. Officials administered whip-pings to troublesome boys. Only children of good social stand-ing attended, whereas other "plebs" went to the public school. The two groups feuded bitterly and frequently. According to Riis's autobiography, the Latin school "prided itself upon being free from commercial taint," so there was little stress on mathematics and much on the rote learning of languages and religion (pp. 84–85). Nikolai Grundtvig, a Danish bishop, social critic, and educational reformer, labeled the sterile and anachronistic Latin schools institutions of death and "scholastic houses of correction."[8]

Jacob's Latin school records revealed his disinterest in formal schooling and restlessness with strict regimentation. On 11 September 1861 his master wrote that "J. Riis and L. Berg showed such unseemly behavior that I found it advisable to dismiss them from the class room." During the following school year, his father Niels noted at various times that Jacob was inattentive, had forgotten his book, and had "neglected a written assignment." On 19 March 1864 Riis angered the rector, Pastor Koch, by forgetting to bring his New Testament to school.[9]

Jacob never became proficient in mathematics, Latin, or Greek and preferred to learn by personal experiences and by reading about the things which interested him. He loved to help his father do work for the local newspaper. Niels helped him learn English and encouraged him to read Charles Dickens's paper *All the Year Round,* to which he subscribed. Jacob read often the tales of Hans Christian Andersen and books by Dickens and James Fenimore Cooper. The heroics of Leatherstocking, Uncas, Chingachgook, Natty Bumppo, and other characters from Cooper's novels "first set my eyes toward the west," he later declared. One of his picture books showed several people sleighriding in New York. Filled with Cooper's tales, he imagined that the people were on a buffalo hunt or about to ambush some Indians.[10]

When Jacob was twelve years old, he attempted to reform the habits of a family who lived in a squalid building which he named Rag Hill. He had observed the "shiftless" tenants and ragged children who lived in this dark and blighted area, which contrasted with the surrounding green hill and open fields. On Christmas Eve he gave one of the families the equivalent of twenty-five cents on the condition that they would clean up their home. Wary of the charity, the head of the household went to Jacob's father to be certain that he could keep the gift. Niels Riis consented, and according to Jacob the tenants of Rag Hill thereafter changed their filthy habits. In this action his idealistic eagerness to improve the lives of the poor merged with his patronizing belief that the values of his class were universal virtues.

Jacob Riis was a spirited youth who got into frequent fights. One of his rivals was a young man whom he nicknamed Liar Hans. Hans skinned cats for a living, tanning them and then selling them to women who wore them as fashionable chest protectors. One day Jacob was walking near his house with his dog Othello when he came upon Hans, who was carrying a sack of dead cats. After the two exchanged insults, they began fighting, Riis with a horsewhip and Hans with a dead cat which he swung by the tail. Hans cornered his opponent, but Carolina Riis heard Othello's barking in time to rescue her son. Much of Riis's formidable energies went into his recreation. After he missed his opportunity to fight the Germans in 1864, he spent many hours hunting and later took fencing lessons. On some winter days he skated all day long on a frozen lake which townsmen created by damming the Nibs River. He liked to skate at top speed and then open his coat to glide with the wind.[11]

Interlude in Copenhagen

In 1865 Jacob took a part-time job after school as a carpenter's apprentice. One day while at work at the lumber yard he became infatuated with his employer's stepdaughter Elisabeth Gortz. During the next few weeks, while concentrating on Elisabeth's golden curls and girlish figure, Jacob cut off part of his forefinger with an axe, scarred his shin with an adze, and fell off a roof. Still he pursued his courtship despite the opposition of Elisabeth's guardian and even joined a dancing class to be near her. At a ball which the class sponsored, Jacob and Elisabeth's stepfather got into a heated quarrel. Afterwards Mr. Gortz refused him permission to see his stepdaughter again. As a result, Jacob decided to go to Copenhagen to work for a builder there. Niels Riis reluctantly consented but hoped that the dreary work would soon prod his son into furthering his education toward a literary or professional career.

During the 1860s Copenhagen was growing, but so were its social and economic problems. Many displaced persons who had fled Holstein and Schleswig after the war with Prussia swelled the city's population to nearly 200,000 by 1870. Almost 7 percent of these people accepted state relief. Workingmen's societies built model tenements to assuage the discomforts of overcrowding, but economic stagnation and unemployment remained. Socialistic labor unions began to form to demand that the government nationalize the means of production.

Jacob Riis took little interest in Copenhagen's problems; he concentrated on his trade and took advantage of the big city's social and cultural attractions. Once he attended an art exhibit at Charlottenborg Palace and talked at length with a plainly dressed man. Afterwards his older brother Sophus, who also lived in Copenhagen, told Jacob that King Christian had been their guide.

Jacob saw Elisabeth only briefly during the four years he spent in Copenhagen. When her family visited Copenhagen, he discovered where they were lodging by surreptitiously riding on the back of their coach. He called on them and purposely left his gloves behind as an excuse for a second visit. Mr. Gortz returned them by mail, along with a bluntly worded note stating that Riis was not to make a second visit.

In 1868 at the age of nineteen, Riis earned a certificate of entrance into the carpenters' guild and returned to Ribe. He soon found that there were few jobs open to a carpenter. Plummeting farm prices and inefficient farm units had brought about a depression in the rural areas of Denmark. Agricultural trade with England and other European countries decreased in the face of competition from Russia and the United States. Riis began to see himself as a burden rather than as a help to his family. His personality, normally cheerful and optimistic, began to become somewhat melancholy and cynical.[12]

Going to America

In the spring of 1870, Riis decided to emigrate to the United States to find work. Many factors entered into this decision. He had hoped to marry Elisabeth, but the sixteen-year-old girl refused his proposals. Thus, his life in Ribe was barren both economically and romantically. He had distant relatives in Philadelphia, and friends of his family moved to New York. His adventurous spirit was eager to confront unknown vistas. He told friends that he had no desire to return to Copenhagen and added, "I must admit that it was hard to leave the old haunts at home but it did not last very long. . . ."[13]

Riis left Ribe just after his twenty-first birthday. Friends gave him about forty dollars, but he used most of it to help pay for the cost of his trip. On the morning of his departure, Jacob went to Elisabeth's house to say farewell, but she was asleep. His mother accompanied him to the stagecoach that would take him to Copenhagen; Niels Edward Riis, unenthusiastic about his son's plans, stayed home.

On 4 May 1870, after arriving in Copenhagen, Riis wrote to four of his friends, thanking them for their monetary gifts. He told them that he would go to Glasgow, Scotland, before taking a steamer to New York. "I shall get a chance for a squint at the Scottish fleshpots . . ." he announced. He said that he would remember the eleventh commandment, "Thou shalt not let thyself be bluffed." He jokingly stated that he expected all Americans to be pirates and iron-eaters. Finally he apologized to them for having been so disspirited during the previous months.

On 18 May 1870 Jacob Riis left Glasgow on the steamer *Iowa*. Most of his fellow passengers were Swedes and Germans. Riis later remembered that their "strange burdens of featherbeds, cooking-pots, and things unknowable . . ." both fascinated him and made him feel lonely. One man carried a knapsack that served as a pillow at night and contained cheese, pumpernickel bread, and "interminable" coils of sausage. For two weeks he endured bad food, crowded quarters, and a stormy voyage. Then for twenty-four hours the *Iowa* lingered by New York harbor waiting for the fog to lift. On Whitsunday morning, 5 June 1870, just as the sun came out, Riis landed at Castle Garden by the Battery.[14]

Riis's Danish background had instilled in him a love of

nature, a belief in the efficacy of hard work, and a recognition of the importance of family and religion in developing moral virtue and character. He retained these values throughout his life and later romanticized his birthplace in a book entitled *The Old Town* as a sanctuary which ever "remained home to one whose cradle was rocked there . . ." (p. 109). Before he emigrated to the United States, however, he held a more enigmatic attitude toward Ribe. The very things he loved most, the rustic simplicity, unchanging traditions, and bucolic peacefulness, conflicted with his restless and adventurous spirit and thus lured him to another country where he could satisfy this drive.

2

A NEW HOME

From 1870 until 1877 Jacob Riis lived near the edge of poverty. Hunger, homesickness, and humiliation were frequently his lot as he drifted from job to job. The many setbacks that he encountered educated him to a realization of the limits to the promises of equality and opportunity. Through it all, however, he retained hope for a good life. He had many advantages over most of the immigrants who traveled to New York's shores. Many of these came from a peasant background and were ill-equipped to overcome the cruelties of their new environment. Riis came from an educated family and possessed talent in his carpentry trade and a flair for writing. Short but powerfully built, he had great physical stamina. His deep-rooted values and pride in his Nordic cultural heritage cushioned the shock of moving to a strange land. Confident that he would fulfill his aspirations for wealth, status, and service, he decided to make the United States his permanent home. During these years he was so busy earning enough money to survive and later to provide for a family that he failed to develop a deep social consciousness. Later, however, after he had obtained a modicum of personal security, he paid increased heed to the suffering of other rootless individuals caught up in the maelstrom of New York's slums.

His suffering gave him a basis for sympathetic understanding of their plight.

When Riis arrived in New York, the city reflected and personified America's expanding industrial might. Within its boundaries lay the institutional agencies of the new order, the financial and commercial establishments, the chaotic stock market, the plants and mills and the sweatshops. To the Empire City flocked the human agents of industrialization, workers from Europe and American farms, captains of business and industry, and a nascent managerial class of technicians. Almost a million people lived on Manhattan, and a half-million others inhabited the four other boroughs of what later became Greater New York. Half of these residents were foreign-born. They lived often in overcrowded, squalid tenements that contrasted starkly with the gilded homes of the very rich. Prevailing over this diversity of cultures was a dynamic and materialistic mood. People came to New York with high hopes; and if most failed to satisfy their dreams, at the least they found excitement. New York in 1870 had no electric lights, telephones, subways, typewriters, skyscrapers, automobiles or movie theaters; but there were billboards, baseball games, bars, brothels, massive traffic jams, and people of every imaginable variety and nationality. The sprawling young metropolis was half provincial and half world capital.[1]

Lean Years

In New York during the early days of June 1870, Riis suffered from his ignorance of American customs. One of the first things he did was get a bath and a haircut. For this service an innkeeper charged him two dollars. When he vehemently disputed the high price, the proprietor threw him out. Riis complained in his thick accent to a nearby policeman, but the officer just told him to move along. Walking up the streets of Manhattan, he noticed a navy revolver in a store window and used half of his remaining funds to purchase it. He strapped it conspicuously around his coat until a policeman warned him to remove it.[2]

It took Riis five days to find a job. Neither the Danish consul nor an acquaintance of his family was in New York to help him, as he had hoped. Finally, on 10 June 1870 he agreed to work for Brady's Bend Iron Works Company in western Pennsylvania. Riis received free passage to his new job. On the way to Brady's Bend, all but one of his fellow passengers jumped off the train, but Riis believed it his duty to honor his contract, despite misgivings as to his fate. When he arrived, his employers assigned him to a construction gang to build huts for the miners. He was soon bored with the carpentry work. As he put it in his autobiography, "I was tired of hammer and saw" (p. 36). Deciding to test his skill at mining, he toiled on his hands and knees in a narrow shaft until a large rock suddenly fell on him, knocking the oil lamp from his hat and leaving him in darkness. Stunned and frightened, he fled for safety. The next day he returned to the carpentry shop.

In mid-July 1870 Riis read that France had declared war on Prussia, and he decided to return to Europe to fight Denmark's old enemy. Receiving a meager ten dollars as final payment from Brady's Bend Iron Works, he had to pawn his watch and trunk of extra clothes in order to pay for his fare to New York. (Within five years after Riis left Brady's Bend, the mining community collapsed in the wake of the panic of 1873, leaving a ghost town.) Arriving back in New York City, Riis asked the Danish consul for free fare to Denmark and then asked the French consul for permission to join a volunteer unit of soldiers. Both men turned him down.

Days of futility followed. Riis had to pawn his revolver and boots to pay for a room. On the second night his land-lady evicted him. Penniless, he wandered around Manhattan carrying his sole possession, a gripsack containing a linen duster and a pair of socks. Near midnight he came upon a house where a society of Frenchmen were having a party.

Sensing a final opportunity to get overseas, he rang the bell. "A flunkey in a dress-suit opened," he wrote in his autobiography, "but when he saw that I was not a guest, but to all appearances a tramp, he tried to put me out" (p. 52). After Riis excitedly pleaded his case, two Frenchmen ejected him physically from the house and slammed the door shut. He walked the streets all night, and at noon the next day a monk at Fordham University found him near exhaustion and gave him some food. His Lutheran training having left him suspicious of Catholics, he later declared in his autobiography that he expected the cleric to ask him "to abjure my faith, or at least do homage to the Virgin Mary" in payment for the aid (p. 53). Later that day Riis found temporary work picking cucumbers for a truck farmer, and then made another unsuccessful effort to join the French unit of soldiers. He worked for two days in a clay bank; but when he left, his boss refused to pay him his wages.

Leaving the metropolis again, Riis spent two days journeying to New Brunswick, New Jersey, by train and by foot. His only food was field apples, and he slept on a churchyard gravestone. At a brickyard near Rutgers University he found work which earned him $22 a month plus sleeping quarters in a wagon. Most of his coworkers were Germans whom he hated. They called him "Bismarck," celebrated Prussian victories over Louis Napoleon, and once even dragged Riis's wagon into the river while he was asleep inside it. After six weeks Riis quit and returned to New York for a third visit to the French consul. The consul insulted him by treating him as if he were a beggar. Riis later recounted in *The Making of an American* how he grabbed the man by the nose, "and in a moment we were rolling down the oval stairs together, clawing and fighting for all we were worth" (p 64). His contentiousness caused him much discomfort but also had some rewards.

In the days that followed, Riis came in contact with New York City's slum areas and into conflict with the police. Winter was approaching, and so jobs were scarce. Brickmaking, for instance, ceased until spring. During the day Riis searched for work. At night he went into the run-down neighborhoods of the East Side such as Mulberry Bend and Five Points and slept in ashbins or in tenement doorways. He refused to beg for food, but once a cook at the gaudy Delmonico's restaurant gave him some rolls and bones.

One cold and rainy night Riis sought free lodging at the Church Street police station house. A sergeant took him to a room which he described later as "jammed with a foul and stewing crowd of tramps." During the night someone pilfered his most prized possession, a locket containing a curl of Elisabeth's hair. When Riis protested, the sergeant forced him outside and started to kick him. At that moment a stray dog, who had befriended Riis and followed him to the station, bit the policeman. The sergeant seized the animal and beat it to death against the steps of the station house. When the sergeant left, Riis began hurling stones at the police station. Two officers appeared and escorted him bodily to the Jersey City ferry. He left New York vowing vengeance on all police lodging houses.[3]

After wandering through New Jersey for a few days doing odd jobs and sleeping in barns and cattle cars, Riis's luck changed. In Camden a policeman arrested him in a freight yard for trespassing, but in the morning the officer gave him enough money for fare to Philadelphia. After crossing the Delaware River, he met with the Danish consul in Philadelphia, Ferdinand Myhlertz, who bought Riis clothes and allowed him to live with his family for two weeks. Contacting friends in Dexterville, New York, a suburb of Jamestown, the consul arranged for Riis to go there to obtain work. The young immigrant thankfully accepted the offer.

Spending the winter of 1870–1871 in Dexterville, Riis worked at a succession of difficult jobs. He made cradles at a furniture store, chopped down trees, repaired a steamer, and chipped ice from the surface of a lake. Despite the scarcity of employment opportunities, he enjoyed living within the small Danish community at Dexterville. Occasionally he attended

parties and joined in the playing of what he later termed
"particularly energetic kissing games," which the young people
played after the Lutheran pastor forbade dancing at these
events. When Riis could find no regular work, he hunted
squirrels, rabbits, and birds, and at night trapped muskrats for
which he received 20 cents per skin.[4]

Riis considered himself a young man of culture rather
than a common laborer, and so while he lived in Dexterville,
he arranged to give two lectures a week to a society of Scan-
dinavian workingmen. Full of confidence, he chose to speak
on the formation and development of the earth and charged
ten cents admission. Sacrificing scientific exactness for interest
and suspense, Riis made the talks into a mystery story and
frequently sketched pictures of prehistoric animals on the
blackboard. His talks came to a sudden and ignominious conclusion one evening when he became confused while discussing
latitude and longitude. A retired sea captain shouted out that
Riis was a simpleton. Soon everyone in the audience walked
out on him.

Tiring of Dexterville in the spring of 1871, Riis moved
on to Buffalo, where he continued to have trouble in his deal-
ings with his employers. He worked briefly in a lumberyard
and a cabinet shop, then took a position at a planing mill.
When Riis began working overtime, his boss kept cutting his
wages. Finally he quit when his employer exclaimed that
laborers should receive no more than ten dollars a week. After
working on a railroad gang for a week, he went back to his
carpentry trade at a Buffalo shipyard.

During this time Riis also attempted to earn money as
a writer. In 1871 he wrote essays about Denmark, but no
magazine would accept them, with their unpolished English
phrases. In his autobiography he later stated: "I lacked words
—they didn't pour . . ." (p. 90). Riis also applied for work
at Buffalo's two newspapers, the *Courier* and the *Express*. His
interviewers poked fun at him. Remembering the work he did
for his father on Ribe's newspaper, however, Riis continued
to think about becoming a reporter.

In his spare time Riis designed a model of a window reflector which allowed homeowners to identify visitors without first opening their doors. When he demonstrated the model to a company official in Buffalo, the man scoffed at the idea. Soon the company began marketing the reflector but gave no money to Riis.

The twenty-three-year-old immigrant, still unfamiliar with the subtleties of American enterprise, spent a year as a salesman. On his first venture he traveled into western Pennsylvania and Ohio gathering orders for furniture. When he returned to his headquarters in Jamestown, New York, he discovered that his company had misquoted their prices and could not honor the orders. Instead of receiving commissions totaling $450, Riis got only 75 cents.

Undeterred, Riis began selling flatirons. Late in 1872 the Myers Manufacturing Company in Pittsburgh, Pennsylvania, assigned him to be their agent in Illinois. During a six-week sojourn in Chicago he foolishly loaned some money to fraudulent dealers and lost his sample of irons. Worse yet, he discovered upon his return to Pittsburgh that his own company had cheated him. Riis later wrote in his autobiography: "In the utter wreck of all my hopes I was alone again" (p. 114).

Further bad news came from Ribe. On 26 March 1873 Niels Riis informed his son that Elisabeth was engaged to a cavalry officer. He advised Jacob to abandon the idle romantic dreams of his youth and to build upon his religious and moral training. "To be in America and not to be influenced by the business life and the restless search for money would be impossible," the father warned. Yet he was confident that his son would develop interests other than "those things that rust and moths can destroy."[5]

Riis did not lose hope, however. He continued to dream of marrying Elisabeth and of making enough money to bring her to America. On Christmas Eve of 1872 he had pasted a clipping of a poem on the inside of his diary. The poem's title was "Never Give Up!" and it contained the advice that " 'tis wiser and better always to hope than once to despair."

All during the winter as he made a slow trek through Pennsylvania toward New York City selling barely enough irons to live, Riis repeated the lines of the poem to himself and copied them into the pages of his notebook.[6]

When Riis returned to New York City in 1873, the metropolis was in the throes of a severe depression; the agencies of public and private charities were unprepared to meet the crisis. Existing relief programs were inadequately funded, uncoordinated, and philosophically at odds with one another. In the wake of the economic collapse, municipal officials cut back on existing work projects, an action which affected thousands of laborers. On 13 January 1874, when ten thousand unemployed workers attended a mass meeting, the city administration, which had granted permission for the rally, ordered the police to disperse the group with clubs. They did, arresting thirty-five men. For a year the Department of Charities and Correction had been operating at half its normal budget under the taint of corruption from the regime of Tammany's boss, William Marcy Tweed. In 1874 the department ceased distributing any outdoor relief at all. At the office of the Association for Improving the Condition of the Poor (AICP), the most prestigious private relief agency, applications for aid increased fivefold in one year, while there was no corresponding rise in the group's budget. Robert M. Hartley, the head of the AICP, criticized the free food, clothing, and coal centers which some newspapers and other private groups had started. Hartley opposed their unscientific methods and their encouragement of tramps and laziness. Anxious to reform the character of the poor, he hung to his principles, even though they were irrelevant to the existing conditions.[7]

From Runabout to Newsman

Riis was too proud and stubborn to accept direct relief at the free centers or to solicit the temporary aid of private philanthropy. Still bent on bettering his lot, he enrolled in a telegraphy course at a business school and attended class in the afternoons while he sold flatirons and copies of *Hard Times* by Charles Dickens in the mornings and evenings. For a brief time he took work as a newspaper editor but quit when his employer could not pay him. He liked the work, however, and when he discovered that the New York News Association was looking for a reporter, he eagerly applied for the job. Intercession by the principal of his business school secured him a trial assignment. The agency sent the hungry Riis to cover a luncheon at the Astor House. His story won him a position as a reporter.[8]

Riis's newspaper work was very hard and tiresome, but it gave him a modicum of security and offered him excitement and incentive. The New York News Association assigned him to work with two other men in covering all city events except those features which came under the special departments. Often working from ten in the morning until after midnight, he covered a territory which extended from Harlem to the Bowery. His superiors paid him according to the quantity of his work, so Riis usually handled multiple assignments each day. He welcomed the heavy schedule as a means of taking his mind off Elisabeth and acquainting him with the many wonders of life in the urban metropolis. Finding a vocation in tune with his temperament and skills rooted Riis more firmly as an American. He had found a place to fix his star for the future.

On 20 May 1874 Riis began working for the South Brooklyn *News*, a small weekly paper which Democrats operated for their political advancement. A few weeks later the owners made him editor, but after the fall election they decided to abandon the debt-ridden paper. In January 1875 Riis bought it from them without the presses for $600; he paid $75 in cash and promised the balance on credit. At the time of the transaction all that was left of the *News* was its name and the type.[9]

Riis transformed the South Brooklyn *News* into a financial success by offering his readers a blend of local gossip and crusading editorials. In six months he was out of debt, despite the severely depressed economic conditions which still existed in New York. Laboriously he managed the four-page weekly almost by himself, writing and editing all the articles, soliciting advertisers, publishing the product, and even carrying the copy to the presses. News that Elisabeth's fiancé had died spurred him to earn enough money to be in a position to ask for her hand in marriage. In his editorial columns he generally supported local Democrats, and he denounced the scandals of the Ulysses S. Grant administration. In return the Democrats arranged for him to become a court interpreter of German and Danish, and for a brief time Riis received $100 a month for doing an average of three days of work. Soon the Democrats were irate at the editor's refusal to denounce the Republican police chief; and Riis lost his sinecure in court, making his conscience clean once again.

One of Riis's reform crusades backfired. After a grocer told him that many customers refused to pay their bills, he published a list of the debtors, labeled them deadbeats, and concluded that they should pay promptly or leave the community. The grocer, in an effort to salvage his own popularity, turned against the obtrusive editor and called him a troublemaker. Riis made enemies during this episode, but the circulation of the *News* continued to spiral. He was happy to appeal to the curiosity of his neighbors as well as to their hearts and minds.

In December 1875 Riis went back to Denmark to marry Elisabeth. She had first been angry with his overtures so soon after her beloved cavalry officer died, but then she accepted his proposal, even though she did not love him. Riis sold the *News* back to the Democratic leaders for a 500 percent profit and returned to Ribe on New Year's Eve. Ever interested in earning extra money, he sent his impressions of Europe back to the *News*. In one article, dated 18 January 1876, he recounted how Prussia had seized Schleswig and Holstein "by fraud and usurpation" twelve years earlier. On 5 March 1876 he married Elisabeth at the Domkirke. During the summer they returned to Brooklyn, where there was a substantial Danish-American community, and Riis again became editor of the paper he had once owned.[10] During his early married life, Riis's religion played a formative role in shaping his ideals and opinions. He maintained a deep faith in God, which served as a source of his optimism; yet his beliefs were independent from rigid dogma. He personalized Christian teachings into axioms which were amenable to his practical mind. A man of action who took pride in his bellicose personality, Riis said that one of his favorite Biblical stories was Peter's slicing off the ear of a priest's servant. Once after a revival meeting at the Methodist church to which Jacob and Elisabeth belonged, he told Reverend Ichabod Simmons that he wanted to become a minister. "No, no, Jacob, not that," Simmons answered, according to Riis's autobiography. "We have preachers enough. What the world needs is consecrated pens" (p. 135). On another occasion Reverend Simmons's successor criticized Riis for selling the *News* on the Sabbath. That afternoon Riis saw the minister hurl a rock at a hen to chase it from his garden. In an editorial he drew parallels between the rock-throwing and the selling of Sunday newspapers. During services the following week, the minister demanded that the sacrilegious editor meet with him and the deacons and retract his statement. Riis replied that he never transacted business on the Sabbath.

Riis resigned as editor of the *News* after engaging in frequent feuds with the owners, and he decided to try his skills at advertising. He bought a stereopticon and showed pictures of famous places and people interspersed with advertisements for local merchants. Sometimes he set up his equipment inside a store window; on other occasions he operated outdoors by hanging a canvas curtain between two trees. Occasionally taunters threw eggs at him, and for a brief time Riis hired guards to protect him. The job gave him freedom, but he soon became interested in a larger scheme.

In the summer of 1877 Riis and a friend, Ed Wells, decided to publish a city directory for Elmira, New York. They journeyed to Elmira at a time when violent railroad strikes were occurring throughout the Northeast. Soldiers and policemen were guarding the city's railway station and bridge when the two entrepreneurs arrived. Setting up their stereopticon and curtain near the bridge, they intended to solicit money from spectators for advertisements in their city directory. Unfortunately the policemen believed that they were signaling the strikers with their gadgets and forced them to leave town. On their way home Riis and Wells stopped briefly in Scranton, Pennsylvania. They merged into a crowd that had formed near the railroad's company stores. The mayor of Scranton urged the crowd to disperse, but someone struck him with a brick. Guards began to fire into the crowd. Riis, upon seeing a man near him fall to the ground bleeding, turned and fled.[11]

Landing a Job on the *Tribune*

When Riis returned to Brooklyn late in 1877, out of money and unenthusiastic about further advertising schemes, he decided to become a reporter. He had had seven lean years financially, but he had gained experience and traveled widely as a writer, speaker, promoter and businessman. As editor of the South Brooklyn *News* he had shown himself to be somewhat of a reformer. During the summer of 1877, he wrote about the blessings of rural life. He said, "Greater than all its physical advantages, its health-giving air, the colors of blending beauty, is its moral effect on the mind and body."[12] Ironically, soon afterward he began a vocation that culminated in his making the city and its problems his primary task and purpose in life. After several newspapers turned him down, he found work on the New York *Tribune*. The paper's editor-in-chief, a neighbor named William F. G. Shanks, who had had a hand in exposing the scandals of the Tweed Ring, hired him on a trial basis.

The new job had many drawbacks, and Riis's anxiety to do well sometimes backfired. The *Tribune* gave him routine assignments that the other, more experienced reporters did not want. One winter evening his task was to learn the effects of a storm's damage on Coney Island. Unable to obtain transportation to the scene of destruction, Riis based his report upon eyewitness accounts of others. He included an anecdote concerning a cat which allegedly floated to safety inside a kitchen stove. Riis was elated with his exclusive story until the following day when his superior criticized him for writing an inaccurate account based upon circumstantial evidence. Riis rarely repeated the mistake.

After six months Riis almost quit his job. His salary was inadequate to support his family. A day after he wrote and then destroyed his letter of resignation, he received a promotion to the position of police reporter, for both the *Tribune* and its adjunct the Associated Press. Riis wired his wife: "Got staff appointment. Police Headquarters. $25 a week. Hurrah!"

In later life Riis took pride in his efforts during his first years in the United States, as if he believed suffering to be necessary to deserve the laurels of success. When someone asked him why he had not depended on philanthropy when he was poor, Riis replied that he had not wanted charity. "A little starvation once in a while even," he concluded in *The Making of an American,* "is not out of the way" (p. 300). He wrote that any man would "get shaken into the corner where he belonged if he took a hand in the game" (pp. 35–36).

It was a mistake for Riis to generalize about the social mobility of immigrants from his own experiences, but he was correct in attributing his own survival during his first seven years in America to his family background, his optimistic and hardworking character and, above all, his good fortune. There was substantial upward mobility, however, among rural Americans moving into new middle class positions which industrialization had created.[13] Riis, in his beliefs and values, had more in common with this native-born subculture than he had with ethnic groups that constituted the so-called new immigration from southern and eastern Europe. His knowledge of rudimentary English and his skill at a trade gave him tools which most of these immigrants did not possess. His moral and social upbringing instilled in him a code of conduct, a high sense of place, and a great deal of ambition. He did not consider himself of the lower class even when he was penniless and when most of his efforts ended in futility. Finally, at critical junctures in his life, when it seemed as though he might abandon the advice of the poet who penned "Never Give Up!" people revived his spirits. Myhlertz, the Danish consul, got him settled in Dexterville. His business school principal and a neighbor helped him to become a reporter. And Elisabeth decided to marry him after all.

3

THE EMERGENCE OF A REFORMER

For more than eleven years beginning in 1877 Jacob Riis was a reporter for the New York *Tribune* and the Associated Press Bureau. His exuberance and sensitivity fitted well with the requirements of personal journalism which flowered during the final third of the nineteenth century. As a newspaperman Riis developed writing skills, personal friendships, contacts with philanthropic organizations, and firsthand knowledge of New York's immigrant ghettos which he gradually turned to use as a spokesman for change. For Riis journalism served as a vehicle for securing a higher place in American society, for protesting slum conditions, and for thrusting him into contact with people who shared his concern with the decaying city. His burgeoning interest in reform, flowing in many directions, led him to work with volunteer groups who were caring for paupers, with patrician gentlemen anxious to clean up the machinery of urban government, with housing experts who were planning an assault on slum tenements, and with settlement workers striving to promote brotherhood among America's social groups.

New York Police Reporter

Riis's beat as a reporter on Mulberry Street included the Police Department, the Board of Health, the coroner's office, the Fire Department, and the Excise Bureau. He operated from a room located in the midst of an East Side slum area across from police headquarters. Working the night shift, Riis shared his quarters with a dozen representatives of rival papers. His colleagues called him "the Dutchman" because of his accent, and for a week they frustrated all his efforts to uncover an original story. They pilfered Riis's memoranda and falsified reports which led him off to cover nonexistent events. After two weeks Riis scored his first exclusive story. His position was still in jeopardy, however. Soon afterwards, the *Tribune* suspended him for failing to report that the police were about to solve a case involving grave robbers, a story that appeared on the pages of the *Tribune*'s competitors. Riis insisted that the other newsmen were spreading false rumors, and charged that some of them were deliberately frustrating police work in order to prolong the sensational case. He won his job back after he wrote an exclusive report on a fire that occurred near his home. Shortly afterwards facts came out about the grave robber mystery which exonerated Riis. From then on, he declared in *The Making of an American,* he and his colleagues "settled down to the ten years' war for the mastery, out of which I was to come at last fairly the victor, and with the only renown I have ever coveted or cared to have, that of being the 'boss reporter' in Mulberry Street" (p. 202).

Riis was a newsman during a period which he labeled the "heroic age" of journalism. Mass circulation dailies paid handsome salaries to star reporters who hunted down stories and then wrote graphic accounts of what they saw. Later these two functions tended to become separate, but during Riis's career a reporter was both an investigator and a writer.

In 1883 Joseph Pulitzer bought the New York *World* and helped turn journalism into a big business. Combining sensationalism and editorial crusading, Pulitzer increased the net worth of the *World* thirtyfold within a decade. In 1883 lurid headlines cascaded from its pages—"Love and Cold Poison," "Baptized in Blood," "A Bride but Not a Wife," "Screaming for Mercy." These proclaimed a new era in journalism. When Edwin L. Godkin of the *Evening Post* pronounced Pulitzer's style to be vulgar, the owner of the *World* replied, "I want to talk to a nation, not to a select committee." Other newspapers copied Pulitzer's techniques and even outdid him in irreverence and slanted news. Reporters wrote humorous accounts of murders; columns appeared with titles such as "Divorce Mill." The *Sun* printed "FRAUD" on the forehead of a picture of Rutherford B. Hayes. Another paper continuously referred to Grover Cleveland as "His Corpulency." Competition among the dozen New York dailies encouraged the trend toward emotionalism. And until the methods of big business usurped the traditions of personal journalism, reporters were the stars of the new system.[1]

Limits to the freedom of reporters existed, of course. The Associated Press often prodded Riis to reduce his editorializing and to stick to the facts. He later wrote in his autobiography that "good or bad, I could write in no other way, and kept right on" (p. 223). It was commonplace for editors to censor material that might upset potential advertisers or that conflicted with their political inclinations. Unable to publish realistic accounts of labor disputes or social injustices on their own merits, reporters had to sell their stories on human interest. Yet there were pitfalls to this tactic. A favorite anecdote of Riis's concerned a rookie reporter who wrote a vivid account of a needless fire in an uninspected tenement shop. "In venomous hisses and spurts, the flame shot into the overhanging darkness," the dispatch read, "while from every window and door poured forth a dense sulphurous smoke, the deadly, suffocating breath of an imprisoned fiend." Editorial changes cut the story to read: "Pat Sheeny's grocery was destroyed by fire last night. Loss, $250; uninsured." Despite the shortcomings, however, Riis convinced himself that reporters had opportunities unequaled in other professions to influence public opinion.[2]

Like most successful journalists, Riis possessed, in addition to intelligence and physical endurance, a romantic and imaginative mind. To remain somewhat invulnerable to the daily disasters that he witnessed, a reporter needed a shell of practical hardheadedness, but to spot the highly marketable possibilities for poignancy in a story he needed the ability to place himself vicariously in the lives and minds of others. Roger S. Tracy, who knew Riis well, later wrote that his friend had a probing mind and kept his optimism within realistic bounds. He concluded that "Riis was an extremely emotional man and very affectionate in his disposition. A tendency to sentimentalism had been tempered and controlled in some degree by the cynicism of skepticism that seems always to be developed by newspaper training. But these two apparently conflicting mental attitudes made him a pretty accurate judge of men and motives." He called Riis a poet who could take a mere item of news and write a story "brimming with pathos, humor and sympathetic insight. . . ."[3]

Riis understood well that his most successful articles were the ones which appealed to the emotions, to fear or guilt or compassion. He later wrote that "a petty tenement-house fire might hide a firebug, who always makes shuddering appeal to our fears; the finding of John Jones sick and destitute in the street meant, perhaps, a story full of the deepest pathos." In turning crime news into taut drama, the reporter portrayed human conflict, the drama of suffering, revenge, passion, and a redeeming heroism. The difference between ghouls and good police reporters, he stated in his autobiography, was that the latter caught the "human drift" and not just the "foulness and the reek of blood." Then even a murder story, Riis believed, could "speak more eloquently to the minds of thousands than the sermon preached to a hundred in the church on Sunday" (pp. 204–6). Mulberry Street thus took on the dimensions of a universal morality play.

Riis's newspaper articles covered a wide spectrum of

topics. Within a space of three months, for instance, he wrote features on fire escapes, billy clubs, unclaimed property at the police station, tramps, cranks who roamed the Bowery, murder weapons, and criminals at large. In an article about the street cleaning department, he wrote that city workers annually carted off over twenty thousand carcasses of dead animals, mainly horses and cats, to a factory that manufactured glue, shoe leather, and buttons. Eleven days later he composed a compelling story about New York's foundling asylum. He described how desperate women abandoned their infants in front of churches, in ashcans, or at the homes of the wealthy, but that almost all of the babies ended up at the city's asylum unless the morgue claimed them first.[4]

On 15 July 1883 the New York *World* published a feature story by Riis entitled "Jail Sermons in Stones," about messages which he found on cell walls. Most of the entries which prisoners etched in stone were sad and fatalistic, he found. Many were Biblical maxims, but some were humorous and a few pornographic. Riis recorded the advice that he found above the signature of Slippery George: "Keep cool, or they will put you down stairs, and it's a h--l of a bad place, take my word for it. I was there."

In his articles Riis put much stress on biographical sketches in order to underscore his belief that even in the slum people retained some dignity and unique spirit. He searched both for bizarre personalities to demonstrate the slum's variety and for commonplace archetypes of its grinding poverty. He found little to laugh about in the tenement environment, but when possible he gave his articles a touch of humor or pathos. He made much of a French nobleman living in a barren attic and an Indian chief who worked as a clerk. He wrote "Some Oddities in Low Life," printed by the New York *Mail and Express* on 18 May 1885, which described an elderly Harvard graduate who gave pennies and trinkets to children and sang "some queer old ditty that sounded like an echo from beyond forgotten graves." Once the man entered a barber shop "and composed his trembling frame in a chair with a weary sigh. When the barber's 'nex' called his turn he was dead."

Other stories by Riis were more macabre. In August 1885 he wrote that when the icy river thawed in the spring over a hundred dead bodies washed ashore. A month later he reported how a sawmill cut a woman in half after she fell from her roof. In March of 1886 Riis told of a felon who assaulted a man with a wooden leg, fracturing his skull. On 11 June he discovered that a boy died when a wooden Indian fell on him.

In writing his articles, Riis sought out phrases that would attract immediate attention, subtleties that differentiated his stories from the steady stream of others, and didactic morals to leave with his readers. In one of them he wrote that history seemed to move in cycles or streaks with great numbers of fires, murders, accidents, and sensational events occurring in rapid succession. Moral epidemics seemed to feed upon themselves. "Is the world itself the great perpetuum mobile," Riis asked, paraphrasing Henry Ward Beecher, "and for fear of going too fast must it retrace its steps now and then?"[5]

Because of his connection with the Associated Press, numerous newspapers printed Riis's articles. In addition to such New York dailies as the *Tribune, World, Mail and Express,* and *Morning Journal,* his work appeared in other parts of the country. He wrote a few columns for the Green Bay, Wisconsin, *Advance* entitled "Gotham Doings." They contained commentary on politics, slum conditions, events in Denmark, and society gossip. Riis castigated Tammany for swelling its voting strength with tramps. Concerning the book-burning Anthony Comstock, he wrote that "with all his morality, [he] is by no means exempt from some of the common weaknesses of the flesh." He told his readers that Jay Gould, whom some people viewed as a "sort of malicious ogre or moral vampire," gave a check to the widow of a former employee which equaled three years' salary. In these and other sketches, Riis, somewhat of an aspiring entrepreneur himself, reaffirmed traditional American values.[6]

After 1880 when Riis began working the day shift, he became better acquainted with the workings of the Board of Health. The motives for his close relationship with public health officers were both personal and professional. He preferred their company to the inane banter and card playing of most reporters, and from them he gained valuable material about the hazards of slum life. One of his good friends was Roger S. Tracy, who worked as a sanitary inspector and statistician. He first met Tracy in 1881 while covering a smallpox epidemic and within a few months began spending an hour or two with him each afternoon. Riis's didactic style gave life to the statistics which Tracy provided him with, and the resulting articles of exposure shocked his readers and made a compelling case for reform. Other journalists covered the health department and wrote about slum conditions; but Riis had the rare ability to bring to life in writing the sounds and smells and moods of the tenements and, most of all, the feelings of their residents.

Riis later attributed the origins of his reform impulses to his contact with members of the Board of Health. His genteel, reform-minded acquaintances there shared his disgust for machine politics and his fear of a burgeoning, anarchistic, contagious slum tide. Part of that growing group of middle class technicians who would manage the legislative fiats of the coming Progressive Era, they had faith in science, reason, progress, and the cultural superiority of Anglo-Saxon institutions. Riis was a reformer for many reasons: moral crusades assuaged his sense of outrage at injustice, meshed well with his vocation, and brought upward mobility and prestigious status as palatable by-products. Roger Tracy's role was to reenforce Riis's humanitarian instincts and arm him with more refined weapons with which to joust with his antagonists.[7]

Riis was very proud of those stories of his which portrayed the miseries of slum life. On 11 June 1883 he published "Pestilence Nurseries" in the New York *World*. While describing the accidental death of a man who fell from atop a tenement house, Riis editorialized against the greed of landlords. When warm weather came to New York, he wrote, the crowded and unventilated tenements became Black Holes which drove dwellers to their roofs for air. The duplicity of owners and the stupidity of tenants frustrated most of the efforts of the Board of Health to ameliorate the situation, Riis sadly concluded.

Riis hated the slum because of the ruinous consequences the environment had upon the health, habits, and morals of the people who had to live there. In *The Making of an American* he called the Mulberry Bend area a pigsty full of depravity, with "foul alleys and fouler tenements" unfit for humanity (p. 235). New York's inadequate water reserves created such shortages that it was easier, he observed, to obtain cheap beer than good water. Often during certain hours only basement spigots of tenements worked, and people had to carry water in pails up to their rooms. New York's system of sewage and garbage disposal was hopelessly obsolete. H. L. Mencken's remark that Baltimore during the 1880s smelled "like a billion polecats" was applicable to New York. When the Association for Improving the Condition of the Poor asked tenants to report violations of city ordinances, the organization received a deluge of letters about the poor sewage facilities. One person complained that "the stink is enough to knock you down."[8]

While Riis feared the consequences that the slum wrought for its residents, he had no personal fear of entering East Side neighborhoods. He wrote that a sober citizen who minded his own business and walked with dignity and authority encountered very little trouble. Residents of Mulberry Street called the bespectacled Riis "Doc," partially because of the many times he chased after fire engines and ran to the scene of accidents. Taking leave of Mulberry Street after work to go to his house in Brooklyn, he pitied those who stayed behind. Proclaiming in his autobiography that he could never reside in the slums, he preferred "to be where there are trees and birds and green hills, and where the sky is blue above" (pp. 284–85).

Riis and Scientific Philanthropy

Riis deeply admired the work of Charles Loring Brace, who in 1853 had founded the Children's Aid Society for the purpose of relocating orphans in foster homes in the country or in small towns. Brace, a minister who had preached in the squalid tenement district of Five Points, wanted youngsters to live where pure air replaced the gaseous stench of sewers, where boys could play in fields and groves rather than in narrow alleys. Brace helped to resettle over ninety thousand children during nearly forty years of work. Riis put more emphasis on reforming the city rather than abandoning it for the countryside, but he believed that Brace's programs did much good for the individual recipients and relieved the city of potentially troublesome youths.[9]

During the 1880s Riis came in contact with, and under the influence of, the Charity Organization Society (COS). The charity organization movement began in England in 1869 and spread to America eight years later. In 1873 New York patricians had founded the Bureau of Charities, a forerunner of the COS, but it collapsed when the Association for Improving the Condition of the Poor refused to cooperate with it, regarding it as a rival and possible usurper of its own authority.

In 1882 Josephine Shaw Lowell founded a COS chapter in New York, in order to coordinate and rationalize private relief work, which had failed disastrously during the depression of the 1870s. Mrs. Lowell, an aristocratic, compassionate puritan who always dressed in black in honor of her husband, who had died during the Civil War, devoted her life to the mission of bringing scientific methods to philanthropy. While a member of New York State's Board of Charities, she blamed most instances of pauperism on heredity, drunkenness, improvidence, and vicious indulgence. She recommended hard labor for the "idle" poor and special asylums for the feeble-minded and insane. She opposed public outdoor relief. During its first year in existence, the COS registered information about thirty-four hundred families. The agency provided no direct relief but investigated applicants to establish their need, then referred them to another charity or to an employer. At first the COS attempted to attract volunteers to provide friendship and moral suasion to their wards during personal visits. Within a decade, however, the stress went toward the training of professionals to handle the casework.[10]

The values which Riis had acquired in Denmark harmonized closely with those of Mrs. Lowell. Both the reporter and the philanthropist were moralists who glorified the ethic of self-help and work, hated laziness, and put much emphasis on saving children from the ruinous effects of the slum environment. In 1883 Riis wrote several articles for the New York *World* about the "tramp menace." Intemperate loafers of every nationality inundated New York during the warm weather, he warned, and he claimed that many made fortunes by forcing children to beg for them. On 8 July he concluded that the "first acceptance of alms puts a brand on the man which his moral strength rarely holds out to efface." And on other occasions he often repeated the maxim of Benjamin Franklin which the COS had adopted as a motto to the effect that "The best way of doing good to the poor is not by making them easy in poverty, but by leading or driving them out of it." Summing up his dislike of misguided alms which encouraged pauperism, he wrote, "As to the man who will not work, let him starve."[11]

As a result, during these years Riis supported and publicized the positive programs of the COS, such as their day nurseries, penny savings banks, trade school courses, and wayfarers' lodge. Once when he took some food to a woman who had appealed for assistance, he came upon a member of the St. Vincent de Paul Society on the same mission. He requested the COS to investigate and discovered that the woman had a bank account of eighteen hundred dollars. Because of such experiences, Riis wrote in his autobiography, "I early pinned my faith to organized charity as just orderly charity . . ." (p. 295).

Riis harbored private misgivings, however, about what

he believed to be the harsh and cold methods of the COS. Although he bowed to the assumed expertise of Mrs. Lowell, whom he deeply admired, presuming that his own softheartedness might lead him into error, he believed that preventive and collective solutions to the problems of poverty were as necessary as remedial and individual cures; and he did not share the society's suspicion that most poor people were shirking work. With his optimistic view of human nature, Riis could not concur with Mrs. Lowell's sardonic comment that only the extraordinary individual "*works for a living* when it is not necessary. . . ." In 1886 when the COS hired a detective to investigate beggars and then had two hundred unfortunate loiterers arrested and jailed, Riis ridiculed the project. He also took exception to the patronizing attitude of some social workers as reflected in a phrase of the 1886 Annual Report of the COS that, "If we do not furnish the poor with elevating influences, they will rule us by degrading ones."[12]

Riis kept silent, perhaps because he too on occasion mistook the ignorance of immigrants for stupidity and their endurance of squalid conditions to mean acceptance or condolence of vile habits. In an article published in the New York *Mail and Express* on 26 December 1885, entitled "Tramps Back in Town," he described how in Mulberry Bend during business hours "the lowest class of Italians claim it as theirs, for the traffic in mouldy bread, stale vegetables, rotten fruit, and similar staples of Mulberry Street."

Coming to Hate Tammany Hall

In 1884 Riis deepened his interest in municipal reform as a result of a special legislative investigation of New York City's Department of Public Works. Under the vigorous leadership of Theodore Roosevelt, a youthful second-term assemblyman whose family "had lived for seven righteous generations on Manhattan Island," the committee hearings produced massive evidence of graft, extortion, and malpractice. Attending the sessions for his wire service, Riis publicized the scandals, gained an admiration for Theodore Roosevelt and rekindled his hatred of Tammany Hall machine politics.[13]

New York City had a reputation for political corruption which dated from the eighteenth century. Holding power for most of these years was Tammany Hall, a social society which early in the nineteenth century had allied itself with the Democratic party. Many factors combined to open the way for the triumph of the machine rule: a chaotic and rapid growth, inadequate lines of communication among the polyglot populace, a politically apathetic citizenry, and an inflexible city charter which had hopelessly divided authority. William Marcy Tweed, the most able and infamous of New York's bosses, personified the blatant dishonesty of city politics during the mid-nineteenth century. Tweed won the support of immigrant groups, especially the Germans and Irish, and then by bribery gained control of the city's board of supervisors. This body controlled voting procedures, expenditures, and public improvements, and became Tweed's vehicle for expanding his power and influence beyond his Tammany base. Tweed's organization provided services for the poor and at election time used bribery, intimidation, illegal voting by aliens, and professional precinct discipline to maintain power. Tweed once stated that "This population is too hopelessly split up into races and factions to govern it under universal suffrage, except by the bribery of patronage or corruption. . . ."[14]

In 1870, the year that Riis emigrated to New York, Tweed controlled twelve thousand patronage positions and collected a 15 percent commission from all city franchises. Similarly he exacted tribute from office seekers, saloon keepers, gamblers, and the owners of other enterprises. The previous year the Tweed ring had pilfered over $10 million from the city. In 1870 Tweed spent a million dollars in bribing state legislators to ensure passage of a new city charter which centralized his power.[15]

Boss Tweed's personal power collapsed in 1871, but Tammany continued to dominate New York City politics throughout the remainder of the nineteenth century. Businessmen became alarmed at the city's rising debt and scandalous reputation and organized the Committee of Seventy under the leadership of Samuel J. Tilden, an ambitious, aristocratic Democrat who had previously gotten along with the machine. Their investigations led to Tweed's ouster from office and criminal conviction. Nevertheless, before Tweed went to jail in 1873, his clique had robbed taxpayers of about $200 million. And after one term of patrician rule, New York's voters returned Tammany to power under the leadership of "Honest" John Kelley.

Riis understood the popularity of Tammany politicians, even as he disliked their methods. As an editor in Brooklyn in 1875, he had allied himself with Democratic ward bosses. He realized the advantages in having contacts in high places. For instance, police officials had information which was material for an abundance of stories, and the manner in which they leaked news or issued bulletins could make or break a police reporter. To ingratiate himself Riis wrote many articles concerning the personal bravery of police officers. But he came to learn about the institutionalized corruption and brutality of the New York force which originated in their alliance with Tammany Hall. During the 1880s he commented editorially about it, making many enemies. And he sided with patrician reformers who argued that the long-range interests of the poor were at odds with machine rule. Yet Tammany's political dominance cooled reformers to schemes of municipal ownership and regulation, for these would only strengthen the enemy.

In 1884, the year of the Roosevelt investigation of corruption in New York City, Riis's newspaper work also brought him into contact with efforts to ameliorate tenement house conditions. He covered a series of lectures on New York's housing crisis by Felix Adler, the founder of the Society of Ethical Culture, which affected him personally as well as professionally. Adler's sincerity and seeming purity of purpose impressed him greatly, especially his knack for blending reason and morality, and for intermixing dispassionate argumentation with spirited advocacy of change. Riis said later that the inspiration of Felix Adler spurred him into becoming a zealous enemy of greedy landlords, dishonest public servants, and other defenders of the status quo.[16]

The publicity which arose from Adler's public addresses prodded the state legislature into establishing a fact-finding tenement house commission. Adler served on it and was its most effective member. Riis contrasted his earnest and forceful demeanor with the apathy of the commission's chairman, Joseph W. Drexel, a professional politician who slept during much of the testimony. Using maps and statistics, Adler charged that almost all tenements were unsafe and dangerous to the health of their residents. Ninety percent of them had faulty drainage. Legal loopholes and inadequate inspection procedures to enforce sanitary standards subverted the state housing code. Most alarming, the newest buildings were even more harmful than their older counterparts. Following a model which resembled the shape of a dumbbell, these five and six-story structures were overcrowded and dimly lit and had narrow, inadequate air shafts which were fire hazards and carriers of germs and foul odors, as tenants used them for garbage receptacles.[17]

The report of the Drexel Commission of 1884 produced only insignificant amendments to the housing code, and the state supreme court further set back the objectives of Adler and Riis by nullifying a law which forbade sweatshop manufacturing in the tenements. Theodore Roosevelt had sponsored the bill in the state legislature after touring the homes of Bohemian cigar makers with union organizer Samuel Gompers. The court ruled that the act violated laborers' freedom of contract to earn a living and was therefore unconstitutional. This reactionary decision, combined with New York City's corrupt municipal government, convinced Riis that a widespread campaign was necessary to keep alive agitation for reform and to get the facts to the public so that they would demand change.[18]

Beginning in 1885, Riis's social consciousness became more pronounced. For one thing, he officially became an American citizen, an action consummated by his appearance before the United States District Court of Southern New York. Also his pen became, more than ever, a rapier against injustice. In a New York *Sun* article, appearing on 16 May 1885, about mothers who abandoned their children to the foundling asylum, he wrote: "The rich have other ways of covering up their sins than by scattering the evidence about the streets." Similarly in a story for the New York *Mercury* entitled "A Church with a New Idea," which appeared in print on 23 August 1885, Riis announced that the City Mission and Tract Society was building a tabernacle in the middle of a slum section. In this model program the society planned to allow the residents to control the activities at the building. The column praised the effort but concluded on a note of pessimism. "A reminder of the rough character of the neighborhood is found on the strong wire-screens that protect the colored windows throughout the church against the brick-bats and snowballs of the Fourteenth Ward youths," Riis wrote.

On 14 June 1885 Riis turned a report of a fatal accident into a melodramatic tragedy and used the event to raise social issues. An elevated railroad train had struck Michael Mahon, a handicapped workman. It hurled his body across the tracks and then crushed and mangled it. The police had investigated the accident, but nobody notified Mahon's family. Three hours later a reporter, presumably Riis, found the body in the lumber room of the railway yard. Unable to persuade the company's officials to inform Mahon's wife of the disaster, he carried the sad news to the dead man's wife and son himself. "Their grief would have wrung tears from a stone," Riis reported in the New York *Mercury*. "Life had seemed bright to the little family since he got work again. Now darkness had settled on it forever. But the company's shares were all right."

Having written about New York City's multitude of

problems, Riis began to suggest ways of solving them. On 1 November 1885 he warned the New York *Mercury*'s readers of the danger of boiler explosions in schools and tenements and castigated city officials for their negligence in failing to examine thousands of boilers. On 20 June 1886 he blamed a host of fires on the sale of unsafe kerosene. Having traced the fires to lamp explosions, he then discovered that dealers who sold the petroleum commonly violated the city's safety ordinances. To halt the menace he advocated a tightening of inspection proceedings. On another occasion Riis mourned the fact that New York schools turned away over five thousand children each year for lack of teachers and space. Finally he wrote about the accumulation of manure on New York's streets, due to the seventy thousand horses in the city. Riis suggested that the city license horses and use the revenue to gather up the refuse, rather than continue the haphazard collection by contractors.

On occasion Riis published articles in Henry George's newspaper the *Standard*. In 1886 the single-taxer and author of *Progress and Poverty* (1879) had outpolled Theodore Roosevelt while losing the New York mayoralty race to Democrat Abram S. Hewitt. Preferring Roosevelt's politics to George's, Riis nevertheless admired the author-reformer for publicizing injustices. Writing about police blackmail for the *Standard,* Riis declared that there were so many contradictory ordinances in New York City that policemen held a potential death grip over the city's citizenry. Compounding the problem, Riis believed, was Tammany's domination over political affairs, which precluded any hope for meaningful change.[19]

Family and Settlement

During the 1880s, meanwhile, Riis had to struggle hard to support his growing family. In 1886 there were four children in his home: Edward, nine; Clara, seven; John, four; and an infant son Stephen, who died after a few months. The following year Elisabeth gave birth to their second daughter, Katherine. In 1886 Riis wanted to move from his rented house in South Brooklyn to an area which he had discovered in a rural section of Long Island. He found a part-time job translating life insurance policies into Danish and earned $200, but he still did not have enough money even to buy the lot. Then two friends came to his aid. Ed Wells, a druggist who had joined Riis a decade earlier in the Elmira advertising scheme, lent him money to buy the property. The manager of the Associated Press Bureau signed for the mortgage to the house. Within a year his family moved into their new home, a two-story, white Victorian model. While it was not an architectural triumph, the house contained a private study for Jacob which faced many gardens and a large lawn. Riis felt that in his home he could shut out the slum. He planted a small fruit tree for each child, a red cherry for Ed, a black cherry for Clara, a pear tree for John, and later an apple tree for Kate.[20]

One spring day in 1888 Riis took some daisies to work with him for the children of Mulberry Street. The pleasure which the flowers brought stirred him to write an article for the *Tribune* on 23 June urging others to do the same. Riis explained that "There are too many sad little eyes in the crowded tenements, where the summer sunshine means disease and death, not play or vacation, that will close without ever having looked upon a field of daisies." The idea of giving flowers to the poor was not new. For more than a decade the Children's Aid Society had operated greenhouses and floral missions for this purpose. Riis's newspaper, the *Tribune,* operated a Fresh Air Fund to take slum children to areas closer to nature. Many churches sent their altar displays to sick and elderly families. Yet it surprised Riis greatly when donors began inundating his office with flowers in response to his plea. And it was an oddity for policemen, reporters, and health department officials, following the reporter's bidding, to be distributing the flowers among the children.[21]

From Riis's *Tribune* letter emerged the beginnings of a settlement house. A women's club in New Jersey, the King's Daughters, was especially zealous in sending boxes of flowers to Mulberry Street. As a result, Riis asked the group to render volunteer service in tenement neighborhoods, telling the ladies about children who "would dodge a gentle hand laid upon their heads in kindness, thinking it meant a blow." Such urchins "were not pretty or attractive," he explained to the King's Daughters, but they still had the "child-love of the beautiful and the pure. . . . "[22]

In November of 1889, the same year as the founding of Hull House in Chicago and the College Settlement in east Manhattan, Riis managed to have the King's Daughters endorse neighborhood work at their annual meeting. Five months later their tenement house committee, on which Riis served, found headquarters at the Mariners' Church on Henry Street and established a plan to work with the health department's summer doctors. During the summer of 1890, the King's Daughters furnished nursing care and distributed food and flowers with Biblical sayings. Working closely with the COS, which approved all requests for alms but advised against doling out money to recipients, the King's Daughters were aiding three hundred families by August. The program continued into the fall, and in October the women began plans to obtain a permanent location for a settlement house. Soon the activities of the volunteers and paid staff workers expanded into such services as the provision of nursing care, fresh air outings, social clubs for all members of the family, kindergartens, libraries, and sewing classes.

Riis later minimized the role he played in the founding of the neighborhood settlement that a decade later would bear his name. "Personally I had little to do with it, except to form the link with the official end of it, the summer doctors, etc., and to make trouble occasionally," he wrote in his autobiography (p. 293). Yet he gave frequent speeches at no charge to raise funds for the property, and his prolific pen provided invaluable publicity. When the King's Daughters needed a baby carriage or a wheelchair, Riis would write a poignant plea for donations in the paper. Less puritanical than the ladies, he once displeased them by giving an elderly couple some plug tobacco. On another occasion he raised $300 for a man who owed gambling debts. Soon after he gave the money to the man, he found him in a bar, lectured him, and finally had the police put him in jail.

Riis placed much faith in the social settlement ideal as a means of bringing people of all classes together and of spreading the values of citizenship and decency among the poor. He shared the optimism and romanticism of the settlement founders. Before settlements appeared, Riis, Felix Adler, and Josephine Shaw Lowell were like a band of guerrillas out in the wilderness without a base for expanding their work. Inspired by English experiments in Christian socialism, the settlement movement was a humanitarian, progressive response to the problems of urban immigrants. By his investigative reporting, climaxing in 1890 with the publication of *How the Other Half Lives,* Riis ignited a spark which did much to create and sustain the Progressive movement.

4

HOW THE OTHER HALF LIVES

It was not unnatural, considering his personal ordeals in America, his newspaper career, and his interest in urban reform movements, that Jacob Riis became the preeminent publicist for bridging the chasm between the rich and the poor. For over a decade he had perfected his attention-getting style of writing in the rough-and-tumble world of his Mulberry Street beat. He experimented with photography as a journalistic tool to capture the essence of slum life. An immigrant who suffered many of the indignities of poverty himself, he nevertheless shared most of the values of his middle and upper class audience. All these experiences went into his first book, *How the Other Half Lives*. Merging his vocation with his reform work, Riis became one of the first crusaders for a moral and political awakening to the virulent consequences of urbanization.

The Other Half: Lectures, Photographs and Articles

In 1888 Riis became interested in presenting illustrated lectures on life in New York's slums. The idea came to him during a tour which he took with sanitation inspectors. Riis later wrote that the sights he saw "gripped my heart until I felt that I must tell of them, or burst, or turn anarchist, or something." Remembering the stereopticon displays that he had given a decade earlier in Brooklyn, he decided that photographs would best attract attention to the horrid conditions. His first attempt to speak misfired. After failing to interest his own church in listening to him, he angrily resigned his post as deacon. On 25 January 1888 he made his first address to a club of amateur photographers to which he belonged on the topic of "The Other Half, How It Lives and Dies in New York." The New York *Tribune* reported that Riis was so ingenious in his descriptions and "brought to his task such a vein of humor that after two hours every one wished that there was more of the exhibition, sad as much of it was."[1]

Just as Riis was putting together his lecture, he learned about a German invention of a new flash lighting process that enabled the camera to capture dark indoor scenes that heretofore had been inaccessible to its eye. In February 1888 Riis and three friends tested the idea in the interior of tenements and lodging houses. The experiment's success meant that for the first time he could present indisputable evidence of the squalor in which some people lived. While explaining his discovery to members of the press, Riis excitedly told about a picture that he took inside a cheap lodging house. It reminded him of a slave ship, the New York *Sun* reported him as saying on 12 February. Here a hundred snoring and groaning tramps lay in stacks of rickety beds, polluting the air with their putrid breath.

When Dr. A. F. Schauffler, the director of the City Mission Society, heard about Riis's slides, he asked him to speak at Broadway Tabernacle. Riis's performance on 28 February impressed Schauffler and others in attendance, including the zealous moralist the Reverend Charles H. Parkhurst, and Josiah Strong, author of the influential indictment of urban ills *Our Country*. The audience afterwards donated $143.50 to the Tabernacle. Of even more consequence, Schauffler,

Strong, and Parkhurst helped arrange other speaking engagements for Riis. In a letter of recommendation, Schauffler called the lecture an object lesson. He added that Riis used no material "that could shock the taste of any in the audience."[2]

During the next nine months, Riis traveled throughout the state repeating his address. He accepted fees of from twenty-five to fifty dollars for traveling expenses and remuneration for time lost from his normal job. The pathetic revelations of misery fascinated his audiences. Sensing in this response the possibilities of marketing his material in book form, he secured a copyright to the title "The Other Half, How It Lives and Dies in New York, with One Hundred Illustrations, Photographs from Real Life, of the Haunts of Poverty and Vice in a Great City."[3]

Yet Riis's first lectures were not a total success. Many people questioned whether the conclusions of a mere reporter were worthy of serious attention. One critic who called him a German immigrant wrote that Riis had a "peculiar, rasping voice" that distracted from the presentation. Furthermore, a considerable number of churches still closed their doors to him, saying that his topic was irrelevant to their purpose. In December when one congregation turned down his offer to speak, Riis angrily declared that churches such as this were no more sanctified than newspaper offices.[4]

In 1889 Riis wrote several articles on the theme of the two Americas which he had enunciated in his lectures. Warning the public about the evils that the slums bred, he characterized the more than a million New York tenement dwellers as "that other half, uneasy, suffering, threatening anarchy and revolt, the despair of our statesmen and the joyful opportunity of the politician." The slums were an evil cancer born of public neglect and nurtured by private greed, Riis declared, and they "touch the family life with deadly moral contagion." In graphic and passionate phrases, he guided his readers on a tour of the tenements. "Do not stumble over the children pitching pennies in the hall," Riis wrote; "not that it would hurt them. Kicks and cuffs are their daily diet." He told of one small child whose

job it was to transport beer from a saloon to workers in a nearby factory. One day the lad drank too much beer himself, fell
asleep in a cellar, and was gnawed to death by rats.[5]

In these articles Riis recommended tighter health laws,
better public schools, and the prohibition of child labor as
viable government programs for ameliorating the suffering of
the poor. Finally he urged individuals to support the activities
of private organizations such as the Children's Aid Society.

Also in 1889 Riis received $150 from *Scribner's* maga-
zine for an article entitled "How the Other Half Lives." The
phrase, originally uttered by the Frenchman François
Rabelais, had been used by several New York writers, including John H. Griscom in his bellwether work, *The Sanitary
Condition of the Laboring Population of New York* (1845).
Just as his camera had helped to launch his career as a lecturer,
so had his photographs caught the eye of editors more than his
prose. When the article appeared in December, *Scribner's*
offered to publish an expanded version of it as a book. Riis
later recounted how he and Elisabeth reacted to the news that
he would become an author: "I should have thought I would
have shouted and carried on. I didn't. We sat looking into the
fire together, she and I. Neither of us spoke. Then we went up
to the children." Elisabeth began to weep and asked Jacob if
this meant that she and the family would lose him. Riis em-
braced her and made a silent vow not to become heady with
conceit.[6]

Revising "How the Other Half Lives" into a book was
hard work, but for Riis it was a labor of love and the culmination of his newspaper work. He personalized his experiences of
two decades into impressionistic vignettes and crystallized the
insights he had formed as a reporter. In fact, for many chapters Riis merely expanded upon material which he had used in
previous articles and columns. To accentuate the importance
of his personal anecdotes, he drew upon statistics which he
got from the health and police departments. His tour-guide
descriptions were reminiscent of the writings of Charles
Dickens, one of Riis's favorite authors. From the English

master, who combined the skills of a novelist, a historian, a social critic, and a reformer, Riis learned how to blend humor, indignation, and pathos. Both writers were expert craftsmen in developing a mood of penetrating realism by the use of picturesque and recurring portraits of the commonplace. Having been virtually weaned on Dickens as a child, having sold *Hard Times* on the streets of New York two decades previously, and having read Dickens's account of his visit to the slums of the Empire City in the 1840s—called *American Notes and Pictures from Italy* (1857)—Riis was emulating his mentor in his first book.[7]

Riis began the manuscript in January 1890, and the book appeared in print ten months later. Since he continued working as a police reporter during the day, he did most of his writing at night, after his family had gone to bed. His habit, he later recalled in *The Making of an American,* was "to light the lamps in all the rooms of the lower story and roam through them with my pipe, for I do most of my writing on my feet" (p. 303). In his study he had a desk with fifty pigeonholes, each with a heading such as "The Bend" or "Slum Tenements." On weekends when the work went slowly, Riis often transplanted flowers or pulled up weeds in his garden. He believed that putting his hands in the earth and on nature's harvest helped to put things in their proper perspective. Riis's proofreader rejected his handwritten drafts and urged him to make several drastic revisions in tone and style. He hired a typist but refused to bow to his editor's blue pencil. During 1889 he continued to give lectures but became so burdened with his manuscript that he suffered lapses of memory. He claimed that once while in Boston he became so weighted down with the project that he temporarily forgot his own name. Whether true or not, this incident became one of his favorite stories.[8]

During the 1880s several men had written tracts concerning the malaise of large cities. Among the most popular books were Charles Loring Brace's *The Dangerous Classes of New York and Twenty Years' Work among Them* (1880), Josiah Strong's *Our Country: Its Possible Future and Its Pres-*

1. Jacob A. Riis (from the J. Riis Owre Collection.)

2a. Elisabeth Riis in the Richmond Hill house at a desk which belonged to Riis's father. From the J. Riis Owre Collection.

2b. Mary Phillips Riis about the time of her marriage (From the J. Riis Owre Collection.)

3. Reporter' Office at 301 Mulberry Street, 1887-1888 (This and all subsequent photographs were taken by Jacob A. Riis and are from the Riis Collection of the Museum of the City of New York.)

4a. Mulberry Bend, 1888-89.
4b. Mulberry Park.

5a. Riis titled this picture "Slept in that cellar four years."

5b. Ludlow Street, early 1890's. Riis's title: "Ready for the Sabbath Eve in a coal cellar."

6. Sweatshop in Ludlow Street Tenement.

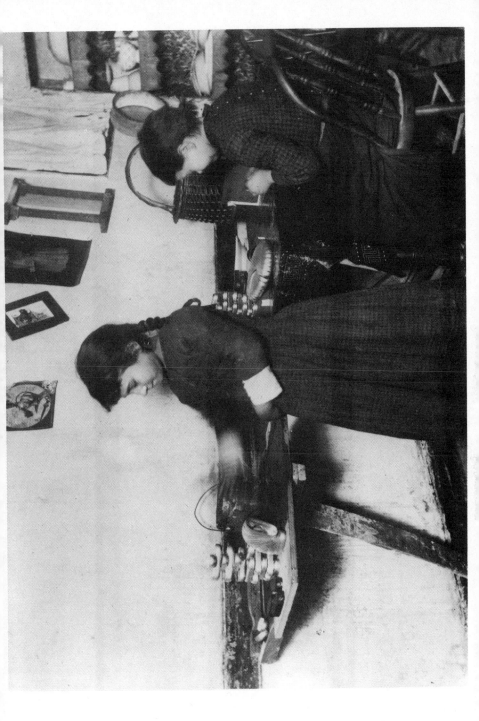

7. 'Little Suzie, whose picture I took while she was pasting linen on tin covers for pocket flasks . . . with hands so deft and swift that even the flash could not catch her moving arm . . . .'' Jacob Riis in *Children of the Poor*.

8. Lodgers at Oak Street Police Station.

ent Crisis (1885), and Samuel L. Loomis's *Modern Cities and Their Religious Problems* (1887). Each noted the enormous growth of urban industrial centers and regretted the trend away from the the values of a rural society. They viewed the rising tide of immigration with concern and emphasized the sinful and devious aspects of urban life. Brace had spent his adult life relocating orphans away from New York. Strong warned that cities menaced civilization, whereas Loomis found them a natural habitat for crime, drunkenness, and sexual immorality since their impersonality was incompatible with the traditional ties of family, church, and community and fraught with temptations for the weak. Similarly in 1887 J. O. S. Huntington wrote in the *Forum* that in the tenements "The bad almost inevitably drag down the good; and the good have not the chance to lift up the bad." While large segments of the populace shared these fears, almost all Americans were anxious to learn about the cities. The popularity of books with this theme augured well for Riis.[9]

Prior to 1890 most social critics had contrasted the pure country with the depraved city, whereas Riis's concept of two Americas centered on the disjunction between the rich and the poor. "The half that was on top cared little for the struggles, and less for the fate of those who were underneath," Riis wrote in *How the Other Half Lives*, "so long as it was able to hold them there and keep its own seat." He had many of the antiurban biases that were so common at the time. He extolled the virtues of rural Denmark, even though he had fled from its boring ways twenty years before. An admirer of the work of Josiah Strong and Charles Loring Brace, Riis nevertheless counseled his readers to accept, not abandon, the city and "make the best of a bad bargain" (pp. 1–2).[10]

Brace and Strong criticized the urban milieu rather than the economic system which spawned the slum. Henry George's *Progress and Poverty* (1879) and Edward Bellamy's *Looking Backward* (1888), two widely read radical critiques of American society, usually scared rather than converted their affluent audiences. Going further than Brace's philanthropic solutions but stopping short of Bellamy's advocacy of socialism, Riis demonstrated the urgency of a workable middle path that utilized all resources. Everyone had a stake in combating the slums, Riis stated in *How the Other Half Lives,* because they bred crime, epidemics, paupers, moral decay, and corrupt government. To remove this blight would require a moral crusade and a multifaceted assault combining charity work, individual regeneration, governmental action, and shrewd business enterprise. Once people answered all problems with "law and order," he proclaimed, but "with our enormously swelling population held in this galling bondage, will that answer always be given?" (pp. 2–4).

The Immigrant Quarters

Riis subtitled his book *Studies among the Tenements of New York.* His focus was on the effect that bad housing had on immigrant families, especially the so-called children of the tenements.[11] "All life eventually accommodates itself to its environment, and human life is no exception," he wrote. He warned that without sufficient space to move, fresh air to breathe, or esthetic pleasures to enjoy, people would lose their capacity for any "gentle thought and aspiration above the mere wants of the body. . . ." By the standards of the slum a respectable neighborhood was one that had a trace of greenery and no more than four saloons to each block. Yet in the midst of these degrading circumstances Riis wondered at the countless personal struggles of heroism "against fearful odds" to overcome the oppressive milieu (pp. 120–22).

Riis traced the genesis of the tenement to the spacious homes of New York's former knickerbocker aristocracy, who sold out to real estate dealers early in the nineteenth century. Reacting to the new conditions of industrialization and immigration, the owners subdivided the floors, partitioned the rooms, and constructed rear tenements "in the old garden[s]

where the stolid Dutch burgher grew his tulips or early cab-
bages . . ." (pp. 6–7). By the 1840s the tenement districts in
east Manhattan were already squalid and overcrowded. After
viewing the scene, Charles Dickens castigated the buildings as
leprous and unspeakable, worse than in London. During the
1880s, 290,000 people lived on 1 square mile of land, often 20
in a room, paying more for their dilapidated quarters than
others paid elsewhere.[12]

Using his favorite device of acting as a tour-guide, Riis
recreated Mulberry Bend, which lurked in the shadows of his
newspaper office and was to the reporter the apotheosis of
evil and neglect. During the 1860s governmental officials had
declared that almost all of the Bend's 609 tenements were a
menace to public health. But in 1889 they still stood. Riis
wrote that "the whole district is a maze of narrow, often un-
suspected passageways—necessarily, for there is scarce a lot
that has not two, three, or four tenements upon it, swarming
with unwholesome crowds" (p. 43). Sections of the Bend had
appropriate sobriquets such as Kerosene Row, Bone Alley,
Bottle Alley, Thieves' Alley, and Bandits' Roost. Murder and
abuse were common in this locale, with absentee landlords
conspicuous among the criminals.

In graphic detail Riis took his readers into a back alley
which was "just about one step wide, with a five-story house
on one side that gets its light and air—God help us for pitiful
mockery!—from this slit between brick walls." One wall had
no windows; a fire escape straddled the two sides, touching
each. He stated that the sun "never shone into the alley from
the day the devil planned and man built it." In a typical
dwelling were a darkened hallway and the odors of poisoned
sewage, a saloon was adjacent. "Here is a door. Listen! That
short hacking cough, that tiny, helpless wail—what do they
mean?" Riis asked. Another child dying. "With half a chance
it might have lived but it had none. That dark bedroom killed
it," he concluded (pp. 31–34).

Summer in the tenements was the worst time of the year.
The heat made indoor life almost insufferable, and the crowded

quarters caused epidemics. Riis told of a woman who attempted to kill her own child after she could obtain no food with which to nourish the infant. On another occasion Riis and a doctor visited a three-room flat that housed six adults and five children who slept on straw-filled boxes. Near the stove a baby lay dying from malnutrition and a lack of fresh air. From the physician's thermometer Riis learned that the temperature of the room was 115 degrees. The pains of life and the shortage of good water drove people to the plentiful taverns, often the only cheerful and "humanly decent" place on the block. Yet Riis believed that the saloons undermined decency by breaking up families, corrupting youngsters, and further pauperizing the downtrodden. He concluded that it "saps the very vitals of society, undermines its strongest defenses, and delivers them over to the enemy" (pp. 48–49, 124–29, 159–63).

In the fourth ward there lived a colony of blind beggars in an area which residents named Blind Man's Alley. Daniel Murphy, their landlord, made a half-million-dollar profit from his occupants, and then in his old age he lost his sight also. When the Board of Health forced him to repair his property, Murphy protested that his tenants were "not fit to live in a nice house." Once every June the city distributed twenty thousand dollars to the blind. On that evening the sightless beggars sang and drank and played their fiddles in celebration. Riis recounted that on this occasion, "Even the blind landlord rejoices, for much of the money goes into his coffers" (pp. 24–26).

Riis's descriptions of living conditions shocked most of his readers but commanded their attention, and his personal sketches of slum residents gained their affection. With vivid strokes he described the multitude of cultures and personalities among New York's polyglot population which he called "this queer conglomerate mass." Concerning the mixed crowd of Italians, Irish, Germans, eastern Europeans, Poles, Chinese, Bohemians, and other national groups, Riis declared with considerable exaggeration that "the one thing you shall vainly ask for in the chief city of America is a distinctively American community. There is none; certainly not among the tenements" (pp. 15–16).

Measuring immigrant societies against his own cultural traditions, which had more in common with the upper class than with the "other half," Riis's yardstick of approval corresponded in part to how well an ethnic group adopted American habits and values. Although he showed much compassion for the plight of immigrants, the Danish-American author was somewhat cavalier in describing their manner of living and used simplistic clichés in characterizing groups. To Riis the Italians seemed clannish, the Bohemians easygoing, and too often the Jews worshiped at the altar of greed. He desired the Americanization of the immigrant, and so he was insensitive at times to habits that were barriers to this goal. Yet he did not so much denigrate ethnic customs as social patterns that were exaggerated or even created by conditions in the American ghetto. The dislocations of the slum caused many foreign-born residents to cling tenaciously to old-world customs. Often their offspring mocked them and abandoned respect for all primary-group ties. Both of these extremes Riis thought to be dangerous.

Riis devoted a chapter of his book to the Italian immigrants. He pilloried the padrone system whereby financiers lured peasants to the United States with false promises of opportunity and then exploited their ignorance by locating them in vile tenements and hiring them out to employers for a pittance. Many Italians became scavengers and ragpickers for contractors who paid officials for the privilege of inspecting the refuse at the city dump. The Italians made less trouble than the Irish, he said, and were usually "gay, light-hearted and . . . inoffensive as a child" (p. 41). They seldom protested against their wretched housing but were clannish and preferred to avenge feuds privately than to call upon the police. Italian society had a closeknit, hierarchical structure with well-defined obligations and rights. Riis understood the need for this tight organization for maintaining order, stability, and status in the face of a hostile and atavistic environment. Nevertheless, while admiring certain Italian customs, he felt it necessary to pry apart others to make the Italians better Americans. For instance, he praised the colorful religious festivals which symbolized hope and unified the community, but he condemned the rowdy Sunday card playing and the frequent vengeance murders which occurred in the Italian districts.[13]

Riis's pen captured the colorful and picturesque culture of the Italian communities, the swarms of laughing children, the earnest hucksters and peddlers with their fish and sausages and fruit and vegetables, the lively gossip of the women, and the fragile dignity of the old patriarchs. He admired the warm ingenuity and zestful nature of the people, even though he thought their habits were somewhat sloppy. He wrote that "When the sun shines the entire population seeks the street, carrying on its household work, its bargaining, its love-making on street or sidewalk, or idling there when it has nothing better to do, with the reverse of the impulse that makes the Polish Jew coop himself up in his den with the thermometer at stewing heat" (p. 43).

Riis's portrayal of New York's Jews was paradoxical because he admired the premises of their ethical code but believed that Jews were, on the whole, too materialistic. Revealing his religious prejudices, Riis wrote that despite the exhortations of Christian preachers, the Jews were "stubbornly refusing to see the light." In the Jewish neighborhood, he stated, thrift was "at once its strength and its fatal weakness, its cardinal virtue and its foul disgrace" (pp. 77–78). Children labored almost from birth, and families packed in lodgers in the hope that they could turn from the exploited to the exploiters. Riis praised the work of Jewish philanthropic organizations such as the Baron de Hirsch Fund and the United Hebrew Charities, but he added that the ignorance of the immigrants often frustrated such admirable programs as farm colonies and vocational schools.

Many Jewish immigrants from Russia, Poland, and other eastern European countries worked in tenement sweatshops. Riis described how the typical sweater in the clothing industry took advantage of the plentiful labor supply and the financial distress and isolation of his employees to circumvent factory and child labor laws. With "merciless severity" the sweater smothered "every symptom of awakening intelligence in his slaves" (p. 90). During a visit to a two-room apartment, the author came upon a family of five who worked from daybreak until nine at night, sewing, finishing, and ironing trousers. They sold them to a manufacturer at a profit of 5 cents a dozen. Supplementing this income by taking in boarders, the family earned $25 a week and paid $20 a month rent for the two rooms. Riis concluded: "At the least calculation, probably, this sweater's family hoards up thirty dollars a month, and in a few years will own a tenement somewhere and profit by the example set by their landlord in rent-collecting" (p. 94).

Rivaling the clothing sweatshops in abasement were the tenement cigar factories. Legions of workers, primarily Bohemians, made cigars by stripping tobacco leaves, breaking bits into filler, and then wrapping it up into a finished product. Landlords held this class of tenants "in virtual serfdom" by binding their rent to the terms of their employment. The exploitation of the Bohemians, according to Riis, constituted "a slavery as real as any that ever disgraced the South" (p. 101). Entire families labored from seventy-five to one hundred hours a week each. Riis reported that a typical household received only $11 for the three thousand cigars they made each week, and then they had to pay $12.25 a month rent to the manufacturer. Such outrageous and barbarian treatment, Riis predicted, would make it not unnatural for the Bohemians, a gregarious and passionate people, to rebel against the system which perpetrated the injustices upon them.

Of all the ethnic groups which Riis analyzed, he had least sympathy for the Chinese, perhaps because he saw little hope of assimilating them into American life. "Between the tabernacles of Jewry and the shrines of the Bend," he wrote, "Joss has cheekily planted his pagan worship of idols, chief

among which are the celestial worshiper's own gain and
lusts." Riis was unable to understand the mysterious Chinese;
he needlessly concluded that "In their very exclusiveness and
reserve they are a constant and terrible menace to society. . . ."
Even their cleanliness he compared to a cat which lived by
cruel cunning. Riis ridiculed their pigtails and fan tan games
and decried the way the Chinese trapped white girls into
their lairs with opium. He urged the police to use the "harsh-
est repressive measures" against this vice. On the other hand,
he suggested that the government allow Chinese women to
come to America in order to transfer the Chinamen's lusts for
white girls. Undesirable and useless as they were, he concluded,
"they are here, and . . . having let them in, we must make the
best of it" (pp. 67-76).

Riis's commentary on New York's black residents mixed
compassion with condescension. This dichotomy sprang from
his partial acceptance of racist stereotypes and concurrently
his deeper commitment to the premise that environment was
the controlling factor in personality development. In the past
Riis had sometimes portrayed black men as strong but dim-
witted. In 1885, writing of a man who got up unhurt after he
fell head-first from a third-story window, he foolishly stated,
"No one but a Negro could possibly have performed that
feat." [14]

In *How the Other Half Lives* Riis presented an image of
the black man as cheerfully working at menial jobs for which
"his past traditions and natural love of ease" perhaps fit him
best. He wrote, however, that "his ludicrous incongruities,
his sensuality and his lack of moral accountability, his superstition and other faults . . . are the effect of temperament and
of centuries of slavery. . . ." What happened, he concluded,
was that the black people emulated the worst characteristics
of their former masters, as evidenced by their love of expen-
sive luxuries. He looked with horror on the mixing of black
men and white women at lewd dance halls that were "the
worst of the desperately bad." Than the mingling of "the
utterly depraved of both sexes, white and black, on such

ground, there can be no greater abomination," Riis concluded (pp. 111–17).

Despite the misgivings which Riis harbored as a result of his inaccurate and simplistic understanding of black culture, in *How the Other Half Lives* he expressed admiration for the Negro's religious faith, his love of citizenship and his desire for education. And he came out squarely against the closed system of housing which black people faced when they immigrated to New York. Landlords, in their lust for profits, deliberately and brutally drew color lines and heightened racial tensions, Riis wrote, in order to make "the prejudice in which he traffics pay him well" (p. 110). He rejected the myth that Negroes were inherently dirty, pointing out that black tenements on 99th Street were cleaner than the Italian ghettos. If vile surroundings debased men, Riis believed, then good housing could uplift them.

One group whom Riis despised fitted no exclusive ethnic or social category: the tramp. Borrowing the rhetoric and using the statistics of the Charity Organization Society, Riis fulminated against paupers who eschewed work for panhandling. Such men contributed nothing to society and consumed all of their energy in inventing ways to deceive the public. Some of them even mutilated children whom they used to gain alms, he claimed. On seventeen separate occasions one lady requested money to give her deceased husband a proper burial. In *How the Other Half Lives* he declared that "There is enough of real suffering in the homes of the poor to make one wish that there were some effective way of enforcing Paul's plan of starving the drones into the paths of self-support: no work, nothing to eat" (p. 191). Riis recommended the outlawry of begging, except for the blind. He believed that labor bureaus, workhouses, asylums, and private philanthropy could take care of the needy.

The Wrecks and the Waste

All immigrant groups in the tenements shared common problems, and the weak perished. Riis cogently told of the toll in wasted lives. In 1889, 140,000 people were jammed into the city's jails, workhouses, almshouses, foundling homes, insane asylum, or charity hospital. In addition, 14,000 men each night slept in unsanitary lodging houses. One of ten New Yorkers ended up in Potter's Field, the burial ground of paupers. Riis wrote: "The Potter's Field stands ever for utter, hopeless surrender. The last the poor will let go, however miserable their lot in life, is the hope of a decent burial" (p. 185).

Children were the most helpless against the slum. Life denied most of them the joys of childhood or the benefits of formal education. Many worked almost from infancy to help their family keep from starving. Young girls often labored eighty hours a week to earn a paltry two dollars and had to pay fines for tardiness and other mistakes. Orphans who escaped the founding asylum often became "street Arabs" or runaway vagabonds, who lived or died in the streets by their cunning. Gangs of young toughs were common on every corner. They offered the sons of immigrants a source of identity, companionship and pride, but Riis lamented that their objectives were usually crime and bravado.

With intolerable conditions in existence and with the gap ever widening between rich and poor, Riis held up the specter of revolution if reform was not forthcoming. "The sea of a mighty population, held in galling fetters, heaves uneasily in the tenements," he warned, and the time for counseling patience or preaching a hollow Christianity had passed (p. 226). Churches had to cease being slum landlords and accessories to an inadequate system. They needed to take up the social gospel in order to keep the faith and save themselves. The only possible paths were justice or violence. Riis warned the wealthy of the consequences of inactivity in an oft-quoted parable:

A man stood at the corner of Fifth Avenue and Fourteenth Street the other day, looking gloomily at the carriages that rolled by, carrying the wealth and fashion of the avenues to and from the big stores down town. He was poor, and hungry, and ragged. This thought was in his mind: "They behind their well-fed teams have no thought for the morrow; they know hunger only by name, and ride down to spend in an hour's shopping what would keep me and my little ones from want a whole year." There rose up before him the picture of those little ones crying for bread around the cold and cheerless hearth—then he sprang into the throng and slashed around him with a knife, blindly seeking to kill, to revenge (pp. 199–200).

In contrast to Riis's optimistic temperament, a foreboding tone pervaded the book. In part Riis did this for shock value rather than as a prediction of doom. Hoping for a moral awakening, he nevertheless knew well the failures of a half-century. The foes of change were ignorance and apathy. The floodtide of immigration rendered useless today the palliatives of the past, he wrote. Often do-gooders faced the resistance of the poor themselves, whose short-term necessities conflicted with their long-range interests. Merely to survive, many families had to take in boarders, send their children to work, act as strikebreakers, or even steal. Slum dwellers, he wrote, were often "shiftless, destructive, and stupid, in a word they are what the tenements made them." He cited an example of a benevolent owner who installed new plumbing, faucets, and wooden closets in his tenement. The occupants used the wood for fires, pawned the faucets, and flooded the building when they pulled up the pipes. After that debacle, the owner became "a firm believer in the total depravity of tenement-house people." The tragedy, Riis said, was that the landlord could have turned his model tenement into a profitable enterprise if he had been a better teacher and manager (pp. 207–8).

In *How the Other Half Lives* Riis called for an end to the economic policy of laissez-faire, which he branded as a smokescreen for selfishness. Private rights had to bend to public interests. Should not laborers have the right to decent housing, even if it infringes on the property rights of others, Riis asked. He pointed out that some absentee landlords even resided in Europe. "It is easy enough to convince a man that he ought not to harbor the thief who steals people's property," he stated; "but to make him see that he has no right to slowly kill his neighbors, or his tenants, by making a death-trap of his house, seems to be the hardest of all tasks" (p. 205).

The final chapter of *How the Other Half Lives* examined "How the Case Stands." Riis concluded that the health and security of all Americans depended upon decent housing. He wrote that if there was a revolution of the poor, "no human power may avail to check it." Cognizant that tenements would not disappear since suburban housing was too costly and impractical for most workers, he called for governmental regulation to make it "unprofitable to own a bad tenement." The state had the duty to tear down the worst buildings and force owners to remodel others. And private enterprise, spurred by moral purpose and self-interest—"philanthropy and five per cent"—should build model tenements. In order to underscore his theme that reform was more than a matter for the idealists, Riis concluded his book with this admonitory poem by James Russell Lowell: "Think ye that building shall endure/Which shelters the noble and crushes the poor?" Thus, slum conditions constituted a clear and present danger to the established institutions, whose military arsenals were scant insurance against a bitter harvest (pp. 215–22, 226).

Impact of How the Other Half Lives

How the Other Half Lives received favorable critical acclaim and quickly gained great popularity, thereby establishing Riis as an expert on urban life. James Russell Lowell told the author that "I had but a vague idea of these horrors before you brought them home to me."[15] Through his dramatic and anecdotal style, Riis had brought the slum to life, made it comprehensible and therefore not quite so fearful. *How the Other Half Lives* was extremely timely in unraveling the mysteries of the big city in a manner that reenforced the traditional values of love, justice, and moral responsibility that were rooted in small communities. Riis defined the slums as the symbol and gauge of society. Their inhabitants were neither immoral dolts who deserved their fate nor happy and noble people. Rather, they were what environment made them, potentially dangerous but, more hopefully capable of becoming good citizens. Riis wanted to wipe out poverty before the culture of the slum affected younger generations and hardened into permanent patterns for individuals, families, communities, and ultimately, the nation. He called on Americans not to construct a new system but to modernize their methods to realize the goals of the past.

How the Other Half Lives reached the public during the same year as did a book about the manners of New York's upper class, Samuel Ward McAllister's Society As I Have Found It. McAllister's portrayal of opulence and ostentatious display reenforced Riis's central theme of poverty in the midst of plenty. Reviewers contrasted the two books and repeated Riis's warning of an impending storm. The True Nationalist wrote: "The bullet-proof shutters, the stacks of hand-grenades and gatling guns of the sub-treasury" show that society foolishly chose to arm itself rather than reform "our cursed, unclean and disgraceful tenement-house system. . . ."[16]

Reviewers also compared How the Other Half Lives with two other contemporary books, John Peter Altgeld's Live Questions and William Booth's In Darkest England. Altgeld's book, a reprint of his speeches and articles, focused on the problems of workingmen in Chicago. Although it concentrated more on labor-management relations than did How the Other Half Lives, the tone of Live Questions was similar to that of Riis's book. In Darkest England, which William T. Stead ghost-write for the leader of the Salvation Army, was a comprehensive study of the slums of London and an indictment of public apathy toward the victims of industrial progress. Riis believed that it sparked sales of his own book. Most reviewers agreed with Lyman Abbott of the Christian

Union that Riis's work was the more graphic and effective, largely because of the realistic photographs of the Bend, the lodging houses, the sweatshops, back alleys, and, most of all, the chilling expressions of the poor. Booth himself admired *How the Other Half Lives,* and his magazine *War Cry* reprinted some of its more poignant passages.

A reviewer for the *Critic,* however, called Booth's treatment of London's poor more sympathetic and noted Riis's "lack of broad and penetrative vision, a singularly warped sense of justice at times, and a roughness amounting almost to brutality."[17]

Riis's portrayal of the Chinese and, to a lesser degree, other ethnic groups warranted criticism. While not unsympathetic toward immigrants, *How the Other Half Lives* contained racial slurs which others could use to support nativistic shibboleths and restrictionist legislation. Ironically, the racial stereotypes, which detracted from the book's veracity, probably widened its appeal with middle class readers. Riis's goal of Americanizing the immigrant perhaps blinded him into too great a desire for cultural homogeneity. Other humanitarian reformers, faced with the magnitude of their problems and the frustrations in improving the quality of urban life, made similar charges. The gentle Jane Addams mentioned the "pathetic stupidity" of so many tenement house residents in her autobiographical *Twenty Years at Hull-House* (1910). In *Civilization's Inferno* (1893) Benjamin O. Flower, the muckraking editor of *Arena,* referred to Boston slums as "reservoirs of physical and moral death. . . ."[18] But while Booth and Flower emphasized sin as the root of human misery and degradation, Riis held the cause to be largely environmental and thus amenable to public treatment.

Within Riis's mind warred two contradictory impulses regarding ghetto residents, one benign and the other backward-looking. On the one hand, he rejected explanations of poverty based upon inherent biological differences among races. Since all people were basically alike in potential, Riis argued, tenement ghettos were unnatural aberrations. Their residents were decent human beings whose aspirations were the same as native Americans but whose poverty sprang from inequality of opportunity. On the other hand, he believed in the cultural superiority of Anglo-American institutions and in an upright code of conduct. Describing habits of ghetto residents which he found loathsome, such as sloth, vice, clannishness, intemperance, and superstition, he explained that they were vestiges of Old World ways or spurious by-products of the slums. But at times his indictments of ethnic customs revealed a class and race snobbery. This trace of condescension toward "this queer conglomerate mass" became less pronounced later in life, but Riis never totally suppressed it.

More important than the shortcomings of *How the Other Half Lives* were its beneficial consequences. Ushering a generation of examination into all aspects of American life, the book educated great numbers of middle and upper class Americans about the seamier side of the American scene but also the human side of that scene. It evoked the compassionate lump in the throat, the tears of sorrow or perhaps guilt, in the place of vague uneasiness. In the words of Sam Bass Warner, Jr., he "painted a colorful landscape of the lower East Side, so that poverty became an interesting subject for social tourism. . . ." Patrician organizations such as the People's Municipal League of New York, which prior to 1890 had been interested primarily in honest government, began compiling remedies for slum conditions. *How the Other Half Lives* stirred the conscience of a generation of young activists, many of whom worked to blot out the ills which Riis described. Louis H. Pink, a settlement house worker and housing expert, John Jay Chapman, an innovator in neighborhood redevelopment, and Ernest Poole, an author, social worker, and socialist reformer—all three men and many more attested to the book's effect in jolting them out of their complacency. Riis also set conditions for a new emphasis on realism in fiction. After *How the Other Half Lives,* the public searched out books such as Stephen Crane's *Maggie: A Girl of the Streets* (1893) and William T. Stead's *If Christ Came to Chicago* (1895). Establishing Riis as an expert on urban problems, the book opened up new opportunities for his espousal of the gospel of reform. And hereafter his utterances had a new authority.[19]

Thus, fame came to Riis because he was able to make life in the slums knowable to affluent Americans. Almost a half-century after the publication of *How the Other Half Lives,* James Ford concluded that "Jacob A. Riis probably had greater influence than any other publicist [during the 1890s] in calling attention in a graphic manner to the evils of slum dwelling. . . . " Riis believed that if people knew the facts about the tenement house ghettos, they would act to eradicate the evils. Otherwise, their ignorance, apathy, and shortsightedness threatened the health, morals, prosperity, and political system of the nation. *How the Other Half Lives* was a book "whose time had come in 1890," to quote historians Charles N. Glaab and A. Theodore Brown, but it also has a timeless relevance. Despite the author's limitations as a social scientist, Sam Bass Warner, Jr., concluded, Riis conveyed the message that every city dweller deserved "a decent house, a decent job, a decent school, fresh air, clean water, and safety against fire, epidemic, and crime. He never lost sight of these basic urban rights of being human."[20]

5

THE PUBLICIST OF SLUM LIFE

Jacob Riis spent the first four years of the 1890s as a publicist for reform, stirring the conscience of interested Americans with articles and speeches about the crisis conditions of city slums. In his activities as a news reporter, Riis tended to hasten from one scene of distress to another, and then another, always seeming in search of a new, fresh, exciting story for his readers. He paused to lend a helping hand to the sufferers, but the requirements of his profession caused him to leave the scene before he had absorbed a complete understanding of what he saw and wherein the solution lay. Nevertheless, the ubiquitous nature of his job enabled him to gain perspectives into poverty which other reformers missed. During these years he deepened his understanding of the role of government in bettering the life of common people, from contact with fellow reformers whom he met on his lecture tours, such as Jane Addams and Richard T. Ely. He examined welfare programs to ameliorate want in Denmark and Great Britain. Out of these experiences Riis emerged advocating a series of practical programs to reconstruct a more equitable urban environment.

Dean of Mulberry Street

In November 1890 the forty-one-year-old Riis commenced work at Charles A. Dana's New York *Evening Sun*. Previously he had broken ties with the New York *Tribune* and the Associated Press Bureau, selling stories to any newspaper that wanted them. The *Evening Sun's* salary offer of fifty dollars a week was less than he had made by freelancing, but he supplemented his income by occasionally writing feature stories for other newspapers. He briefly considered giving up the whirligig world of police reporting to concentrate his energies on books, magazine articles, and lectures. But the steady salary and the opportunities that Mulberry Street gave him for good copy caused him to stay.[1]

The owner of the *Evening Sun,* Charles A. Dana, had pioneered in the sponsorship of personal journalism. Cynical, fiercely independent, and competitive, Dana searched out bizarre articles which contained vignettes of life's passions. A good human interest story, the editor believed, captivated his readers' attention as much as great political events. Once Dana's chief assistant and alter ego John Bogart told a young reporter that "When a dog bites a man, that is not news, because it happens so often. But if a man bites a dog, *that* is news." During the 1880s and 1890s Dana employed such journalists as Arthur Brisbane, David Graham Phillips, Samuel Hopkins Adams, Julian Ralph, Will Irwin, and Richard Harding Davis to work for his morning and evening papers. His hiring of Riis was an indication of how well the police reporter had mastered his craft and increased his status.[2]

To relieve himself from some of the time-consuming duties of reporting, Riis in February 1891 hired an assistant, Max Fischel, to be his messenger and news gatherer. Fischel, a boyish and energetic Jew who idolized Riis, worked well in tandem with his boss. Riis saw in him the image of his younger self. Whereas most other reporters used assistants only for petty assignments, he treated Fischel as a junior partner and trusted him enough to write articles straight from his notes.

Lincoln Steffens, a correspondent for the New York *Evening Post*, wrote that "Riis was growing old, but he had found and trained his boy, Max, to see and to understand as Riis did; and Max could see." When the two men covered an event together, Max usually collected details and statistics while the older man stood back from the scene and studied it for perspective and color. Commenting years later on a disaster which they reported, Fischel stated: "We found an excited, wailing crowd. I was so busy trying to get the facts that I lost sight of him for a moment. Suddenly I looked up the block and saw Jake standing on a doorstep—just standing. He was listening to the moans of the crowd as the sounds moved up and down the street. The moans of those poor people made his story."[3]

Riis's reform sentiments conflicted with the usual editorial policy of the New York *Evening Sun*, but despite their political differences the brusque Dana and effusive Riis admired and respected each other. The editor allowed the reporter a wide latitude and lightened his duties during lecture tours. Recounting Dana's last day at work before retiring, in *The Making of an American*, Riis remembered that the "old chief" met him on the steps of the *Sun's* office and exclaimed: "Well, have you reformed everything to suit you, straightened out every kink in town?" Riis replied that his greatest disappointment was Dana's newspapers, which were as reactionary as ever. Dana shook his hand and laughed. Thirty years previously, when the tattered immigrant had first applied for work at the *Sun*, Dana had turned him down with an extended hand which contained a dollar in it, a present which Riis haughtily spurned (pp. 371–74).

In 1891 Riis scored his most important triumph as a reporter; his investigative journalism helped avert a cholera epidemic and brought about a pure water supply for New York City. In August Riis noticed a health department bulletin which mentioned the existence of nitrates in the city's water reservoir at Croton Watershed. He promptly wrote an article warning the public to boil all water before consuming it, and then he hurried to the source of the trouble. During a week-

long investigation he discovered that people bathed in and
dumped their sewage into streams which flowed into the Croton
River. Taking many pictures of the polluted water, and combining them with lucid prose, he sent off a story entitled "Some
Things We Drink," which appeared on 21 August in the
Evening Sun. When skeptics claimed that the water purified
itself, Riis produced health department testimony purporting
to show that cholera bacilli could live for a week in water. He
concluded that inaction might result in an "inconceivable
calamity." As a result of his personal campaign, the state
purchased land near the Croton River and adjacent streams
to prevent disease and a possible plague.[4]

When Lincoln Steffens became a police reporter in 1892,
Riis introduced him to the brutality of New York's methods
of maintaining order. Showing Steffens the interior of Mulberry Street station, he told his new friend to make the police
fearful of him or else they would not respect him. They spotted
two policemen carrying a man who had obviously been the
victim of a beating. "That's a prisoner," Steffens remembered
his colleague as saying. "Maybe he's done something wrong,
that miserable Russian Jew; anyway he's done something the
police don't like." Riis explained that Alec Williams, the
enforcer on police chief Thomas Byrne's staff, frequently
flogged his adversaries with a nightstick. Hang around William's office every morning, he told Steffens, and listen to the
stories of the prisoners who left with broken heads. Many
were unionists whose only crime was striking against intolerable wages and working conditions. No paper would print the
accounts, Riis added, but Steffens would understand the system. At that moment "Clubber" Williams slammed shut his
office door. Riis gave out a loud laugh, but its tone was not
one of merriment. As Steffens looked at his companion, he
remembered in his *Autobiography,* "There was bold rage in
his face, as he left me, banging out of the building" (pp.
205–7).

Deeply admiring Riis as the dean of his trade, the skeptical Steffens nevertheless wondered at his colleague's faith

that the forces of good would triumph in the city. Steffens was a democrat who once said that "Not many educated individuals are as wise as the mass of men." Yet he felt that the people had to earn good government, that a few reformers could not provide it as if it were charity. When Steffens attempted to vocalize his political theories, Riis replied that abstractions were irrelevant to New York's needs. Steffens later wrote: "I could think aloud more clearly with my mother-in-law than with Riis and other reporters. She was neither religious nor cynical." Steffens's analytical mind contrasted with Riis's, whose beliefs sprang from his heart and who insulated himself against the worst tales of depravity. Vice and crime and corruption were important to Riis primarily as illustrations of an imperfect and dangerous environment and thus as moral parables. Once Max Fischel started telling him about a police raid on homosexuals. According to Steffens's *Autobiography,* when Max used the word "fairies," Riis became confused and asked what the word meant. Rejecting the explanation, Riis shouted out "Not so. There are no such creatures in this world." He left the room and refused to write up the account (pp. 223, 241, 257).[5]

Publicist for Progressive Change

During 1891 Riis expanded his lecture schedule and gave illustrated talks about a wide variety of urban needs and problems, including housing, child labor, parks and playgrounds, immigration restriction, and the abolition of sweatshops and police lodging houses. Because of the limitations of his job, he spoke most often in the New York area. In May, however, Riis addressed members of the General Conference of Charities in Boston on the evils of tenement sweatshops. He emphasized the inhumanity of a slave labor system which bred disease, drove out better competitive businesses, and thwarted labor unions. He implored health departments to end the worst abuses immediately, and he advocated a constitutional amendment that would wipe out all sweatshops. In July Riis took part in the Chautauqua summer university in southwestern New York, along with such noted celebrities as the Spencerian philosopher John Fiske, the historian John Bach McMaster, the Reverend Edward Everett Hale, and the feminist Julia Ward Howe. In November he spoke in Washington, D.C., to a convention of "Christians at Work." In his address he castigated wealthy Americans who ignored the poor, but praised such patrons of charity as Mrs. William H. Vanderbilt, whose husband had allegedly said, "The public be damned!"[6]

The most direct method that Riis employed in his campaign of education about the slums was the guided tour. On 27 November 1891 he escorted three British noblewomen, including Lady Henry Somerset, on a personal inspection of New York's poverty areas. Lady Somerset, the president of a London temperance society, was the vice-president of the King's Daughters, the organization which Riis had persuaded to found a social settlement. Starting out at 10:30 P.M., the group visited Mulberry Bend. When Riis pointed out the opium dens of the Chinese, the women "looked upon the scene with sternness and pity mingled in their faces," according to the account the next day in the New York *Evening Sun*. The reporter then showed them the rear tenements and back alleys which he had made notorious in *How the Other Half Lives*. Spotting peddlers sleeping in trash basements, Lady Somerset cried out "Horrible, oh horrible." At two in the morning, the foursome arrived at the Mulberry Street police station and observed the lodging quarters. Riis had intended to continue the tour, but the ladies were too tired and discouraged to go on.

During 1892 Riis turned his attention to the enormous problem of child labor in New York. On 18 March 1892 the *Evening Sun* carried the feature "Real Wharf Rats," in which Riis portrayed Italian children living under the wharf at the city dump. They existed on the refuse that they could scrape together from the offal of society. During the summer Riis gave six lectures in New York, Ohio, and Michigan, in which he claimed that child labor was "eating into the vitals of the nation" and related that a million children in New York alone halted their education out of the necessity to work for their families. At the same time *Scribner's* magazine began printing chapters of his new book *The Children of the Poor,* which described in dreary detail the plight of youths who lived in the tenements.

The theme of *The Children of the Poor,* which appeared in book form in October 1892, was the debilitating effect of the slum environment on its human offspring. Its tone was at once more militant and more hopeful of improvement than that of *How the Other Half Lives* had been. "The story of inhuman packing of human swarms, of bitter poverty and of landlord greed, of darkness and squalor and misery, which these tenements have to tell, is equaled, I suppose, nowhere in a civilized land," he wrote. Yet he was cautiously optimistic in his prognosis that Americans were responding to the problem. He pointed to the establishment of institutions that were beginning to replace the saloons and the street as formative influences upon children—nurseries, kindergartens, social settlements, industrial schools, neighborhood clubs, playgrounds, and Fresh Air Funds.[7]

Some of the book's statements provoked bitter criticism from within New York's tenement districts, especially Riis's attack on unrestricted immigration of untrained persons into New York and doubts he cast on the legitimacy of certain labor unions. Radicals dismissed as naive Riis's faith that men of good will could salvage the American political and economic system. Some members of College Settlement, for which the author did volunteer work, resented his characterization of tenement dwellers as breeders of paupers and criminals. Riis told them that he had directed his indictment at the perpetrators of the environment, not its victims.[8]

Riis liked *The Children of the Poor* better than his first book. It was more solidly rooted in quantitative data and received better reviews than had *How the Other Half Lives,* but it never sold as well. Perhaps, for most people, one guided tour of the slum was enough.

Speaking about the exploitation of innocent children during his spring lecture tour of 1893, Riis met many humanitarian reformers who shared common purpose with him. In the Middle West Riis spoke at Hull-House and many other settlement houses, churches, and colleges, and began friendships with settlement workers Jane Addams, Julia Lathrop, and Florence Kelley, who like him were advocates of making the health and happiness of the individual the foremost purpose of government. In Madison, Wisconsin, Riis met Richard T. Ely, a tight-laced economics professor who advocated stronger governmental control over private enterprise. Ely introduced speaker Riis to the members of his Congregational church. On 29 March 1893, in response to a complimentary letter from Endicott Peabody, the energetic and puritanical headmaster of Groton School in Massachusetts, Riis offered to address his students. After spending a weekend at Groton in May, he told his host that he considered Peabody and his wife among his "cherished friends."[9]

Riis told Peabody on 1 April 1893 that his role as an urban reformer was simply to demonstrate "the *facts* as the foundation for other and wiser minds to build upon. . . ." Slowly he came to realize, however, that his articles were more cogent if they were didactic, that is, if they ended with specific proposals for action. Therefore, he supported the aims of experts such as health officials, social workers, labor leaders, settlement workers, and enlightened businessmen. Blending their conclusions with his own preconceptions, Riis began to formulate a unified blueprint of positive programs to reconstruct the slums.

Home to Denmark

For three months during the summer of 1893, Jacob and Elisabeth and their four children vacationed in Europe. For

Riis it was the first trip to Denmark since his wedding, although he had kept in close touch with his family. Arriving in Copenhagen in June, they visited Elisabeth's mother, who was living modestly since her husband had lost most of their money and then died. Jacob had despised Elisabeth's stepfather since childhood and told his sister Emma that "I am glad that I should not see that man more." When he arrived in Ribe, he found that little had changed in two decades. The watchman still cried the hour, and the same country doctor made neighborhood calls in his ancient buggy.[10]

During his European trip Riis inspected the slum conditions in London. In an article entitled "London's East Side," which the *Evening Sun* printed on 19 August 1893, he described the overcrowded flats, dark alleys, and repugnant filth of the English tenements. He admired model tenement projects but complained that the British made almost no attempt to regulate living conditions. When Riis noticed people living in damp, windowless cellars, he told his guide that New York's health code prevented such practices. According to Riis, the guide responded with surprise, "I thought yours was a free country." Riis replied: "So it is. Freedom to poison yourself or your neighbor excluded."

The memory which Riis cherished most about the European trip was his reunion with his father. Niels Riis had shown his son the Dannebrog Medal, symbolizing service to country, which King Christian had presented to the old schoolmaster. Unknown to his father, Jacob had been instrumental in getting the Danish government to consider bestowing the honor. Four months after the reunion of father and son, Niels died. When Jacob heard the sad news, he wrote that he felt "like a man who has suddenly lost his background and stands alone in an open desert." He lamented that his mother would live only for the past; her "connection with today is broken, never to be mended." His father had been his friend and counselor in manhood. Riis concluded that "He was, as it were, the link between the past and the present for me." He had taught Jacob to love family, church, and nation and the language of America.

Riis thanked God that in 1893 he had taken his children to him.[11]

Riis's Danish background remained important to him all his life and conditioned the directions of his activities. At home his family observed many Danish customs, such as a Christmas Eve festival of caroling and eating the traditional old-country dinner of roasted goose, apple cake and risingrod. More important to his public life was his desire to maintain primary-group ties of family and community values which he esteemed from his youth in Denmark and romanticized as he grew older. Finally he studied with interest welfare measures of the Danish government and the practices of private charities. In 1873 Denmark had established old age pensions and factory inspection and had taken action to reduce child labor. During the 1890s other welfare measures followed, such as unemployment compensation, state accident insurance, and labor-management arbitration courts on the model of Bismarck's Germany. Measured against these advances in social justice, the prevailing American credo of laissez-faire seemed hollow and hardly God-ordained.[12]

Battling against Police Lodging Houses

In 1893 Riis's advocacy of the abolition of police lodging houses led him to serve on the Committee on Vagrancy of the Conference of Charities of New York City. The group's purpose was to study proper methods of providing shelter for the homeless. Riis's interest in lodging houses dated from his nightmarish experience at Church Street police station in 1870, when a tramp had stolen his gold locket and a sergeant had insulted him and killed the stray dog which had been his companion. Often after that he had photographed and spoken out against the menace of these squalid quarters. In 1891 Riis gathered together and published information about wayfarers' lodges in Boston, Philadelphia, Baltimore, London, and Paris.

Unlike New York, these cities attempted to separate from criminals young boys and men temporarily down on their luck. New York's system encouraged tramps to migrate to the city, Riis charged, and disregarded rules against overcrowding and accepting intoxicated lodgers. When critics claimed that his accusations were unfounded and that he was seeking publicity for self-serving motives, Riis took his camera to the Oak Street police station and photographed six youths bedded up with forty hardened tramps and thieves. He termed the system a parody upon Christian charity which furnished homes only for the unworthy and said that the police should not mix philanthropy with criminology.[13]

When typhus raged in New York in 1892, Riis and other reformers petitioned city officials to close down police lodging houses in order to head off an epidemic. Riis took pictures to the Academy of Medicine, but the rooms remained open. Health officers tightened their inspection of private low-cost flophouses, but Riis assumed correctly that until the city itself cleaned up the police lodging houses, the private abuses would remain. In *The Children of the Poor* he told of a visit that a sanitary inspector made to a cheap lodging house. The proprietor reluctantly assented to some suggestions for improvements, but he became indignant at the demand for clean sheets. Riis wrote that "He lost all patience and said, with bitter contempt, 'Well, you needn't tink dem's angels!' "[14]

Josephine Lowell, the president of the Charity Organization Society (COS) and chairman of the Committee on Vagrancy, shared Riis's hatred of New York's lodging house system. As an alternative, her organization ran a workyard for men and a laundry for women and provided room and board for able-bodied paupers on the condition that the registrants labored for three hours, bathed, and abstained from smoking or drinking. To encourage self-reliance, the COS decreed that nobody could use the facilities more than six days a month without special permission.[15]

Both Mrs. Lowell and Riis desired the abolition of the police lodging houses and the strict regulation of private rooms, but they disagreed on whether the city should take responsibility for providing shelter for the deserving poor. In 1886 the New York legislature had passed an enabling act for the establishment of municipal lodging houses; but the city government had never implemented it. Riis wanted the city to put the law into effect and pointed out the success of a similar plan in Boston. Mrs. Lowell opposed public facilities and wanted the COS to expand its own workhouses. She feared that municipal stations would soon sink to the level of the police lodging houses. "With our *rotten* city government, how can any city institution be decent?" she asked Riis.[16]

In the face of the refusal of New York administrators to enforce the Municipal Lodging House Act of 1886, the Committee on Vagrancy endorsed Mrs. Lowell's proposals. The tone of its report was negative, and its emphasis was directed toward nongovernmental institutions. The committee recommended an end to police lodging houses and the sending of professional vagrants to farm colonies. The COS leased property for a new wayfarers' lodge, which opened in December of 1893. While Mrs. Lowell viewed this action as the most desirable end, Riis praised it as expedient only until the city would meet its proper responsibilities. At least people received clean clothes, a decent bed, and food, "so they did not have to go out and beg the first thing," he wrote in his autobiography (p. 252). Yet if the private philanthropy properly discouraged mendicancy, Riis realized that it did little to prevent people from falling below the poverty line. And he feared that their rigid standards would end up with decent people being treated as tramps. Pressure from the Committee on Vagrancy caused the police to close down some lodging quarters, but twelve of them remained as a blight upon efforts to improve the situation.[17]

Riis's disagreement with the COS over their relief standards demonstrated his ambivalent and somewhat jaundiced attitude about private philanthropy. What he lamented was the patronizing attitude that some charity workers had toward the poor. The way to gain the confidence of slum tenants, he believed, was to trust them, not preach sermons to them. Reformers had to come over to the ghetto, not down to it. As much as he hated Tammany politicians, he realized that they lived with and understood their constituency. Riis later wrote in *The Battle with the Slum:* "Certainly you do not want to reform men by main strength, drag them into righteousness by the hair of the head, as it were" (pp. 283–84).

Lincoln Steffens later remembered that in private Riis often denounced the harsh and impersonal methods of the COS, but then he would "go right off to support it publicly with an eloquence that must have derived some of its force from the passion of his rage at it."[18] Riis summarized his position this way in *The Making of an American:* "I am a believer in organized, systematic charity upon the evidence of my senses; but—I am glad we have that one season in which we can forget our principles and err on the side of mercy, . . . and no questions asked. No need to be afraid. It is safe. Christmas charity never corrupts" (pp. 11–12).

Portraits from Mulberry Street

Often Riis's newspaper articles produced results that directly benefited the subjects of his stories. For example, he wrote a feature on a French Canadian woman named Mrs. Ben Wah who was the widow of an Iroquois Indian. He quoted Mrs. Ben Wah as stating that poverty was not a disgrace but very inconvenient. She had little desire to live, Riis wrote, but did wish that she had a parrot to keep her company. Within days someone donated a parrot for her. It did not surprise the reporter, for regularly he received at his office wheelchairs, parcels of clothes, and other items of relief for the poor. But it buoyed up his faith in human nature.[19]

The New York *World* described Riis as "an easy mark" and his office on Mulberry Street during the 1890s as "the Mecca of a constant procession of visitors," ranging from

prominent citizens to humble East Siders who "on one pretext
or another are seeking a little 'temporary aid'. . . ." One of
Riis's acquaintances, Dexter Marshall, later described the reporter as a man of little pretension. "He dresses as plainly as it
is possible for a man to dress," Marshall wrote. "His trousers
bag at the knees; his hair is unkempt, frequently his fingers are
splotched with ink or smudged with lead pencil dust."[20]

Even though most of Riis's writing at this time examined
urban problems, he still on occasion wrote about sensational
murders and mayhem in a style which pandered to the instincts of shock. As late as 4 August 1896 he published "A
Brutal Murder" in the *Evening Sun,* which described the victim, Annie Bock, as "ostensibly an honest wife, [but] professionally a woman of the streets." An assailant had cut
Annie's throat "with two quick slashes, one which severed the
jugular vein!" Then the criminal had smoothed over the
pillows of her bed with his bloody hands. "The mark of bloody
fingers was on the dead woman's naked body, too," he wrote.

Riis realized that newspaper work at Mulberry Street
depended largely upon the unearthing of personal tragedy.
Once one of his competitors gained an exclusive story about
an entire family which died after eating diseased smelt. For
a week Riis searched for something to top the smelt story.
Then the Board of Health received a report that several
people came down with a sickness after eating ham. Suspecting
trichinosis, the enterprising reporter followed the victims to
the hospital. He later admitted that when doctors discovered
"one of the little beasts curled up and taking a nap in a shred
of muscle," it seemed to him "the sweetest creature alive."[21]

Riis later compiled his best articles in a book entitled
*Out of Mulberry Street: Stories of Tenement Life in New
York City* (1898). Focusing on the human response to tenement conditions, he presented vignettes of both appalling
tragedy and comic relief, of personal heroism and private
surrender to grief. *Out of Mulberry Street* revealed Riis's
mastery at making ghetto life real for Americans who heretofore had visualized immigrants only as a fearsome mass of

shadowy figures. Although Riis sometimes employed a syrupy style, his best articles combined pathos and compassion. In "John Gavin, Misfit" he told about a father of six children who shot himself after he became sick, lost his job, and faced eviction from his tenement dwelling. Two of the most humorous stories were "Sarah Joyce's Husbands" and "Spooning in Dynamite Alley," whereas other chapters, such as "Heroes Who Fight Fire" and "Rover's Last Fight," were overly melodramatic. Perhaps the strangest story, and most condescending, was "Nigger Martha's Wake," which described a hatpin duel between two prostitutes. As a unit, the book had a very somber tone; accidents, suicides, unrewarding toil, murders, and suffering outnumbered the lighter moments. In one article he called the slum a "maelstrom that sucks under all it seizes" (p. 115). Counteracting this mood was the reporter's cautious optimism which caused him to stress the innate decency and goodness of people who were struggling against a hostile environment.

Many of the stories were about Christmas, which symbolized to Riis the spirit of love. In 1893, in fact, he wrote a book entitled *Nibsy's Christmas,* which invoked this same theme. The opening chapter in *Out of Mulberry Street,* "Merry Christmas in the Tenements," contrasted the ornate, week-long celebrations in Denmark with the drab habits of the Bowery. In Ribe a thousand candles lighted the Domkirke, revealing a Christ-thorn of red berries. The badge of the Bowery, "the great highway of the homeless," was withered holly. On Christmas Eve people of all faiths and races went to an ancient Baptist church which Riis called "a missionary outpost in the land of the enemy. . . ." One Jewish woman in tattered rags took her children to enjoy the festive church pageant. She tried to be inconspicuous, but her offspring applauded and sang without shame. Wrote Riis, "She is the yesterday, they the tomorrow. What shall the harvest be?" (pp. 1–14).

In most stories the central characters were children, whose purity of spirit ill-fitted the tragic fate that awaited them in the slums, as the forces of environment stunted their minds and made mockery of their dreams. In "Death Comes to Cat Alley" Riis described a wagon carrying off two infants, one dead from malnutrition and the other barely alive and headed for an orphans' asylum. Only the very hardy survived at the asylum, even though they received adequate care, he wrote, since "the babies know that they are cheated, and they will not stay" (p. 85).

Youths had to adopt a shell of hardness to survive in the city, Riis believed; but in a story which he called "The Kid" he attempted to demonstrate that adolescents retained a spark of their inherent goodness. Of a delinquent who had attacked two policemen during a gang fight, the "kid" was "an every-day tough," Riis wrote, "bull-necked, square-jawed, red of face, and with his hair cropped short in the fashion that rules at Sing Sing and is admired of Battle Row." The youth refused to cooperate with the authorities who had arrested him. On the way to court he broke away from his guard. Dashing into the street, he saved a child from a railway car. He was gentle with the baby, the author exclaimed, but when the policemen reached him, his sullenness and defiance returned (pp. 147–50).

In these articles Riis's sympathy and understanding of immigrants seemed more apparent than it had been in *How the Other Half Lives*. He especially praised the dignity and moralism of the Jews. He believed that their thousand-year struggle against oppression and bigotry gave them a special quality of intellectual vigor and motivation which brought excitement to their lives and maintained them in crises. One of his articles was about a cloakmaker who went on strike against his oppressive employer. The man had no reserve funds for his large family, Riis stated, but he had faith that his God and his neighbors would sustain him until he regained his job and won his dignity (p. 34).

Echoing the prejudices of his time, however, Riis continued to slur and stereotype the Chinese and black slum dwellers. He condoned the immigrants' common hatred of "John Chinaman." In "A Heathen Baby" he wrote: "Piccaninnies have come [to the police station] before this, lots of them, black and shiny, and one papoose from a West-Side wigwam; but a Chinese baby never" (p. 80).

The chapter which best combined Riis's powers of description with his moralistic optimism was "Paolo's Awakening." Paolo was an eight-year-old Italian boy whose father had drowned on the way to work at an island dumping ground. The family was so poor that it could not afford "the luxury of grief," Riis wrote, and soon Paolo went to work at a sweatshop. Paolo lived with his mother and uncle and many brothers and sisters in the basement of a rear tenement. They shared two rooms, one dark as "twilight even on the brightest days" and the other "a dark little cubbyhole, where it was always midnight, and where there was just room for a bed of old boards, no more." During his few moments of pleasure, Paolo rummaged for scraps and chased rats at the city dump and built castles from sand and clay. One day a teacher noticed the artistry of Paolo's castles and persuaded his mother to allow him to attend an industrial school. Paolo became the best pupil and won a medal for sculpturing a bust of his mother. On the way home from his graduation, Paolo died in a train collision. Riis viewed the incident as a triumph rather than a tragedy, however. He wrote: "Brighter skies than those of sunny Italy had dawned upon him in the gloom and terror of the great crash. Paolo was at home, waiting for his mother" (pp. 180–81).[22]

Soon after he finished editing *Out of Mulberry Street*, Riis received an offer from Richard W. Gilder to write an article on the brighter side of slum life. He responded that writers of fiction could do the best job at this and added that he had no imaginaion for inventing stories. "I can't invent," he later remarked. "The smallest detail of a story has to be there before I can write it." He told Gilder, however, that he would attempt to find a true story that satisfied him. Riis wrote: "The brightness comes from the children and I will seek it there."[23]

6

JACOB RIIS AND THE DEPRESSION

In 1893 the general economic collapse in the United States had calamitous consequences for the tenement districts of New York City. The severe depression that ensued throughout the rest of the decade shattered the preconceptions which Jacob Riis held concerning the care of paupers and caused him to reevaluate his attitudes about public relief. It strengthened his commitment to positive governmental action to reconstruct the slums, which he viewed in social terms as a way of life rather than merely a set of squalid surroundings. Regarding Tammany Hall as the chief perpetrator of these unjust conditions, he actively worked for the machine's defeat in the New York mayoralty election of 1894. As the desperate economic conditions lingered on for four years and political leaders seemed powerless to find a way out of the morass, Americans of all classes began to listen with a new urgency to the messages of reformers such as Riis.[1]

Painful Reevaluation of Poverty

During the winter of 1893–94, the depressed economic conditions upset the institutions of private charity. Less than one fourth of the manufacturing establishments in New York were operating at full capacity. A hundred thousand people in New York City alone were unemployed. As relief applications at the COS trebled, charity leaders at first blamed the crisis on ill-advised almsgiving, and declared that free food and lodging were luring tramps to the city. Only slowly did they realize that emergency programs to deal with the distress were essential to public safety. The Association for Improving the Condition of the Poor (AICP) warned that "the turbulent elements of riot and discord would appear" if the situation deteriorated without abatement.[2]

Riis wanted New York's municipal government to combat the depression by expanding public works projects, but he opposed measures of direct relief because that would create "a horde of tramps." He also rejected the premise that government had the obligation to guarantee full employment, in the belief that such a program would aggravate the crisis by causing outsiders to swarm to New York. On 21 December 1893 Riis urged city officials to hire workers to demolish condemned property under the auspices and authority of the Small Parks Act of 1887. He also urged the stepping up of all public projects that would create jobs. In 1895 he supported a plan to allow citizens to plant vegetable gardens on vacant lots, thinking that this would foster self-reliance and relieve distress.[3]

Riis's opposition to soup kitchens and other institutional forms of direct relief seemed to be out of keeping with his compassionate nature and his belief that social forces created conditions of poverty. Anxious for an active governmental role in preventing the *causes* of poverty, Riis still clung to an obsolete theory of dealing with the *consequences* of poverty which he viewed in terms of dependency rather than insufficiency. Nevertheless, his mind worked more on a personal than an economic level; and since he had private doubts about the maxims of the COS, he handed out money from his own pocket to many people in distress.[4]

Riis's primary response to the economic collapse was to mobilize private groups into action. He supported the East Side Relief Work Committee, which hired three thousand men and women to clean up the slums and make clothing. The committee spent $120,000 before disbanding in April 1894. At that time John Bancroft Devins, a COS official, reorganized the committee into the Federation of East Side Workers with the purpose of improving the tenement neighborhoods. On another front Riis sought to interest the COS in printing Good Works cards which people could send as condolences to funerals rather than wasting money on ornate display. The cards would be a pledge to give money to charity. Riis got this idea from practices he observed in Denmark and other European countries. Mrs. Lowell's agency declined to solicit money for relief but suggested that the King's Daughters settlement workers experiment with it.[5]

Finally Riis urged city dwellers to move to the country, and supported agencies, such as the Baron de Hirsch Fund, which were attempting to resettle tenants in rural colonies. It was a great disappointment to him that so few people were anxious to take part in these ventures. One winter evening in the midst of the depression, he visited a wretched and unheated flat. A mother and daughter were without food and were huddled in bed in a fruitless effort to keep warm. A year earlier Riis had helped them obtain a homestead in Woodbine, New Jersey, but shortly afterward the two women moved back to the more exciting atmosphere of the city. Riis could not understand this and told his friend Lincoln Steffens that he must be a poor judge of human nature.[6]

The response to the depression by New York's municipal government and by private charities was ineffective in combating the distress. Public works projects increased only inappreciably. The Department of Charities and Correction distributed aid to the blind and free coal to the poor but ceased doling out food and clothing as a result of pressure from the COS and the

AICP. Yet these two groups reached less than 10 percent of the unemployed with their woodyards and sewing projects. The East Side Relief Work Committee was a modest success but an ineffective response to unemployment on a large scale. The depression led to a reevaluation of poverty in America. Throughout the nineteenth century most charity workers accepted the premise that America's abundance made it possible for all able-bodied persons to be free from want. Therefore they viewed poverty in terms of dependency, laziness, or other defects in character. Their immediate solutions were alms to the helpless and character training to the others. During the depression economic realities squashed this simplistic formula, and the perceptive reformers came to view poverty in terms of insecurity and insufficiency. Jane Addams declared that when the poor met up with the delay and skepticism of philanthropic agencies, "These do not appear to them conscientious scruples, but the cold and calculating action of selfish men." In the wake of the hard times, however, many caseworkers softened their attitudes and allowed empirical evidence rather than their ingrained philosophy to dictate their actions. In fact, in 1896 the COS dropped the word "deserving" in referring to cases of needy recipients.[7]

Riis's ideas changed in the wake of the depression, even though he had recognized earlier that health and housing regulation by government was necessary to restrict practices that dehumanized individuals and loosened family ties. After 1894 he emphasized more than ever before that social control by experts in government was necessary to root out exploitation and to create a climate where all people enjoyed an opportunity to use their talents. The depression caused him to lose faith that natural economic laws would provide an adequate urban environment. Riis admired the emphasis on planning and coordination which the COS applied to philanthropy, but he came to realize that the institutions of private charity were inadequate in times of emergency and that their responses to poverty were palliatives rather than solutions. Thus, he lobbied for statutes regulating the working conditions and rights of laborers and for experiments in limited municipal ownership of utilities. Yet the thrust of his philosophy was moral and personal, and the forms of social control by government which he advocated had as their primary purpose the fashioning of a more creative and useful citizenry rather than the creation of a revolutionary political or economic system.[8]

Practical and undogmatic, Riis distrusted political theorists who attempted to respond to urban problems only within the framework of a rigid system. He doubted whether such things as small parks and a tenement house code would appeal "to the Anarchists, the Socialists, or the other theorists who have each his own cure for all society's ills ready-made, and who would rather see the patient die than have him relieved according to any other formula than their own." In 1895 he complained that the poor lacked proper books, citing the deaths of two suicide victims, a girl who had been reading salacious love stories and a man who had been reading Thomas Paine's *Age of Reason* and works by the agnostic Robert C. Ingersoll.[9]

Riis's fundamental concern was for the individual, the human being's moral, ethical, physical, and intellectual development. He believed that human nature was essentially benevolent but maintained that a decent environment was necessary to allow the goodness in man to blossom. Over and over again on lecture tours, he defended his optimism as the most practical reform philosophy. "The pessimist is the most useless being on earth," he said, "for his theory, like the theory of heredity, is not a working theory." In rural America, as well as in Denmark, the bonds of family, church, school, community, and nation had guided the maturation process of the young. In New York City Riis found that man had polluted and desecrated the beauty of nature, and the slums were destroying the traditional institutional and primary-group bonds of society. Poverty made irrelevant the ideals of citizenship and the moral blandishments of religion. Neighborhood ties broke down as people fought desperately to escape starvation. Riis said later that one of his main purposes in urban reconstruction was "to

arouse neighborhood interest and neighborhood pride, to link
the neighbors to one spot that will hold them long enough to
take root and stop them from moving." He hoped that schools
could become community centers, replacing the saloon and the
streets as the formative factors in slum habits.[10]

Thus, Riis's programs of social, economic, political, and
humanitarian reform aimed to beautify the environment and to
reestablish the position of the home, the school, and the neighborhood in the lives of the poor. Housing reform was the most
urgent priority, he believed, for proper family life could not
survive intact in foul and overcrowded tenements. Riis wanted
school buildings to be open in the evenings, on weekends, and
during the summer for recreational, cultural, and civic use.
He joined organizations which advocated public kindergartens,
vocational education, and special farm and truant schools for
errant children. Working with several settlement houses in
New York City, Riis believed that the social settlement movement was conducive to expanding opportunity, molding good
citizens, and cementing class harmony. Calling settlements the
best example of practical Christianity, he admonished organized religion to wipe the soot from its windows and take up
the gospel of service. Finally he advocated more small parks
and playgrounds for the poor. A supporter of the philosophy
of creative play, he believed that recreation and freedom to
move freely were necessary ingredients for proper citizenship.[11]

City Hall Critic

Riis saw to his dismay that New York's problems were
multiplying despite the many indications of public concern; and
slowly he came to realize that what was needed even more than
persuasion was planning, pressure, and power. Public officials
had not implemented small parks and tenement house legislation passed during the previous decade. In 1892 the Department of Buildings preempted the investigative functions of the

Board of Health over the objections of public health experts. Two years later the Democratic governor Roswell Flower vetoed a public works program which the state legislature had passed with the intention of softening the effects of the depression. Flower explained lamely that the bill would have encouraged "prodigal extravagance."[12]

Riis expressed his dissatisfaction with the city's management of the public school system in an article entitled "The Making of Thieves in New York." He wrote that New York's pupils attended "foul, dark class-rooms, where they grow crooked for the want of proper desks." He charged that authorities "bid them play in gloomy caverns which the sun never enters, forgetting that boys must have a chance to play properly, or they will play hookey. . . ." There were so many rats in the buildings, he reported, that the children could hardly hear above the squeaking. When a Tammany official denied the statement, the newspaperman threatened to send him a specimen. Proper schools, Riis believed, could teach the children of immigrants American values and principles, rather than turn out "queer manikins stuffed with information for which they have no use. . . ."[13]

Reform was a natural response to industrialization and urbanization, Riis declared on 8 February 1894 during a forum on child labor and working conditions for women at Cooper Union in New York. Sharing the dais with labor leader Samuel Gompers, ethical culture advocate Felix Adler, patrician reformer Joseph H. Choate, Bishop Henry Potter, and Father Thomas James Ducey, he pledged to use all necessary measures to win over the apathetic, the stubborn, and the irresponsible. Throughout the rest of the year, he publicized police and tenement house investigations in an effort to expose, during a mayoralty election year, the degradation of Tammany Hall machine rule.[14]

The Lexow Committee investigation into New York's police force was the result of a personal crusade by the Reverend Charles H. Parkhurst, a fifty-year-old Presbyterian who was the president of the Society for the Prevention of Crime.

The tall, curly-haired minister was amiable and wryly humorous in private, magnetic and messianic from the pulpit, and singleminded and fearless in his opposition to vice and corruption. In 1892 Parkhurst had accused Mayor Hugh J. Grant and the Tammany-controlled Board of Police Commissioners of tolerating a network of graft and immorality. A grand jury rebuked him for attacking police officials groundlessly without proving his charges.[15]

As a result, Parkhurst began to search out incriminating evidence. Hiring a private detective to guide him to New York's unlicensed saloons, gambling dens, and brothels, the minister disguised himself as a pleasure-seeker and gained an unforgettable personal education. At one place he watched eight naked women dance lewdly and play leapfrog with his guide. He fled another establishment in horror when a young boy tried to hold his hand under a table. On the following Sunday Parkhurst revealed his experiences to his congregation. New York's Chamber of Commerce, dominated by businessmen hostile to Tammany, persuaded Republican Boss Thomas C. Platt to sanction a legislative investigation of the police department. Parkhurst was not enthusiastic about the ensuing Lexow Committee inquiry. He did not look kindly on politicians, whether from New York or Albany.[16]

In response to Parkhurst's charges, Riis and Lincoln Steffens visited police chief Thomas Byrnes, who bore the brunt of the criticism. A member of the Society for the Prevention of Crime, Riis sympathized with Parkhurst's goals. Yet he greatly admired the colorful and efficient Byrnes and had often glorified the work of his detectives in capturing notorious outlaws. Riis opened the interview by asking whether the police would continue to allow saloon owners to violate the Sunday liquor laws. Byrnes snapped back that he thought the New York *Evening Sun* was on his side. According to Steffens's autobiography, Riis replied, "Never you mind the *Sun*. Say what you are going to do. That's the news of the day, and the *Sun* prints the news." Byrnes then made a speech to his inspectors, admonishing them to enforce the closing law (pp. 215–20).

Riis opposed police raids on brothels, however. Such action would only drive the prostitutes into the tenements and therefore corrupt others. Instead, he put his hope into reforming the minds and morals of the fallen women.[17]

On 9 March 1894, amidst a carnival atmosphere, the Lexow Committee opened its hearings. Reporters came from as far away as Oregon, and at times the inquiry received more publicity than the Pullman strike in Illinois or Jacob S. Coxey's march on Washington. Newspapers in rural America played up the theme of sin in the big city; nativists and anti-Catholic groups exploited the hearings for their own purposes. For a fee children guided tourists and reporters through back alleys past rowdy houses and Chinese opium dens. In his autobiography Steffens called New York "a provincial moral community" to which Parkhurst had successfully appealed "with fine blind faith" (p. 247). To an Englishman New York was like "a lady in ball costume, with diamonds in her ears, and her toes out at her boots." The hearings lasted until December. The Lexow Committee published a six-thousand-page report, packed with testimony about police blackmail and graft. Payoffs took place between large businesses and city officials all the way down to prostitutes and organ grinders who gave money to their neighborhood patrolmen. A policeman had to pay $200 to $300 merely to join the force, and promotions to the rank of captain cost from $12,000 to $15,000. The poor suffered the most from the system of blackmail, as the police worked in alliance with landlords, strikebreaking employers, fraudulent insurance companies, and other racketeers.[18]

Riis reported the unfolding scandals vigorously. He had known about the seamy side of police work, the broken heads and the stale beer dives. Still, the extent of the corruption shocked him. Steffens later wrote, with some exaggeration, that "The power to conceive evil in its vicious form failed Riis always." In September 1894 Riis castigated Chief Byrnes as a man of iron who had feet of clay, a man who had built his power on bargains with thieves. He charged that "The detective staff plotted with the pawnbrokers on the one hand and the bunco men on the other to 'do the guys!' " Recommending complete reorganization of the department, he suggested that trained soldiers might have to keep order in the interim. No criminal convictions of a lasting nature resulted from the Lexow Committee's inquiry, but it had a great effect on the November mayoralty elections in temporarily discrediting Riis's enemy Tammany Hall.[19]

Also in 1894 a series of articles by Edward Marshall on the slum holdings of Trinity Church led to the formation of a state tenement house committee under the chairmanship of Richard W. Gilder. A close friend of Riis, Gilder was the managing editor of the *Century* magazine. Small, frail, and unassertive, he was a patrician writer of genteel poetry, whose appearance did not fit the part of a watchdog of the pubilc interest. Gilder was so prudish that he once censored a line in a story that mentioned "a little blue mark over the brown nipple" of a man. Nevertheless, he approved of realism in nonfictional articles and sought out Riis's work. The gentleman editor harbored a hatred for injustice and had a vicarious dislike of slum life. [20]

Riis served on Gilder's committee as an unofficial adviser. He suggested that the group draw up an ethnic map of New York, compile statistics on the effect of inadequate housing on social habits, and consult with health officials, trade unions, settlement workers, and, above all, representatives of the poor. He recommended that the committee study urban planning in other cities, including the "Glasgow idea" of municipal socialism. Finally he succeeded in convincing the committee to view the tenement problem as more than merely a housing crisis and thus endorse increased recreation facilities, kindergartens, and the like.[21]

The findings of the Gilder Tenement House Committee of 1894, in Riis's words, reeked with unpleasant information. Six hundred pages long, the final report was an exhaustingly comprehensive compilation of New York's housing ills. It emphasized the high disease rate in tenement neighborhoods, the lack of space and parks and playgrounds. The Gilder committee recommended, among other things, that the Board of Health should have the power to condemn buildings that were unfit for human habitation, with compensation to their owners.

Absent were solutions to the nagging problems of over-crowding and of ensuring an honest and efficient inspection system. Nevertheless, the facts themselves indicted the existing situation and spurred sentiment for change. In many articles Riis echoed the call for the seizure and destruction of the worst dwellings, but he was more reluctant than the committee to compensate the owners, agreeing finally for practical reasons, against his better judgment.[22]

Both Riis and Gilder had great hope that model tenements would provide one solution to the housing crisis. Urging busi-nessmen to combine philanthropy with profit, in his autobiog-raphy Riis asked them to take 7 percent and save their souls "or twenty-five and lose it" (p. 248). The awakened interest led to the creation of the City and Suburban Homes Company, whose wealthy stockholders pledged to place a ceiling of 5 per-cent on the dividends to their $1 million outlay in capital stock. In 1896 under the direction of E. R. L. Gould, the company began constructing safe and sanitary tenements. Nevertheless, few other businessmen followed their example, and model tene-ments had no appreciable effect on alleviating New York's population density. The poor could not afford the few new buildings which the philanthropists erected, as Riis came to realize to his dismay.[23]

As public pressure reached a crescendo in 1894, Republi-cans, reformers, and civic leaders merged in efforts to oust Tammany from power. Allied together were the Reverend Parkhurst's forces, the New York Chamber of Commerce, the Confederated Good Government Clubs, and the Committee of Seventy. Supported alike by upper class tycoons such as John D. Rockefeller and patrician philanthropists such as Robert Fulton Cutting, the Committee of Seventy, which later became the Citizens' Union, hoped to bring rational planning to urban government in the interest of honesty and efficiency. The group established a permanent municipal research bureau, and their long-range goal was a new city charter for greater New York.[24] In the 1894 election these men gave their support to William L. Strong, a Republican banker and dry goods merchant who promised to carry out substantial reforms if elected. Riis and his friends in charity and settlement work supported Strong almost to a man. On 4 November 1894, two days before the election, the Reverend Parkhurst prayed at the Madison Square Church that the spirit of God would "so possess this vast metropolis . . . as to lift us momentarily out of the tainted atmosphere we are breathing and [open the door] to a nobler future of American dignity, prosperity, and power."[25]

William Strong won. For three years Tammany was out of power. Riis seemed no longer to be a voice crying in the wilderness. Sensing that his optimism had been justified, he prepared to do battle to implement the programs he had long advocated: the abolition of police lodging houses, an equitable tenement house code, and better parks, playgrounds, and schools for the poor.

On 1 January 1895, the day that Strong took office, Riis wrote to his sister Emma in Denmark concerning the significance of Tammany's demise. "It begins to look as if I were going to win my war," he declared. The new year seemed to augur a new era of moral purpose in municipal government.

Riis and the George Junior Republic

During the 1890s Riis's interest in the children of the poor caused him to support a novel educational experiment in training delinquent and dependent youths, the George Junior Republic. For five summers beginning in 1890, William R. George, a strong-minded, eccentric businessman in his mid-twenties, had been taking the most incorrigible slum children on summer excursions to Freeville, New York, in conjunction with the New York *Tribune's* Fresh Air Fund program. Exhilarated that the trips liberated youths from the hostile grip of

the slum, George lamented that the escape was temporary and
that the program had the debilitating side effect of making the
campers dependent on charitable alms. When depressed economic conditions ruined his business, George drew up blueprints to transform the Freeville excursion site near Ithaca,
New York, into a permanent self-sustaining school controlled
democratically by the children. Friends and would-be patrons
scoffed at the visionary dream, but Riis lifted his spirits, encouraged George to pursue his plans, and talked others into
opening their minds and wallets to him.[26]

On 5 September 1895, Riis wrote in the New York *Sun*
about the hundred and fifty boys that were returning from a
two-month stay at Freeville. "The roughest of the rough were
picked, the ones whom the Fresh Air Fund rejected because
they were too untidy and too troublesome to go as its boarders,"
Riis stated. A skeleton crew of youths were staying with George
to create a year-round junior republic. The school's motto was
"Nothing without Labor." Riis told his readers that all participants had to work for a living, that if one refused, "he was
adjudged a pauper by his compeers, was fed on pauper fare,
water and bread, and made to sleep on straw."

The group survived the bleak frosty winter of 1895–96,
living in crude quarters. The ordeal, which "Daddy" George
compared to General George Washington's encampment at
Valley Forge during the War for Independence, assured the
project's success. By the summer of 1896, an impressive array
of humanitarian reformers, civic clubs, and religious groups,
from both the Freeville area and New York City, had agreed to
aid the project. Among those on the school's advisory council
were Riis, the editors Lyman Abbott and Albert Shaw, the
civic-minded ministers Charles Parkhurst and Josiah Strong,
and Wisconsin economist John R. Commons. Assisting George
at financial, bureaucratic, and political tasks—which the
schoolmaster had little use for anyway—was a Board of
Trustees headed by the able and dedicated Thomas Mott
Osborne. By 1896 students were deciding most of the school's
internal political, economic, penal, and social policies. They

conducted elections, formed political parties, ran a police force
and court, managed a hotel, restaurant, and workhouse, bid
for labor contracts, and worked on or supervised labor gangs.
Each newcomer received enough scrip to see him through an
initiation period, whereupon he was expected to fend for himself. Residents were theoretically free to do what they wanted,
but laziness resulted in poor food, bad quarters, and even jail
sentences. And there were compulsory militia, patriotic singing
during flag-raising ceremonies, and marching drills. Generally,
the youths attended school for a half-day and worked at trades
in the afternoons.[27]

Within two years the George Junior Republic attracted
national attention as a progressive, character-building laboratory for orphans and delinquents, poor and rich, of both sexes,
native-born and foreign-born. Visitors marveled that George's
miniature society was a model from which elders could learn
valuable lessons in citizenship. The radical institutional setting
attracted zealous volunteers, while the school's traditional
principles of frugality, Americanization, and thrift made it
acceptable to conservative patrons. Riis reiterated the school's
use of revolutionary means to maintain traditional values when
he declared: "I believe in it above all as a means of teaching
the boys what boys most need today in our country: respect
for law. . . . It is the contempt for law, which the fellowship
of politics and legislation has brought upon us, that makes
toughs and largely slums. Contempt for law is the beginning
of barbarism. In the issue with the forces of barbarism the
Junior Republic has taken its stand on the side of patriotism
and good citizenship."[28]

It was natural that Riis should endorse the principles of
the Junior Republic, given his personality and pedagogical
beliefs. Earlier he had lauded Charles Loring Brace and the
Children's Aid Society for placing city waifs in rural foster
homes. In *How the Other Half Lives* he praised the Five Points
House of Industry, which sought to relocate invalids and destitute people in the country. In November 1894 he wrote in
Century magazine that the man who marches the superfluous

urban youngsters "off to the mountains to camp under military rule in July or August, will come near to solving the delinquency problem, I think . . ." (p. 115). Like William George, whom he deeply admired for his courage and warmth' toward young people, Riis combined an agrarian romanticism with the attitude that practical education was the surest avenue toward progress. Both men were perfectionists, yet critical of ineffective dreamers; they were environmentalists who nevertheless believed that proper habits and skills could go far in enabling individuals to overcome poverty. Both blamed urban delinquency on injurious conditions which left potentially good youths idle and rootless and susceptible to the corrupting influences of the street. Riis admired the fact that George planted his child-centered social experiment on the firm ground of community self-discipline and individual self-respect.

In short, Riis saw the Junior Republic as the perfect setting into which to transplant slum children who were "waiting to be enrolled in the [American] Republic." Riis wrote that George's camp "enables a young tough to 'figger out' that it 'costs more to be bad den good' and starts him off on the other tack, reaches down through all theories and good intentions to hard pan, and heads off the jail and the workhouse." He added that it was "a practical effort to fit the boy to the things that are, rather than to such as might be in a millenium neither he nor we shall live to see."[29]

Given the nature of the school and the notoriety it received, it was perhaps inevitable that it suffer from growing pains and the slurs of sensationalist critics. Vandalism at neighboring farms was blamed on the pupils, sometimes with cause. Friction developed between year-round residents and summer transients. The former clique tended to dominate government and enjoy George's favor, until finally the summer sessions were terminated. Other problems resulted from overly harsh punishments meted out in the student court and from inequities in the rudimentary capitalist system. Until George intervened, corruption in assigning labor contracts created a cabal of idle "millionaires" living at the Republic's "Waldorf" while less fortunate boys worked in labor gangs. The intermingling of the sexes sparked constant rumors of orgies. Debaucheries were alluded to in a series of spurious articles by a Rochester newspaper which touched off an investigation by the State Board of Charities, which was controlled by an old enemy of William George, Secretary Robert W. Hebberd. George, who shared Riis's anti-institutional distrust of bureaucrats, professional philanthropists, and politicians, tried in vain to head off the probe. Although his school was semiprivate, it received state funds since a large minority of its pupils were wards of the courts. On 16 August 1897 investigators of New York's State Board of Charities allegedly found unsanitary conditions on the premises, a lack of order, cruelty, and evidence of promiscuity in the form of unregulated overnight camping trips. Two months later, following the publication of a derogatory report, the Board of Charities denied funds to the Republic on the grounds that there was an absence of family life and inadequate educational facilities.[30]

In the wake of the damaging report, Thomas Mott Osborne, the chairman of the Board of Trustees, asked Riis and others to revisit the school and tender their advice. Shortly thereafter the Board of Trustees wrote a memorandum to the Board of Charities, explaining that the Junior Republic fostered self-control and order and that the self-government idea had been adopted mainly as a disciplinary ploy against unruly elements. Noting that vocational and academic courses were an integral part of the institution, as well as training in self-reliance, Osborne's committee argued that its critics wanted the school to resemble a prison. Nevertheless, Osborne and the trustees moved to strip George of many of his powers. Thus, they rescued the school from extinction by reducing the status of the flamboyant founder. Riis and most benefactors stuck by the school during its troubles and publicly downplayed its radical features. In speeches Riis stressed how the Republic fostered morality and patriotism in an age when most schools were too secular. And he contrasted the school's

spartan and entrepreneurial emphasis with his own inaccurate
interpretation of socialism, which taught, he said, that people
have a right to enjoy things without working for them.[31]

Thus, the George Junior Republic endured and spawned
a whole network of imitators, some of which still exist. The
assistance and inspiration which Riis provided George at a
critical juncture during the 1890s helped create one of the
most important experiments in progressive education as applied to delinquent and dependent children.

Upward Mobility

Although the depression of the 1890s had little effect
upon Riis's earning power, his large family and his generosity
in support of charitable causes kept his monetary affairs un-
settled and prevented him from saving any money. He wrote
his sister Emma that he had no "wish to be rich and that it
would not help to wish it as it would fortunately never come
true." He apologized for not being able to pledge a more substantial donation to the school where Emma taught. On 1
January 1895 Riis began recording his income and expenditures in an account book. His first entry was five cents for the
cost of the purchase. In October he jokingly wrote that he was
bequeathing the account book in his will to Lincoln Steffens
so that his friend might learn how properly to "conduct his
business with satisfaction to himself and profit to his neighbors
(in trade)." At the end of the year he prepared a balance sheet
for 1895. He had earned $3,500 but spent all of it. "I am now
on the divide," Riis exclaimed, "earning as much as I ever
will, with nothing going into the bank for a rainy day. Well!
It isn't wealth exactly, but all considered isn't it enough?"
Compensating for a lack of funds, he said, were a good family,
true friends, and a place of usefulness in his work. "What
more can a man want?", he concluded.[32]

Riis never allowed financial strains to prevent him from

enjoying the amenities of a comfortable life or expansion of his family. A domestic servant worked at his household, and he enjoyed the luxury of good wine and cigars. In 1895 his wife Elisabeth, whom Jacob called Lammet or the Lamb, gave birth to a son, William. Riis found that William's crying interfered with his writing and complained that the baby "must cut his teeth before the public can expect anything from me." In July he sent the rest of his family to a boardinghouse in Massachusetts and then joined them in August. In October the family relaxed for four days at a resort in the Berkshire Hills. The two vacations became a yearly routine, as were Jacob's lecture tours and hunting trips which he went on without his family.[33]

Riis longed for social status and recognition more than wealth. Historian Robert H. Wiebe has termed him an "aspiring gentleman," a rather pejorative phrase in that it implies a more selfish motive for his reform activities than was the case. Nevertheless, he began thinking seriously about writing his autobiography and harbored a wish to win Denmark's Order of Dannebrog Cross. Of the two Americas which he had described in *How the Other Half Lives,* Riis longed to join the comfortable classes rather than to suffer with the unfortunate. He rationalized that he could best serve the poor by winning entry into the salons of the rich and convincing them to patronize worthy causes. Thus, as he was seeking recognition as a reformer, he muted somewhat the angry words about economic exploitation so as not to alienate his wealthy patrons.[34]

In March 1895 Riis delivered a lecture on behalf of the New York Kindergarten Association. According to the *New York Times,* "a large number of fashionable people" attended, including the wives of J. P. Morgan, John Jacob Astor, and Alexander M. Van Rensselaer. In January of 1896 Dr. Albert Shaw, the editor of *World's Work,* invited Riis to participate in discussions on the promotion of the higher life at the home of Mrs. Robert Abbe II. With self-effacing courtesy the reformer responded: "My principal occupation—albeit my immediate environment has more to do with the lower than the higher life of our town. Still, as tending upward under difficulties, I may perhaps sneak in."[35]

Thus, the paradox of the social critic whose pen opens doors to the "higher" life did not escape Riis; but he did not regard his upward climb in status, coming ironically during a depression decade for the Empire City, as unpalatable to his intellectual honesty. At the time there was no distinct subculture of intellectuals, and Riis would have lamented such a development. The purpose of his writings was to promote harmony among classes, races, and other social groupings rather than to foster class consciousness. Correctly or incorrectly, he viewed the rich as potential comrades of the poor, not as foreordained villainous antagonists.

7

SPEARHEADING URBAN REFORM

When William L. Strong became mayor of New York City in January 1895, Jacob Riis embarked on a three-year flurry of activities to implement the goals which he had set for urban reconstruction. Modifying his gadfly role as a publicist, he worked along three political paths, each of which tested a different reform strategy. He was general agent for the New York Council of Good Government Clubs, served as secretary to the mayor's Advisory Committee on Small Parks, and was a close adviser to Theodore Roosevelt, the president of the Board of Police Commissioners. Organizing Good Government Clubs was for Riis a step toward participatory democracy and neighborhood rehabilitation. Selecting park sites was a demonstration of social control by experts for the public welfare, whereas Roosevelt's actions exemplified dynamic executive leadership.

Riis became disappointed with the mediocre overall record of the Strong administration, which he attributed to the indecision and compromises of the mayor; but he retained his confidence in channeling the energies of local citizenry, municipal experts, and political leaders into service for the city. He found a hero in Theodore Roosevelt, younger and more headstrong even than himself. The veteran police reporter and the incoming civil servant–politician were much alike. Each was conservative in his social habits and convictions while progressive in his political and economic beliefs. Both imagined themselves to be practical, vigorous men of action with an unflappable zest for life and an impish delight in the flamboyant. Concerning Roosevelt's passion for excitement, Sir Cecil Spring-Rice later declared: "You must always remember that the President is about six." He could have as easily made the statement about Riis. At one in their immediate objectives on Mulberry Street, Riis with his urban expertise and Roosevelt with his political acumen complemented each other.[1]

Roosevelt Comes to Mulberry Street

Shortly after the 1894 election, Roosevelt had urged Mayor Strong to appoint Riis as one of his close advisers. A couple of years previously, Roosevelt had attempted to meet the author of *How the Other Half Lives*. He went to Riis's office on Mulberry Street and, finding it vacant, left a note which said: "I have read your book, and I have come to help." Writing from Washington, D.C., where he was a Civil Service commissioner, Roosevelt expressed the hope to Riis that the new mayor would satisfy the needs of both working men and businessmen. "From you," Roosevelt said, "I feel he could get information such as he could not get from anyone else about the condition of our schools and about what can be done towards giving a better chance for respectability and usefulness to the people in the crowded lower wards." Riis cherished the compliment but received no invitation from Strong. He later declared that, in any event, he had harbored no desire for an official position. "I was ever an irregular," Riis wrote in his autobiography, "given to sniping on my own hook" (p. 327).[2]

Nevertheless, in April 1895 Riis was delighted when Strong selected Roosevelt to serve on New York City's Board of Police Commissioners. Several months earlier he had told Lincoln Steffens that only Roosevelt could rid the department of corruption, and he declared that "God will attend to his appointment." Roosevelt, who a decade earlier had enhanced his reputation by heading a legislative investigation into corruption in New York City, accepted the position with some reluctance. In March he declined posts on both the police board and the street cleaning department. But as he was tiring of his Civil Service Commission job and anxious to get back into New York politics, he changed his mind and gave an affirmative answer to Strong's second offer.[3]

On 6 May as Roosevelt walked along the dirty sidewalks of Mulberry Street to his new place of work, he spotted Riis. With great fanfare Roosevelt yelled for "Jake" to follow him. Riis told his friend Steffens to come along. As Steffens later recalled the scene in his autobiography, when the three men arrived at police headquarters, followed by a large crowd of spectators, Roosevelt cried out: "Where are our offices? Where is the board room? What do we do first?" (pp. 257–59). The three other commissioners greeted him and by a prearranged plan elected him president of the police board. Then Roosevelt adjourned the brief meeting and asked the two newspapermen what he should do next. They warned him to treat his colleagues with some deference, or they might make trouble for him. In fact, Democrat Andrew D. Parker and Republican Frederick D. Grant, an undistinguished career politician whose only claim to fame resulted from his being the son of President Ulysses S. Grant, resented Roosevelt's antics. The only commissioner with whom Roosevelt subsequently enjoyed a satisfactory rapport was Democrat Avery D. Andrews.

Riis and Steffens saw much of the new boss of Mulberry Street during his first weeks in office. When he wanted to confer with the two reporters, Roosevelt opened his office window and hollered a cowboy yell, "Hi yi yi!" He referred to them as his cabinet and said that they knew the needs of his job better than he did. When a newspaper hinted that Roosevelt was using his position as a springboard for higher office, the reporters decided to ask him about the charge. After Riis inquired whether he wanted to be president, Roosevelt sprang up with clenched fists and shouted out, "No friend of mine would ever say a thing like that. . . ." Then he relaxed and said that all young men dream of becoming their country's leader but that he would not plot and plan for it but only do the just thing. Utilizing the advice of Riis and Steffens and thankful for the publicity which they showered upon him, Roosevelt reciprocated by giving them inside information and access to private police documents.[4]

Roosevelt's immediate task was to restore confidence in the honesty of the police force. He dramatically canceled the annual police parade until a time when his men would be deserving of public accolade. On 18 May Roosevelt wrote Henry Cabot Lodge that he would move to oust police chief Thomas Byrnes, and within ten days Byrnes resigned. Riis later wrote in his autobiography: "There was not one of us all who had known him [Byrnes] long who did not regret it, though I, for one, had to own the necessity of it; for Byrnes stood for the old days that were bad" (p. 339). Roosevelt forced the most blatantly corrupt policemen, including "Clubber" Williams, into retirement. He hoped that careful scrutiny would lead others to mend their ways, and he took pains to promote men without regard to tenure who displayed conspicuous loyalty and valor.

To build esprit de corps, Roosevelt had the city pay for policemen's uniforms and gave out medals for heroism. Some reformers wanted the commissioner to indict many more men on criminal charges. For practical reasons Roosevelt demurred; and Riis, for more sentimental reasons, agreed with his decision. Riis "was fond even of some of the worst men," Steffens said in his autobiography (p. 261). In fact, Riis said this of Chief Byrnes in *The Making of an American:* "He made life in a mean street picturesque while he was there, and for that something is due him" (p. 313).

During his first two months in office, Roosevelt attracted much attention from the press corps, which realized that his dashing and unorthodox style made good copy. Roosevelt's mannerisms were bigger than life, and his swashbuckling style was good for both his own reputation and the morale of the force. On one occasion he responded to the threat of a riot by assigning twenty-five Jewish policemen to protect a virulently anti-Semitic speaker. This action muted both the speech and the crowd's angry mood. Roosevelt's flamboyance extended even to his dress. In the summer he commonly wore a black silk sash and pink shirts with tassels down to his knees. Arthur Brisbane wrote in the *World* that Roosevelt's teeth "are big and white, his eyes are small and piercing, his voice is rasping." Because of his midnight inspection tours, reporters began calling Roosevelt Haroun-al-Raschid, a reference to the Abbasidian Caliph memorialized in *Arabian Nights*.[5]

On the night of 6 June 1895, Riis accompanied Roosevelt on the first of many such checks of patrol posts. According to the *Evening Sun*'s story the following day, they discovered that all but one group of officers were negligent. Often thereafter the two men ventured forth incognito, in black cloaks and wide-brimmed hats, searching for patrolmen who might be sleeping, drinking, mingling with disreputable ladies, or otherwise shirking their duty. Riis used the tours to alert Roosevelt about slum conditions. Along the way he pointed out the wretched lodging houses and tenements. Since the president of the police board was an ex officio member of the Board of Health, Riis hoped that his friend could spur a frontal assault against the worst evils.[6]

While there was little open opposition to Roosevelt's first forays against corruption, his decision to vigorously enforce the Raines Excise Act, which prohibited the sale of alcohol on Sundays, stirred up a bitter wave of criticism. Neither Riis nor Roosevelt approved totally of the Raines law. The reporter did not disapprove of drinking except when it had harmful social effects. People who sought a drink were not criminals, Riis declared; "Their lives are dreary and barren enough for six days in the week without having all of their desolation compressed into the seventh and drilled into them

again." In fact, he quipped that Carrie Nation, the hatchet-
wielding saloon smasher, would do better to attack frying pans
rather than whiskey glasses, since poor food drove more people to drink than improper morals. Despite these misgivings,
however, Riis and Roosevelt believed that the impartial enforcement of all statutes was necessary to avert corruption
and gain respect for the law. During the previous year the
police under Tammany's control had enforced the law discrim-
inately in order to gain political favors and monetary payoffs,
arresting eighty-four hundred excise violators but winking at
other lawbreakers.[7]

Thus the Raines Excise Act crackdown was perhaps
necessary, but it had undesirable political and social results.
On 18 August 1895 Riis and Roosevelt made an inspection of
the twenty-first precinct and afterwards announced, according
to the *Evening Sun,* that almost all saloons that they witnessed
were complying with the law. Even so, they could not claim
that illicit traffic in liquor had completely halted. Moreover,
the issue eroded Roosevelt's power and turned his attention
from other pressing matters. His position outraged many
immigrants whose custom it was to celebrate the Sabbath with
spirits. Commissioner Parker and Tammany politicians actively worked to undermine the policy. Even Mayor Strong
and the Reverend Parkhurst, whom Roosevelt began calling
"that goose," urged the police force to concentrate more on
crime and less on blue laws. The mayor chided Roosevelt at a
public dinner. "I found that the Dutchman whom I had appointed meant to turn all New Yorkers into Puritans," the
mayor gibed gracelessly, stinging Roosevelt to even greater
zeal. In retaliation and to demonstrate his impartiality to
class, he ordered a raid on the fashionable Sherry's restaurant.
In April 1896 the state legislature amended the Raines Act
to permit the serving of liquor with meals at hotels. Immediately saloons began converting their quarters to satisfy the
wording of the law, serving free meals—which sometimes con-
sisted solely of pretzels, a diet approved by one tolerant judge
—and often using their tiny bedroom facilities as brothels.[8]

Shortly after Roosevelt joined the police board, Riis became a source of embarrassment to him by fostering the illusion that New York City was undergoing an epidemic of crime. The incident began when a new police reporter started writing sensational stories about the daily events at Mulberry Street headquarters. At the request of their editors, Riis and Steffens increased the publicity they gave to minor crimes. This professional rivalry left an impression which Roosevelt feared would do damage to his reputation. After he asked Riis to settle the disruptive, competitive war, the "crime wave" abruptly ended, according to the *Autobiography of Lincoln Steffens* (pp. 285–91).

On another occasion Riis wrote a feature story on the breast feeding of infants. His friend Roger Tracy had discovered that in England and Germany more than 96 percent of infant deaths occurred with bottle-fed babies. In order to supplement these statistics, Riis sought out Roosevelt's opinion on the matter. He quoted the police commissioner as saying "By Godfrey, the woman who won't nurse her own babies, if she can, isn't fit to have a baby anyhow—I always said so."[9]

In 1895 the forty-six-year-old Riis had gray hair and was gaining a paunch, but neither age nor weight reduced his impulsive spirit or his contentious personality. Once, according to Roger Tracy, he knocked a man down for insulting his hero Roosevelt. During another heated altercation a reporter threw him to the ground. Riis would have retaliated, Tracy wrote, except that "his glasses flew off and as he was groping for them others came up and separated the combatants." Proud of his pugnaciousness and moral vigor, he wrote in his account book that his greatest wish for his children was not wealth but for them to have the will to "stand up for the right and fight for it if need be."[10]

Disillusionment with Mayor Strong

By the winter of 1895, Riis's support of William L. Strong
was cooling, as the mayor delayed and compromised on im-
plementing reform programs. On 1 December 1895 Riis
declared that the urban reform movement in New York did not
need new laws so much as the enforcement of existing statutes
regarding tenements, schools, child labor, and parks. Praising
the police work of Roosevelt and the street-cleaning improvement under Colonel George E. Waring, he hoped that their
example would extend to other agencies. Inertia and incom-
petence were nullifying legislation which gave the government
the power to condemn dwellings that were dangerous to life
and health. City ordinances required all children to attend
school and all new schools to have open air playgrounds, but
the lack of facilities made these mandates inoperable. In 1895
New York City's public schools turned away pupils for lack
of space, while fifty thousand children of school age were on
the streets or working.[11]

Riis's unhappiness with the Strong administration resulted also from the continuing abuses of child labor. In April
1895 Riis had testified before the Reinhardt committee on
tenement sweatshops that parents circumvented the existing
minimum age law covering nonfamily laborers by falsifying
their children's birthdates. He supported legislation that would
allow inspectors to demand birth certificates or passports
rather than having to accept the statement of parents. A few
weeks later he asked the mayor to appoint as volunteer factory
inspectors members of the Reverend Charles Parkhurst's City
Vigilance League, to which he belonged. He quoted a three-
year-old ordinance that gave Mayor Strong the authority to
appoint private citizens to such positions. Some of the professional inspectors disliked the idea, however, and nothing
came from the request.[12]

When Mayor Strong took office, Riis had expected the
speedy implementation of the 1887 Small Parks Act, which
authorized the spending of $1 million annually for parks. A

member of the Committee of Seventy's parks and playgrounds subcommittee, he believed the city should provide public areas "for the rest and recreation of the poor," rather than "for the pomp and parade of the wealthy." All during 1895 the Board of Street Opening and Improvement and the Department of Parks quarreled and seemed uninterested, in the eyes of Riis, in using the funds. As a result, in January 1896 Riis and other urban reformers called on the mayor to request approval for specific parks which the Gilder Committee had recommended. Mayor Strong delayed an affirmative reply but asked his visitors to serve as an advisory committee to study possible sites. Settlement worker James B. Reynolds became chairman, and John B. Devins, the founder of the East Side Federation, was its secretary. Also on the committee with Riis were businessman A. C. Kimber and Dr. Jane E. Robbins, a close friend of the Danish-American reformer who worked at College Settlement. After three weeks the committee selected two sites. The city soon seized the property and razed the tenement houses on them, but then delayed putting in the parks. This infuriated Riis.[13]

Realizing that Mayor Strong was operating from the framework of political expediency more than from a dedication to the cause of small parks, Riis tried a variety of tactics to win his support. He had both the Social Reform Club and Good Government Clubs lobby in a futile effort to have the city convert an ancient cemetery into a playground. On several occasions, he wrote later, he sent women to the mayor's office to bargain for his objectives because "They could worm a playground or a small park out of him when I should have met with a curt refusal and a virtual invitation to be gone." Riis concluded that "In his political doldrums the Mayor did not have a kindly eye to reformers; but he was not always able to make them out in petticoats."[14]

During 1895 Riis also became concerned about the fate of the Mulberry Bend area, the three-acre maze of back alleys and dilapidated tenements that had symbolized to the police reporter the shamefulness and rottenness of the slums. In 1869 a report of the Board of Health had labeled Mulberry Street "death's thoroughfare." Riis termed the Bend the "wicked core of the bloody Sixth Ward" which "reeked with incest and murder," a den of darkness which God's beauty never traversed, a pigsty that made animals of men. In an article entitled "What the Christmas Sun Saw," he told of an immigrant woman in the Bend who sang a native song to her grandchild. "The song ended in a burst of passionate grief," he wrote. "The old granny and the baby woke up at once. They were not in sunny Italy; not under southern cloudless skies . . . the wintry wind rattled the door as if it would say, in the language of their new home, the land of the free: 'Less music! More work! Root, hog, or die!' "[15]

During 1894 the city seized the property in the Bend for health reasons and announced plans to replace the tenements with a park; but for a year the city merely collected rents from the Bend's tenants, as there were not enough funds to reimburse the old landlords and then build the park. Mayor Strong ordered all residents out of their homes by 1 June 1895, and soon afterwards the city demolished the buildings, to Riis's great joy. But after the city auctioned off the remnants of the structures, the area remained as the wrecking crews had left it. Thus, during the winter of Riis's discontent in 1895–96 Mulberry Bend's tenements no longer existed, but neither was there a park in their place.[16]

On 23 December 1895 Riis publicly declared that the Mulberry Bend area was a health and safety hazard. He charged that the city used it as dumping grounds, while children played among the filth and rubble and in cellar-holes that contained rats and stagnant water. He attacked the Strong administration for advocating reform on election day but then forgetting its promises. His New York *Tribune* article concluded: "Let me ask you a simple question in arithmetic: if it took us eight years to get the Mulberry slum made into a dunghill, how long is it going to take us, with present machinery and official energy, to get the two tenement blocks over there, where people are smothering for want of elbow room, made into two parks?"

Within days after Riis's broadside, a gang of boys rolled a municipal dump truck into one of the cellars of which his article had spoken. The vehicle crushed several children to death. This tragedy, combined with pressure from reformers, prodded the government into finalizing plans for the park. Workmen leveled the property and planted grass and trees. The formal opening of the park took place on 15 June 1897, several months after it had been in use.

Riis received no invitation to attend the dedication. He had argued with city officials about trespass signs which forbade residents from walking on the grass. In fact, one day he had disobeyed the edict, and a policeman put a cane to his back and ordered him off. Attending the ceremonial opening with Lincoln Steffens, Riis noted with pleasure that policemen allowed the thousands of spectators to gather on the grass to hear the band and speeches by politicians and community leaders. The moment which he cherished most, however, was when Colonel George E. Waring addressed the crowd and led them in saluting Jacob Riis with three cheers.[17]

Roosevelt's Triumphs and Tribulations

During the winter of 1895, Roosevelt incurred the wrath of organized labor when he helped break a strike against the city's street cleaning department. When some city workers struck for higher wages, Colonel Waring, the head of the agency, fired all of the dissidents and used strikebreakers to clean the streets. Roosevelt ordered the police to protect Colonel Waring's new work force. Said Roosevelt: "We shall guard as zealously the rights of the striker as those of the employer. But when a riot is menaced it is different. The mob takes its own chances. Order will be kept at whatever cost. If it comes to shooting we shall shoot to hit. No blank cartridges or firing over the head of anybody." Riis, who deeply admired

Colonel Waring for the efficiency with which he cleaned up slum neighborhoods, defended the administration's position against strikers.[18]

Roosevelt came to believe, as did Riis, that the unionization of laborers was necessary and justifiable; but he countenanced only peaceful union tactics, which put working men at a distinct disadvantage in their clashes with employers. When a group of tailors went on strike, the police commissioner refused to break up their picket lines. But in a cab company dispute, Roosevelt gave police protection to the strikebreaking drivers. When he heard rumors of impending violence, he took Riis with him to a union meeting at Clarendon Hall. Boldly he announced that his force would maintain order at all costs and argued that the unionists would damage their aims if they perpetrated violence. Riis later wrote in his autobiography that the cab drivers responded to these words with sustained applause (p. 333).

The education on slum conditions which Roosevelt absorbed from Riis led directly to the condemnation of a hundred cigar-making sweatshops in the tenements. Riis showed his friend some of these home factories and then pointed out health department regulations concerning sanitary conditions. As organized labor applauded, Roosevelt persuaded the Board of Health to close down the worst violators of the law. Two landlords sued him, but the courts vindicated Roosevelt.[19]

Roosevelt's most valuable contribution to Riis's reform program was his closing of the police lodging houses. In February 1896, during a midnight walk past the Church Street station, Riis related how a policeman had thrown him out of the lodging quarters and killed his canine friend twenty-five years earlier. Roosevelt irately pounded his fists together and announced that he would smash the lodging houses altogether. Within twenty-four hours he emerged from a meeting of the police board with an edict to shut down all police lodging houses. The city transferred applicants for shelter to a barge on the East River. Of this prompt action Riis wrote: "Arbitration is good, but there are times when it becomes necessary

9. Getting books at the Riis House.

10. Girls Returning from Fresh Air Vacation.

11. Mullen's Alley.

12. Street Arabs barelegged on Mulberry Street.

13. Street Arabs in the Area of Mulberry Street.

14. Industrial School on West 52nd Street.

15. Children in Beach Street Industrial School.

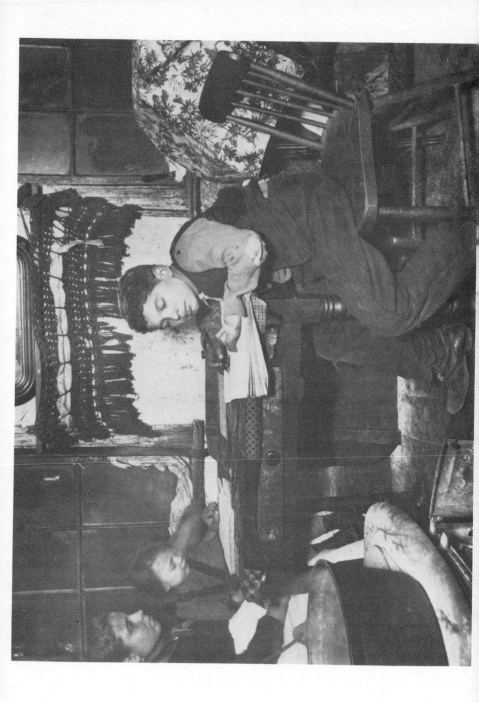

16. Pietro learning to write.

to knock a man down and arbitrate sitting on him, and this was such a time."[20]

Critics of Roosevelt's action denounced as heartless the closing of the free shelters. In March 1896 the city began to improve the facilities of the East River barge and sift the deserving applicants from so-called tramps. As a result, registration fell from ten thousand to two hundred. Riis argued that the adoption of scientific methods of separating the innocent poor from tramps and thieves was the only humane system. He bade the deserving poor use the Wayfarers' Lodge of the Charity Organization Society and lauded two other model houses which the philanthropist D. O. Mills had founded. The Mills lodging houses, dedicated to the promotion of self-reliance, manliness, and good citizenship, provided room and board for thirty-five cents and offered a library, a laundry, and smoking and writing rooms.[21]

During 1896 Roosevelt's enthusiasm for his job began to wane, as the split on the police board hindered his freedom of action. As a result, he began sounding out Republicans in Washington about an appointment as Assistant Secretary of the Navy. In August he told a friend that two of his colleagues were dishonest scoundrels. In December he labeled Grant a fool and Parker a knave. Parker at this time was spreading rumors that Roosevelt frequently attended irreputable burlesque shows and drank whiskey on Sundays at the Union League.[22]

Riis hated Parker for his cynical and dishonest attacks on Roosevelt, and in 1897 he opened a campaign for his dismissal from the police board. Parker encouraged a Tammany newspaper which doled out free soup to the poor to taunt Roosevelt and Riis on their opposition to this kind of aid. After the paper invited Riis to inspect its operations, the police reporter discovered that children were trading their food for beer at saloons which in turn then advertised free lunches for their patrons. Riis criticized this "mushy philanthropy" in an *Evening Sun* article dated 24 February 1897. Parker's claim that Roosevelt attended immoral shows stemmed from activities which took place at Clarendon Hall on the same night as when he and Riis attended the union meeting of cab drivers there. Riis called the charge "utterly contemptible." He called for men of good will to petition for Parker's ouster. In March 1897, in response to this pressure Mayor Strong asked the governor to remove Parker from office, but the Republican boss Thomas Platt interceded to save his job. A month later Roosevelt quit to work in the Navy Department in Washington.[23]

Roosevelt made an impressive record during his two years in Mulberry Street and credited Riis with inaugurating many of his programs. He ended the most flagrant forms of corruption, abolished police lodging houses, and enforced city ordinances impartially. In addition, he made efforts to hire members of ethnic minority groups for the force; and he established a bicycle squad, a telephone communication system, a rudimentary training program, and the beginnings of a civil service system. Roosevelt's friendship with Riis exposed him to social conditions which as a member of the Board of Health he helped to ameliorate. On 18 April 1897 Roosevelt told Riis that "For these two years you have been my main prop and comfort." He called him "the most loyal and disinterested man I ever knew." Six months later Roosevelt summarized his tenure as police commissioner. Writing to Riis on 25 October he said: "When I went to the Police Department it was on your book that I had built, and it was on you yourself that I continued to build. Whatever else I did there was done because I was trying, with much stumbling and ill success, but with genuine effort, to put into practice the principles you had set forth, and to live up to the standard you had established."

Despite Roosevelt's trumpetings, his accomplishments in refurbishing the police force were less important than the effect the slum had on the social philosophy of the future governor and president. The inner workings of the police department had a life of their own, characterized best perhaps by the pragmatic slogan "If you want to get along, go along." Despite

Roosevelt's good work, the recognition that Tammany would probably be back in command soon made ephemeral the results of the brief reform interlude.[24]

For Riis, Roosevelt's tenure in office had been Mulberry Street's golden age. He admired Roosevelt from his first day in office, and the younger man rapidly became a hero to the police reporter. "I had Roosevelt at last in my own domain," he later declared in a laudatory biography entitled *Theodore Roosevelt the Citizen* (1904). "For two years we were to be together all the day, and quite often most of the night, in the environment in which I had spent twenty years of my life. And these two were the happiest by far of them all. Then was life really worth living, and I have a pretty robust enjoyment of it at all times" (p. 131).

Agent for Good Government Clubs

During the summer of 1896, Riis began work as the secretary and general agent for the Council of Confederated Good Government Clubs of New York. Founded in 1893, the clubs ostensibly were nonpartisan groups dedicated to "efficient city government without regard for state or national politics." Their members, who gained the appellation of "goo goos," were united more by their hatred of Tammany and opposition to lawlessness than by their agreement on positive alternatives. Their main activity had been campaigning for the election of William L. Strong. In February 1896 Riis had spoken to the organization about goals for civic improvement. When he finished, members of the group asked him to direct their program of lobbying for governmental action. After he convinced himself that he would still have enough time for journalism and lecturing, Riis accepted election as their general secretary for six months beginning in July at a salary of $166 a month.[25]

Riis's long-range goal was to mobilize neighborhood

cells to root out their local problems and investigate and lobby for solutions to citywide problems. The clubs, he hoped, would serve as a vehicle to carry out his reform ideas. His specific job was to funnel out assignments of research or direct action to the more than twenty local clubs within the confederation.

Upon taking office Riis asked each club to provide him with information on membership, projects, time and place of meetings, territorial boundaries, and the success of past programs. The results of the poll were disappointing. Some clubs met formally only once a year and had not even decided upon projects. Almost all members were businessmen and professionals, a constituency that was atypical of New York's populace and one not anxious to fundamentally alter social or economic conditions. The representative of Club O wrote Riis that "Most of the members are prominent lawyers and doctors —too prominent in fact. We haven't a working man left, though we had a few once." Only an insignificant number of clubs were serving the needs of the poor. One of these was Club X, whose secretary reported that his members were lobbying for a new school, investigating complaints of code violations, and patrolling a park against "toughs" who "amuse themselves by attacking unoffending foreigners." Riis encouraged these community projects.[26]

At the city level Riis assigned each club the task of becoming a watchdog of a municipal agency. For instance, Club A checked into street cleaning; others investigated public schools, rapid transit, parks, and the police and fire departments. Riis wanted the clubs to demand better enforcement of the law and to draw up blueprints for new initiatives. By 16 December he noted in the *New York Times* that city officials were improving but added that a battle still "had to be waged against stupidity."

As a coordinator and administrator, Riis spent the bulk of his time issuing assignments, lobbying for proposals, and serving as a liaison between the clubs. For example, on 5 August 1896 Richard W. Gilder wrote Riis about a fire which occurred in a tenement paint store operating in violation of the law. As a result, he had one of his clubs compile a list of other unlawful establishments. Two months later he inaugurated a similar survey of hazardous tenement bakeries. Quite often Riis obtained the cooperation of public officials in his work, but he discovered that bureaucratic entanglements and the absence of governmental power were sometimes more responsible for neglect than the villainy of men in office. For example, the Fire Department, which issued bakery permits to tenement shops, was anxious to maximize safety standards but had no power to ensure that owners complied with their regulations. The Superintendent of School Buildings allowed clubs to meet on school property during afternoons and evenings, but the bleak and gloomy rooms discouraged many youths from participating in the programs. Most school officials supported a plan by Riis to provide free eye examinations for all pupils, but opposition from physicians caused the program to fail. The Department of Public Instruction welcomed the support of the Good Government Clubs in obtaining educational appropriations and in advocating a truant school for children, but these programs met stiff resistance from legislators in Albany until the winter of 1896–97.[27]

Riis achieved better results in pressuring the Board of Health to take action against tenement house abuses. During the summer of 1896, he escorted health officials on a tour of tenement hallways. As a result, the health department ordered ten thousand landlords to install proper lighting in their halls and staircases. And during 1896 and 1897, the city tore down almost a hundred rear tenements, including Gotham Court, which Riis had described as a notorious headquarters of sickness and suffering. "Directly or indirectly, I had a hand in destroying seven whole blocks of them as I count it up. I wish it had been seventy," his autobiography stated (p. 349). The owners of the condemned property raised a loud protest but suffered very little. Riis complained that Gotham Court's landlords, who had been murdering tenants for years, received compensation totalling $19,750, more than a hundred times the value of the property. Some critics charged that the policy of razing these buildings accelerated overcrowding and put extra burdens on the poor. Riis answered that there was sufficient housing available elsewhere. He estimated that twelve thousand people lost their homes and claimed that there were thirty-seven thousand vacant apartments in Manhattan. His statistics were approximately correct, but most of the poor could not afford to move into the apartments which were unfilled.[28]

During his year as general agent, Riis worked closely with the Public Education Association of New York City (PEA), which had been formed as an offshoot of Good Government Club E by women whose sex disqualified them from membership in the parent organization. In many ways Riis was the spiritual founder of the PEA, which was to outlive Club E by more than a half-century and become the most important force for progressive education in New York. Both Riis and the PEA believed that education was the cornerstone of urban reconstruction; both dedicated themselves to making public schools into community centers. After William Strong's election, they lobbied together for a state law that allowed the mayor to appoint new members to a restructured school board. In 1896 the Board rebuked Riis's request to open schools at night for use by clubs. But a year later it approved a pilot program whereby the PEA supervised club activities in two public schools. This was the opening wedge for comprehensive recreational, cultural, social, and educational evening and weekend programs.[29]

On several occasions Riis attempted to interest the Council of Good Government Clubs in the issue of public ownership of utilities. Praising European experiments in municipal socialism, he requested one local club to study its feasibility in New York. Most members did not warm to the idea; but in April 1897 Riis personally endorsed the Association for the Public Control of Franchises. This group, which attracted such distinguished patrician reformers as E. R. L. Gould and

Edwin R. A. Seligman, declared that the city had a right to control natural monopolies and public facilities such as streets, waterways, wharfs, and docks.[30]

In June 1897, after a year in office, Riis resigned his post as general agent in order to concentrate his reform efforts on the small parks movement. He had persuaded Mayor Strong to establish an Advisory Committee on Small Parks with himself as secretary. The nearness of the 1897 elections was causing the clubs to devote more time to politics than to reform. Riis acknowledged the value of activities to block Tammany Hall's return to power but decided that his most valuable service to reform would be on the mayor's Small Parks Committee.

Soon after Riis severed his connection with the Good Government clubs, they atrophied and never became the laboratories for community planning and nurseries of political action that he had hoped. Lacking a base of working class strength, they disintegrated into hollow mockeries of participatory democracy. Most of the patrician members were amateurs in politics who had vocational and cultural interests that took higher priority than uplift work. In 1905 George Washington Plunkitt of Tammany Hall asked sarcastically: "Do you ever hear of Good Government Club D and P and Q and Z any more? What's become of the infants who were to grow up and show us how to govern the city?"[31]

Perhaps what was remarkable was not that they faded away but that Riis was able to make such good use of them while he was their agent. Even though they did not become centers for neighborhood unity, the clubs helped bring about valuable programs of urban renewal. Pressure from the clubs strengthened the health department's campaigns against sweatshops and ill-lighted tenements. The clubs helped win approval for a truant school and forty-three new public schools, all of which would contain playgrounds and facilities for community clubs. Some of their members drafted model legislation for judicial reform and tenement house regulation and for a new charter for Greater New York. In 1897 the state legislature approved the consolidation of Queens, Brooklyn, and Staten Island with Manhattan and the Bronx, and the new charter which went into effect on 1 January 1898 contained many features which were identical to the model charter.[32]

During 1897 Riis again talked of quitting his job as a reporter. Only the certain income caused him to stay, and he decided to leave Mulberry Street when his children began going off on their own. In July, perhaps to test their independence, he sent one of his sons to a ranch in the West and allowed his daughter Clara to travel alone to Ribe, Denmark.[33]

Riis wrote very few magazine articles during 1897, but he continued to lecture and again attended the Chautauqua summer festival. Short of money, as usual, he called his account book for 1897 "The Mystery." On 24 July 1897, shortly after he left his post with the Good Government Clubs, Gilder sent him a check for $150 for a Christmas article. Six days later Riis returned it along with a friendly note that nevertheless made it clear that he wanted $200 for the piece. Before he started his account book entries for 1898, Riis wrote: "Perhaps I will have better luck this time."

Parks for the People

In June 1897 Mayor Strong selected Abram S. Hewitt and Riis to become chairman and secretary respectively of the Small Parks Advisory Committee. Hewitt was an aloof aristocrat, a Bourbon Democrat without much social conscience. In 1886 he had campaigned successfully for mayor with a pledge to save New York City from the "ideas of anarchists, nihilists, communists, socialists, and mere theorists." Once, on a visit to an insane asylum, Hewitt stretched out on a cot and said, "Well, I suppose I could get used to it." Unlike Riis, he advocated a literacy test for immigrants and a fourteen-year residency requirement for citizenship. Strong balanced the other members with reformers, business leaders, and public officials. When Hewitt accepted the post, he told Riis that "naturally you will have to do most of the work."[34]

On 10 June, when the Small Parks Advisory Committee convened for the first time, Riis argued that the group should examine the entire question of the functions of parks and the steps necessary to achieve those ends rather than merely select park sites. Remembering the "Keep off the Grass" signs at Mulberry Bend Park, he persuaded the other members to emphasize playgrounds and recreation as the primary purpose of the parks. When the committee members reassembled a week later, Riis brought with him topographical maps which he had drawn up with the help of health officials. The group urged the mayor to speed up condemnation proceedings on two parks which the state legislature had already approved.[35]

The Hewitt Committee held frequent meetings during the next four months in an effort to make known its findings before a new and possibly hostile administration took office. Declaring that parks were vital for the "physical and moral health of the people," the committee's final report included maps, copies of existing statutes, statistics regarding population density and death rates, long-range goals, and recommendations for over a dozen park sites, including a large recreation complex on Randall's Island. The cost estimate of these immediate recommendations was $3,500,000 for land purchase and conversion. In addition, the report urged the planning of parks at the outer reaches of the city before rising land prices would make it less practical.

The spirit of the report embodied the philosophy of the creative play movement to which Riis was an enthusiastic subscriber. Riis peppered the wording of the report with phrases from Friedrich Froebel, the German philosopher and father of the play movement. And he quoted an English maxim to the effect that athletics could cure crime. Thus, parks would deter vandalism and fighting by neighborhood gangs, the report stated, as boys would have "something better to do than smashing lamps and windows and getting themselves arrested." The unofficial motto of the Hewitt-Riis report was "Room for all to breathe and for the young to play. . . ."[36]

During the autumn of 1897, Mayor Strong carried out plans for parks at three sites which the Hewitt Committee had recommended. Nevertheless, by the time he turned the report over to subordinates he was a lame duck official. More interested in parks than in politics, Riis hoped that the victorious Democrats would implement his program. On 24 November he sent a copy of the Small Parks Committee report to Nathan Straus, a Democrat who was in line for an appointment to the park board. Riis said that he would "rejoice to see Tammany earn the credit for doing the work we planned; and it shall have no more staunch and loyal supporter than myself in such a course." Straus thanked him for his interest and replied that Tammany had always been the friend of the poor.[37]

The attitude of the new mayor, Robert A. Van Wyck, disappointed Riis. The two men met together in January 1898. The mayor declared that he approved of the report in principle but regretted that the city had a shortage of funds. Then he said ominously that he could find no provision in the city charter for a small parks committee. Riis replied that its members had been acting as unofficial advisers. Then they had no power, Van Wyck said. On another occasion Riis and representatives of five groups, including the Y.M.C.A., the Social Reform Club, and three athletic associations, petitioned the city for playground equipment. Van Wyck denied their request, saying "Vaudeville destroyed Rome."[38]

Riis had better fortune in persuading the New York School Board to establish play areas. In 1898 the board voted to maintain eighteen playgrounds during the summer, and the number was increased by thirteen in 1899. That same year the Board of Education expanded evening school activities by supplying books, games, athletic equipment, and supervisors. The trend toward making the schoolhouse a neighborhood center was gaining support, and finally there was some answer for the East Side lament: "And what shall we do with our nights?" In addition, the school board operated recreational piers, sand gardens in Central Park, and a number of kindergarten centers.[39]

Defeat and Rededication

Thus the labors of the Good Government Clubs and the Small Parks Advisory Committee effected a number of practical results, but Riis was melancholy about the overall results of three years of patrician rule. He told one friend that the failure of municipal reform distressed him even more than national affairs because the problems were so much more immediate. When people became cynical about the promises of progress and accepted corrupt officials on a local level, Riis believed, then they would be apathetic to malpractice on the state and federal levels. In the 1897 mayoralty election, Riis had supported Seth Low, the candidate of the Republican party and of most humanitarian reformers. But he felt that Low's campaign gave too much emphasis to structural changes geared to economy and efficiency and not enough to social welfare. He told Theodore Roosevelt that many of Seth Low's patrician supporters were hypocrites and that reformers had too willingly joined with them. Roosevelt agreed. He singled out Abram Hewitt, the man who had defeated him in the 1886 mayoralty election, as a dishonest and selfish man who took credit for the work of others. But Roosevelt added that "in spite of it good work can often be gotten out of these same pharisees."[40]

The return of Tammany demonstrated how fragile public support was for patrician reform. On the night of the 1897 election, Riis walked through the Bowery and observed the celebrations of the poor over the results. He later wrote in *The Battle with the Slum* that the "mob" was "gorging itself, like a starved wolf. . . . Drunken men and women sat in every doorway, howling ribald songs and curses" (p. 56). Yet Riis did not blame the poor. "It was not the slum that had won; it was we who had lost. We were not up to the mark,—not yet," he added (p. 60). Even though he had not been able to make the William L. Strong administration bridge the gap that existed in New York between the powerful and the poor, he still retained confidence in channeling the energies of local citizenry, municipal experts, and political reform leaders for a multipronged assault on the slums.

8

RIIS AND GOVERNOR ROOSEVELT

Theodore Roosevelt's tenure in office as governor of New York during 1899 and 1900 led to the culmination, in many ways, of Jacob Riis's urban reform efforts. As a close friend and adviser to the governor, he helped bring about tighter governmental regulation of housing standards and tenement sweatshops. During this time his religious faith, his adulation of Roosevelt, his optimism, and his nationalism became more dominant features of his personality. Concurrently, after 1900 the urban reform scene became more professionalized, and its institutions adapted organizational techniques along lines that were somewhat foreign and repugnant to his romantic temperament. After Roosevelt's election to the vice-presidency in 1900, Riis became less intimately connected with New York City's municipal problems and more a national spokesman of a gospel of morality, humanitarianism, and progressivism.

Fervent Nationalist

When the battleship *Maine* exploded and sank in Havana Harbor on the evening of 15 February 1898, the forty-nine-year-old reformer became an ardent champion of an American declaration of war to avenge the deaths of the 260 sailors and to end the Spanish atrocities in Cuba. In Washington, D.C. at the time, for a speaking engagement, Riis stayed on until May to help Roosevelt gather together and outfit a volunteer unit of Rough Riders to go into battle if war came. He supported the attempts of his oldest son to enlist in the army and his second son to enter the Naval Academy. Roosevelt was not able to help him achieve either objective. Poor eyesight, which plagued the Riis family, kept both sons out of the armed forces.[1]

When Congress declared war on 25 April 1898, Riis pondered whether to accept offers from the New York *Sun* and *Outlook* to go to Cuba as a correspondent. The plan was for him to travel with Clara Barton and the Red Cross and learn the extent of the suffering which the Cuban people had undergone under Spanish rule. Caught up in the righteousness of the American cause, Riis needed little prodding, even though he told friends that he hated the sight of violence. He declared in his autobiography that he had had a "wicked and foolish" desire to "get on a horse with a sword, and slam in just once, like another Sheridan" (pp. 378–79). Nevertheless, he reluctantly turned down the assignment. His two youngest children, Kate and Billy, were ill with scarlet fever; and he did not want to burden further his wife. He wrote his sister Emma in Denmark on 4 May 1898 that he would have chosen otherwise if his daughter Clara had been at home rather than vacationing in Ribe.

And so Riis went home to Richmond Hill with matchboxes and other souvenirs, and for a month he prepared notes for his July lecture tour in the Middle West and wrote war dispatches for a newspaper in Denmark. The editor returned the articles unused, because of their chauvinistic excesses. Riis angrily wrote back that the man was jealous of America's might and that he would proudly continue to "shout for the flag in a fight. . . ." For him the war was not only a crusade against despotism but a victory for progressive forces over the caution and greed of Wall Street businessmen.[2]

Arriving home in August from his midwestern trip, Riis made plans for a hunting and fishing expedition at Parry Sound, Ontario, and listened with hope to rumors of the impending gubernatorial candidacy of Roosevelt. In mid-August the leader of the Rough Riders landed with his troops at Montauk Point, Long Island, fresh from his triumph in Cuba. On 9 September Roosevelt wrote Riis: "Good luck on your hunt! Death to grizzly-bear cubs." Riis did not kill any cubs but mistakenly shot a porcupine and impaled his hand on its quills.[3]

After he returned from Canada, Riis eagerly accepted a place on Roosevelt's campaign train which on 17 October 1898 began a whistle-stop tour of the state. Roosevelt was thankful for Riis's vocal support since his political tactics had angered many reformers. During the early fall the Rough Rider had intimated to representatives of the Citizens' Union, a patrician reform organization to which Riis belonged, that he would accept nomination for governor on an independent ticket. Then, after visiting boss Thomas C. Platt and securing the Republican nomination, he refused to accept a third-party endorsement. The Reverend Charles Parkhurst vehemently criticized Roosevelt for forming an unholy alliance with Platt and his machine. Robert Fulton Cutting, the Victorian leader of the Association for Improving the Condition of the Poor, charged that the Republican candidate had become "the standard bearer of corruption and demoralization." Roosevelt believed that the purist political morality of these men was suicidal. Riis agreed, and his presence on the campaign train helped cool some of the sting.[4]

Although Riis's main functions during the campaign junket were symbolic and social, he did make a few short speeches about the leadership ability of the former police commissioner and Rough Rider. He came out for law and order and for tighter controls on immigration to weed out criminals. Neither position was likely to make Roosevelt many enemies in the hinterland. Appealing to moderates and conservatives, he exclaimed at one whistle stop: "I am in favor of stamping out anarchy with a heavy hand. The man who preaches murder, who holds aloft the dagger and the torch, should be treated as a murderer. No reform can be effected while men are fighting." Roosevelt was the main attraction on the stump, but he also took with him seven Rough Riders in full uniform. At each stop a bugler blew a cavalry charge; then Roosevelt told how he won victory in Santiago and would administer a similar beating on the Democrats. His opponent, Augustus Van Wyck, was an honest and respected judge, but Roosevelt called him a pawn of Tammany boss Richard Croker. During a rally at Flushing on Long Island Riis spoke to an overflow crowd which could not fit into the main hall. His speech aroused such lusty cheers, he later wrote, that the noise interrupted Roosevelt's address inside.[5]

During the final ten days of the campaign, Roosevelt's victory was in doubt. Because of this, Republican boss Thomas C. Platt secured an emergency war chest of sixty thousand dollars from John Pierpont Morgan and other wealthy financiers. In addition, Roosevelt took advantage of a dispute within the Democratic ranks. Boss Croker refused to renominate a judge with more than twenty years of experience because the man was too independent. Croker declared publicly that "Tammany Hall has a right to expect proper consideration at his hands." On the final night of the campaign, Riis said that a hundred-vote victory would satisfy him. Roosevelt predicted a wider margin but prepared for the worst. On 4 November he wrote Henry Cabot Lodge that "I have had a very hard campaign, but at any rate I have made the best fight I could, and if Blifil and Black George win, why win they must." Roosevelt lost New York City by 80,000 votes but won by a large enough margin in rural counties to defeat Van Wyck by a plurality of 17,786 votes. It was an impressive victory but one founded in part on the money of big business and the organization of a corrupt and self-satisfied political machine.[6]

On 24 December 1898 Riis published his last Christmas story for the New York *Evening Sun,* for soon afterwards he went into semiretirement as a journalist in order to concentrate more on lectures and reform activities. His fellow news-papermen made fun of the article's sentimentality and "laughed it to scorn," Riis wrote, but it "moved me more deeply than any of the rest." The article concerned "Black Bill," a habitual criminal whom the police had arrested for stealing a purse. While they were searching him, police found a Christmas list for food and gifts for his family. Realizing that the motive for his crime had been pure, Black Bill's captors raised some money, found him a job, and released him on probation to give his family a Merry Christmas.

Riis's sentimentality did not quash his contentiousness, however; rather, the two traits worked in tandem. In a letter to Silas McBee, the editor of the *Churchman,* he denied a request to send a picture of himself to print with one of his articles. He did not approve of "this celebration business" of lionizing reformers. What he needed was "to be sat on instead at short intervals." Riis wrote: "Don't think that humility has anything to do with this, just the reverse. I am just as obstrep-erous as I can be, and as my forefathers the old Vikings probably were. Sometimes I wish I was a Viking—maybe I was once."[7]

Riis's contact with settlement workers, housing experts, social workers, and other urban reformers gave Roosevelt an important pipeline to a group of dedicated idealists whose favor and programs the governor-elect hoped to cultivate. Through his friendship with settlement residents Lillian D. Wald, James B. Reynolds, and Jane E. Robbins, Riis had joined the Social Reform Club, which met on Tuesday evenings to hear lectures and argue practical and theoretical questions far into the night. Only their openness to new ideas, their commit-ment to social justice, and their skepticism of simplistic dogma united the disparate group of members. They welcomed as speakers college professors, labor leaders, enlightened business-men, radicals, and foreign visitors such as the socialists Sidney and Beatrice Webb and the anarchist Peter Kropotkin.[8] A small but significant minority of the Social Reform Club set, including Florence Kelley, Robert Hunter, and J. G. Phelps

Stokes, eventually became socialists. Riis and most of the rest ultimately accepted America's political and economic system, and the sweeping changes they advocated were attempts to lessen class conflict, promote social harmony, and therefore make the system more workable. In 1899 many of them, including Riis, founded the People's Institute in order to promote "the ethical uplift of the community." And in 1900 they organized the Committee of One Hundred to investigate and lobby for municipal reform.[9]

Labor Adviser for Governor Roosevelt

Even before he took office, Roosevelt made Riis a consultant on labor policies. On 22 November 1898 the governor-elect called together Riis, three union officials, social worker James Reynolds, and editor George Gunton, a defender of big business who nevertheless favored an eight-hour day and strong labor organizations. Riis suggested that the most practical course would be the vigorous enforcement of existing health, housing, child labor, and maximum hours statutes. Having seen many well-intentioned laws go unenforced, he had more concern for methods of implementation than with composing new bodies of law. In principle he favored the abolition of tenement sweatshops, but since the Supreme Court had ruled that this was unconstitutional, he favored strict governmental regulation of tenement factories as the most expedient course. He and the other advisers also recommended that Roosevelt centralize the bureaucratic machinery that was responsible for checking the abuses of employers.[10]

Acting upon the recommendation of the six advisers, Roosevelt proposed legislation to place control over labor laws in the hands of the Board of Factory Inspectors. And he urged a tightening of the tenement house code of 1897 so that public officials could inspect and license sweatshops more effectively. He also asked for enabling legislation to allow volunteer deputies to help enforce the law. In the spring of 1899, Roosevelt signed a compromise measure which contained the licensing provisions, added fourteen paid workers to the staff of the Board of Factory Inspectors, and transferred more power to that agency. The bill made no provision for volunteer inspectors and left to the Board of Health the enforcement of the Mercantile Act which put limits on the working hours of store employees. Nevertheless, Roosevelt and Riis expressed pleasure that the new statutes would improve working conditions in the slums.[11]

The governor made clear to Riis early in his administration that he would lean heavily on him for ideas to combat urban decay. In May 1899, for instance, Riis wrote an article entitled "The Battle with the Slum" for the *Atlantic Monthly* in which he declared that "The poor we shall have always with us, but the slum we need not have. These two do not rightfully belong together. Their present partnership is at once poverty's worst hardship and our worst fault" (p. 634). Roosevelt, after perusing the piece, asked Riis on 12 June: "Is there anything I can do in reference to the slum? Can I touch on it in my next message? If so, I will write it with you."

Sometimes practical politics caused Roosevelt to withhold his endorsement of Riis's recommendations. Such a case occurred when the reporter endorsed Florence Kelley to serve on the Board of Factory Inspectors. Mrs. Kelley had formerly headed Governor John Peter Altgeld's inspection system in Illinois and was a leader of the National Consumers' League. Lillian Wald and James Reynolds, leaders in New York's settlement movement which was moving inexorably into the area of economic issues, persuaded Riis to act as an intermediary on her behalf. On 21 January 1899 Riis took Florence Kelley and their mutual friend Jane Addams to Albany but found Roosevelt too busy to see them. Two days later Roosevelt apologized for the fiasco. He wrote Riis that he "was merely informed that you had two ladies to see me and as I was late for an engagement and literally had not one second, I sent down the word I did." The governor told his friend to bring them again but to make an appointment first.

The campaign for Florence Kelley's appointment floundered as a result of the opposition of Boss Platt and the Republican machine. Roosevelt convinced himself that her views and reputation were too radical for the political climate. On 11 February 1899 he wrote Riis: "I shall be overjoyed to see Mrs. [sic] Adams [sic]. Don't have Mrs. Kelley come on; you see I don't really see how I can appoint her—even legally." Using the excuse of her nonresidency, the governor appointed a Republican elevator operator from Albany to the post.[12]

In March 1899 Roosevelt asked Riis to look into a dispute regarding the personnel on the Board of Factory Inspectors. The governor became alarmed when the New York *World* charged that New York's Chief Factory Inspector, Daniel O'Leary, was uninterested in forcing sweatshop operators to conform to the law. He had exposed only four illegal establishments in twelve months, the *World* charged, and in a speech O'Leary had called sweatshop laborers a "degenerate . . . [and] filthy people, undeserving of sympathy." On 24 February 1899 the United Brotherhood of Tailors appealed to Roosevelt to remedy their miserable working conditions. The tailors complained that sweatshops kept down their wages and that their employers kept unsanitary shops and violated the maximum hours law. They invited Roosevelt to inspect their condition personally. Instead the governor appointed Riis to look into their complaints.[13]

Riis entered the investigation with mixed sympathies. As much as he hated the sweatshops, he, like Daniel O'Leary, put the blame partly on workers who submitted to the system rather than strike for their rights. Furthermore, he realized that O'Leary's undermanned staff could not enforce the law properly. Yet Riis also sympathized with the goals of the tailors. Realizing that only strong unions could effectively protect workers against the exploitation of economic masters, he recognized that the sweatshops undermined the influence of organized labor.

Riis decided that he could best carry out his assignment

by observing conditions firsthand on a personal tour. He took with him two officers of the United Brotherhood of Tailors and three inspectors, to shops which the union had picked out as in violation of the law. He did not limit his inspection to sweatshops. In fact, he visited twenty other establishments, asking workers about their working hours and complaints, and examining toilets, closets, and stairways. A week later in a detailed report Riis told Roosevelt that the charges against O'Leary had been groundless. Where violations occurred, the inspectors had already issued orders to remedy the situation. Nevertheless, the report recommended legislation to provide for a team of night inspectors and the licensing of all rooms where manufacturing took place, since the existing law applied only when nonfamily workers labored in a room, and therefore was easy to circumvent.[14]

Roosevelt dismissed the charges against O'Leary; but when the chief inspector's term of office expired in April, he replaced him because he learned that O'Leary was using his staff to perform political errands for Boss Platt. Roosevelt told O'Leary's successor, John Williams, to seek out the advice of settlement workers and reformers such as Riis, Mrs. Kelley, and Reynolds. The job took on new importance in June 1899, when a law went into effect requiring the licensing of all tenement sweatshops. The new code outlawed beds in workrooms and required that no more than one family reside in any flat where manufacturing took place. Williams ignored the advice of reformers, and to their dismay he appointed O'Leary to be the head of the city's Licensing Bureau. O'Leary continued to devote more time to politics than to the new law. In December 1899 at a protest meeting labor leaders charged that O'Leary discriminated against union shops, and Florence Kelley claimed that he had licensed two hundred unfit establishments.[15]

In response to this renewed criticism Roosevelt asked Riis to conduct a second investigation. This time Riis found that the charges by the unions were substantially correct. On 30 December, after he related some of the details of O'Leary's malpractices to Roosevelt, the governor told him: "It is perfectly evident that O'Leary will have to go." Riis recommended a freeze on appropriations for additional paid inspectors until the inefficiency and corruption ended, but he suggested that Roosevelt again attempt to authorize volunteers to do this work. Submitting the report on 15 January 1900, Riis wrote: "I am sorry to add as much as one feather's weight to your cares at this time; . . . but I should not serve you faithfully if I reported otherwise."

No positive action came from Riis's proposals. Constitutionally, Roosevelt had no power to dismiss either Williams or O'Leary unless he brought impeachment proceedings before the state senate, and Republican leaders were opposed to this. On 7 January 1900 Roosevelt received a letter from Benjamin B. Odell, a powerful associate of Platt's whom the New York *World* had described as saturnine-looking with "black hair, black eyes, black moustache and a parchment white complexion." Odell wrote: "Care should be exercised in any action taken with O'Leary, Factory Inspector, as he has been a pretty good friend of ours." Roosevelt obeyed this counsel for caution. His only action was to urge without success legislation to permit unpaid inspectors. In a letter to Josephine S. Lowell the governor admitted that his appointment of Williams had been a mistake, but he claimed that the law permitted him no course of action.[16]

In the spring of 1900, Roosevelt decided to publicize his concern for the enforcement of labor laws by personally visiting tenement shops in the Lower East Side. Such a tour might also demonstrate to reformers that he had not abandoned them. Disturbed by a popular book about "dangerous trades" called *No. 5 John Street* (1899), written for young people by Richard Whiteing, he asked Riis whether such places existed in New York. "If so, I would like to go to them," Roosevelt wrote on 8 May. He asked Riis to arrange the details and to invite Florence Kelley to accompany them. Mrs. Kelley declined the invitation, but James Reynolds went in her place. Joined by a team of factory inspectors, the group set out on the tour on 31 May and visited twenty tenements. As they found conditions that were in violation of the law, Roosevelt and Riis suggested remedial measures to the factory inspectors. Everyone agreed, the New York *Sun* reported on the following day, that conditions were improving. Nevertheless, the continuing abuses of underage workers led settlement workers to form the "Child Labor Committee" two years later. Riis, a member, advised the committee staff to concentrate on lobby activities in Albany. The committee prodded legislators into passing the Hill-Finch Act of 1903, the first effective child labor statute in the history of the state.

Riis also advised Roosevelt on legislation concerning the working conditions of druggists' clerks. In the spring of 1899 the state legislature passed a bill, endorsed by organized labor and social reformers such as Reynolds and Riis, that set the hours of clerks at a maximum of ten a day and seventy a week. Roosevelt approved of it in principle but received unfavorable mail from small druggists who claimed that it would unfairly aid their large competitors. Druggists' clerks also complained that the bill would make them lose their vacation days. The governor decided to hold a public hearing. After the hearing the Secretary of the Druggists' League for Shorter Hours, a Tammany politician named Edward Thimme, charged that Roosevelt was no friend of labor but that public pressure might force him to sign the bill. Angry and confused, Roosevelt asked Riis to seek out public sentiment among the interested parties. After surveying the opinions of clerks and pharmacists, Riis reported that the bill in its present form was too inflexible and would cause harmful consequences for many clerks.

Roosevelt vetoed the bill but promised to draft an improved measure for the next legislative session. When Edward Thimme denounced the veto, Roosevelt dismissed him as a schemer, a "blackguard," and a "blatherskite." In December 1899 the governor said that he would not sign any bill until Seth Low and Riis had personally approved it. Three months later a measure acceptable to all factions became law.[17]

While Roosevelt was governor, Riis frequently asked

him to intercede on behalf of a person in need or a charitable cause. On one occasion he wanted Roosevelt to ask Secretary of the Navy John D. Long for a pass for a sailor to see his family before he set sail on a long voyage. Roosevelt sent the request to Washington. Riis then asked his friend to compose a letter of recommendation for a person whom Roosevelt did not know personally. Roosevelt refused, saying it would open up a Pandora's box of similar requests from other friends.[18]

Several times Riis tried to have the governor lighten the sentences of convicted criminals. He unsuccessfully pleaded for Roosevelt to stay the execution of Martha Place, whom the court had convicted of murdering another woman. On 8 February 1899 the governor told the reformer that "There are some fiends among women, and I hardly think, old man, that we help womanhood by making these exceptions." Undaunted, Riis took up the case of a patrolman who was serving a prison sentence at Sing Sing for shooting a boy in the leg. The youth had refused to cease playing football in the street. The policeman, who had no previous record, had apparently intended to fire a warning shot but the bullet wounded the boy slightly. On 29 December 1899 Roosevelt sent Riis a telegram which read: "Dear Jake:—Happy New Year to you and yours, and as a New Year's gift take the pardon of the policeman, Hannigan." To Roosevelt's chagrin Riis released the telegram to the press, and it caused a brief flurry of adverse publicity. Four months later Riis requested a pardon for a man named Samuels. Roosevelt replied on 4 May 1900 that the prosecuting attorney and the judge who sentenced him told him that the penalty, if anything, was too lenient.

Roosevelt realized that Riis's requests for favors sprang from pure motives and were the result of kindheartedness rather than any desire for personal gain. The service which his good friend rendered as an adviser, pamphleteer, and pipeline to other reformers surpassed in value these occasional annoyances. On 17 February 1900, after Riis wrote a sketch on Roosevelt as a man of fairness and righteousness, the governor expressed his appreciation. He said modestly that "There are rose-tinted glasses over your loyal eyes when you look upon those whom you love and who love you." Ten days later he told Riis: "I regard you on the whole [as] the most useful citizen there is in New York and among my dearest friends."

During the late 1890s Riis kept in close contact with the Charity Organization Society, as that philanthropic agency expanded its interests into areas of social and economic welfare while continuing to function as a watchdog of private relief procedures. He served on their parks and tenement house committees, and on a personal level he secured assistance for people who were destitute. For example, in 1898 he obtained a loan for an immigrant named Viggo Toepfer. Two years later Toepfer had still not fully repaid the money, so Riis sent a personal check for the balance of $22 to John Pierpont Morgan, the millionaire treasurer of the COS.[19]

Lawrence Veiller and Tenement House Reform

In February 1900 Governor Roosevelt's appearance at the Charity Organization Society's Tenement House Exhibition heralded a new era for New York's housing reform movement. For two years the COS tenement house committee had been lobbying for an equitable housing code for New York City. Under the direction of its secretary Lawrence Veiller, a twenty-six-year-old settlement worker and former member of the Bureau of Buildings during the Strong administration, the committee drew up a model code whose main purpose was to end further construction of dumbbell tenements. Riis served on the committee along with other distinguished housing experts such as Robert W. DeForest, Frederick W. Holls, Felix Adler, Richard W. Gilder, and I. N. Phelps Stokes. When the Tammany-dominated Building Code Commission ignored their advice, Veiller convinced the committee to hold an exhibition in order to gain public support for action on the state level.[20]

Riis recognized the futility of hoping for municipal action under the Democrats and actively supported Veiller's tactics. In 1899 he had several disputes with Tammany officials, which convinced him that under their control housing reform would languish. Once when he asked the Superintendent of Buildings to enforce a law requiring fireproof stairways, the official replied that wooden stairways that burned slowly were acceptable to him. During the months before the exhibition's opening, Riis became its primary publicist and submitted photographs and population maps.[21]

The Tenement House Exhibition was a triumph of organization and expertise which attracted over ten thousand visitors. Three papier-maché models, of a dumbbell tenement, an existing block of slum territory, and a model tenement system, highlighted the exhibit. Maps, charts, and photographs demonstrated the disastrous consequences to life and health of overcrowded and ill-planned housing. One of the surveys revealed that two million New Yorkers were crowded into eighty thousand tenements. A pamphlet by Veiller contained recommendations on lighting, air shafts, fireproofing, toilets, room sizes, and other technical details. Riis persuaded the committee to show pictures of European experiments in public housing, even though Veiller did not think the idea would work in New York City. Speaking to visitors at the exhibition, Riis advocated legislation to force landlords to live on the premises of their buildings and to pay fees to sustain a force of sanitary police. When he visited the exhibition, Roosevelt announced his support for a bill to establish a state commission with the authority to write a new housing code.[22]

Riis and Roosevelt worked hard to obtain a state tenement house commission. Riis wrote a barrage of newspaper and magazine articles and worked with Felix Adler, Jacob H. Schiff, and patrician reformers at the People's Institute in planning lobbying tactics. Out of these plans evolved a Committee of Fifteen to investigate tenement house crime and vice. Roosevelt called the legislation "my ewe lamb," and in a special message to lawmakers he termed New York City's tenements a festering, cancerous sore which would poison the body politic and wreak vengeance on civilization if people did not quickly repair the system. In April Roosevelt obtained a $10,000 appropriation for a commission to draw up a code for first-class cities, which included New York and Buffalo. Roosevelt selected Robert DeForest and Lawrence Veiller to become president and secretary respectively of the Tenement House Commission. Using material which the COS tenement house committee had been compiling since 1898, DeForest and Veiller completed their task in four weeks.[23]

Riis, who declined to serve on the new commission, was somewhat critical of its final report. He supported its goals but believed it to be too single-minded in its espousal of a rigid code of restrictive standards. Critical references to the work of the Gilder Committee of 1894 also irritated him. He told Veiller that during the 1890s reformers had gained wide discriminatory powers for the Board of Health and the Board of Factory Inspectors. Veiller replied that the Gilder Committee had worked in an unscientific manner, that destroying slums to build small parks did not improve housing conditions. "There are no rooms in any of the surrounding buildings that are any lighter for this park, because it only touches the front apartments in each building, which already have ample light," Veiller told Riis. Patronizingly, he concluded: "Of course they did as well as they could with the imperfect knowledge they had when they started it."[24]

There was a fundamental difference in style and emphasis between Riis and Veiller. Riis stressed ends and morality while Veiller emphasized means and method. During his tenure with the Council of Good Government Clubs, Riis had combined organization and proselytizing, but essentially he was a propagandist who sought practical answers by intuition and observation more than by systematic analysis. And he feared that the bureaucratization and specialization of reform work would diminish its strength and cut it off from the people. Veiller's methods were a reflection of COS techniques and emphasized efficiency rather than democratic individuality. He was a systematizer who sought to professionalize reform work. A technician, legislative draftsman, and expert at organization, he looked upon Riis as unskilled in these areas. Crediting his older colleague with educating and stirring up public sentiment, he believed, however, that the greatest need was technical proficiency rather than well-intentioned "amateurism." He later described Riis as "a romantic, honest, imaginative, *unscientific*, intense, exuberant person . . ." (italics added). On the other hand, Riis said that he was not against organization *per se* but against the type of theoretician who classified and subclassified people as "mere items in his infallible system. . . . One throb of a human heart is worth a whole book of his stuff."[25]

Rather than viewing Veiller's work as complementary to his own, Riis became resentful of Veiller's implied slurs about his lack of expertise. At the annual meeting of the National Conference of Charities and Correction in Washington, D.C., Riis gave his answer to the advocates of scientific method. He said, "Preserve me from the term 'laboratory work'! A human being in misery is not a bug to be stuck upon a pin for leisurely investigation and learned indexing. . . ." Whereas Veiller put all his emphasis on restrictive housing legislation, Riis continued to preach for a multilevel assault on the consequences of poverty.[26]

The differences between the two reformers became more apparent with the publication in 1900 of Riis's *A Ten Years' War*. If the future belonged with Veiller and the new professionals, *A Ten Years' War* was a glorification and justification of the reform work of the 1890s and a call for private citizens to join the battle rather than to leave it to the technicians. Quoting from the Roman satirist Juvenal and British historian Edward Gibbon and citing statistics provided by the COS, Board of Health, AICP, and Citizens' Council on Hygiene, he nonetheless warned against scientific surveys becoming ends in themselves or substitutes for a moral commitment to combat urban decay. His tone was personal rather than professional, his appeal was to the heart rather than to logic. In a concluding chapter which he appropriately entitled "Reform by Humane Touch," Riis wrote: "When we have learned to smile and weep with the poor, we shall have mastered our problem."

In April 1901, when Governor Benjamin Odell signed the New York Tenement House Act and appointed its co-authors DeForest and Veiller to head up the new department in New York City, which was to enforce the housing code, Riis approved of the centralization of authority into this agency but urged caution against viewing the new law as a cure-all to the problem. On 10 October 1901 he wrote Jane Robbins that the "experts" were closing off housing for those most in need. He told Richard W. Gilder that the poor immigrants in Manhattan would not be able to afford the rent on new tenements that followed the requirements of Veiller. "That is all wrong, and I said so several times to Veiller and De-Forest, but I was overruled," Riis complained. He had always been fond of DeForest but told Gilder that he did not trust Veiller.[27]

Riis's fears about the continuing housing crisis proved accurate. Although the 1901 law outlawed further construction of dumbbell tenements and required existing dwellings to conform with higher standards, the legislation did nothing to create or encourage new construction. Often, in fact, the strict enforcement of the law exacerbated the overcrowded conditions by causing the eviction of tenants from buildings which did not meet licensing standards. Many owners converted their dwellings to lodging houses, a ploy which deteriorated conditions. Racial barriers, absentee landlords, and property speculation all hurt the success of the new Tenement House Department. Deplorable conditions continued. In 1903 the department reported the existence of "vile privies and privy sinks; foul cellars full of rubbish, in many cases of garbage and decomposing fecal matter; dilapidated and dangerous stairs; plumbing pipes containing large holes emitting sewer gas through the houses; [and] rooms so dark that one cannot see the people in them."[28]

Heart Trouble

In 1900 the quick pace of Riis's activities proved harmful to his health. During the winter and spring he had helped with the Tenement House Exhibition, continued work on articles and his autobiography, and had made three lecture trips, one to New England and two to the Middle West. Touring the Chicago slums with members of Hull-House, he confirmed their worst fears by remarking: "The best street I saw today . . . was worse that the worst street I ever saw in New York." This was a familiar litany that Riis often repeated with relish, especially in middle-size cities whose populace viewed New York as a singularly hopeless environment. During Roosevelt's inspection of sweatshops in May, Riis felt the symptoms of heart seizures but shrugged them off as the result of exhaustion from the sweltering heat. On the following day the wedding of his daughter Clara took place. The elaborate preparations had upset his household for months and had caused Riis to complain that it "Isn't our style, I think it is vulgar." The long day, which featured a reception for a hundred guests including Roosevelt, took its toll on Riis's health. A few days later he collapsed on the street. Doctors described the ailment as angina pectoris, and an enlargement of the heart.[29]

On 22 June 1900, as he lay bedridden and suffering from paroxysms of pain, Riis believed that he was dying. Elisabeth telegraphed Roosevelt, who a day earlier in Philadelphia had received the Republican nomination for vice president as William McKinley's running mate. Riis also composed a letter to Roosevelt which said: "You will keep the course and the faith, I know. . . ." Calling himself a "potential invalid," he wrote: "I shall no more be able to go sweat-shopping with you." When he heard of his friend's illness, Roosevelt went immediately to him.

The best way to gain back his strength, Riis decided, was to be close to nature; so he planned a two-month vacation to Lake Wahwaskesh in Canada. Before he left, Roosevelt invited him to Oyster Bay. The two men took a walk through the woods. Roosevelt started out at a very brisk pace, then suddenly slowed down for fear of Riis's health but tried to cover his action with earnest conversation. Riis understood. While in Canada, Riis wrote an article about Roosevelt's father, whom he called one of the first battlers against the slum. Mindful of the upcoming election, he told Endicott Peabody that "The moon looks better behind a cloud on this side of the border than it does in all its silver shine on the other side—less like Bryan perhaps." Feeling much better, he returned to New York eager to continue his reform activities.[30]

Roosevelt's expressions of friendship during his period of recuperation cemented Riis's love and utter loyalty to the man who had stormed into his life five years earlier on Mulberry Street. Shortly before the election of 1900, Riis came upon a Republican political rally in the Bowery. He did not think the speaker was very effective, so he jumped on the platform truck and began telling about the courage and honesty of Roosevelt. Suddenly, he wrote in *Theodore Roosevelt the Citizen,* a heckler yelled out in a drunken voice: "T-tin s-soldier! Teddy Ro-senfeld he never went to Cu-u-ba. . . ." The man never finished the sentence because, to Riis's great joy, someone silenced him with his fists (pp. 239-40).

For the Republicans the November elections were a victory not only for their national ticket but also for the mayoralty contest in New York City. Seth Low, the former mayor of Brooklyn and president of Columbia University, defeated the candidate of Tammany Hall. Low enjoyed the active support of the Citizens' Union, a patrician reform group to which Riis belonged. Like Riis, Low equated the Democrats with corruption and endorsed the platform of the Citizens' Union, which called for the regulation of service corporations, an eight-hour day for city employees, pure water and clean streets, more schools and public baths, and home rule for the city. Of Seth Low's victory Riis later wrote: "Drunk with the power and plunder of four long unchallenged

years, during which the honest name of democracy was pilloried in the sight of all men as the active partner of blackmail and the brothel, the monstrous malignity reached a point
at last where it was no longer to be borne."[31]

On 13 November 1900 Roosevelt accomplished one of
Riis's main goals in relation to charity work, separating police
activities and the care of paupers. In 1897 Riis and Roosevelt had persuaded the Greater New York Charter Commission to transfer this task to the Department of Charities; but
when the state legislature ordered a revision of the charter in
1900, adherents of the old system pushed through an amendment to place control back in the hands of the police. At
a public dinner celebrating the Republican victory, Riis
brought the matter to Roosevelt's attention, and the vice
president-elect convinced George L. Rives, the president of
the Charter Commission, to drop the new amendment.[32]

Riis believed that Roosevelt's governorship signaled a
new era in the relationship between government and the poor.
He stated that Roosevelt had put himself on record against
the slum landlords and sweatshop operators and had given a
fair hearing to people of all backgrounds. He used the power
of government as an instrument of social control to increase
opportunity by reordering the environment. Of his role in instituting these changes, Riis later wrote in his autobiography:
"I was his umpire with the tailors, with the drug clerks, in
the enforcement of the Factory Law against sweaters, and I
know that early and late he had no other thought than how
best to serve the people who trusted him" (p. 382).

Roosevelt, in summarizing his own accomplishments,
told Riis on 4 August 1900 that "It has really been your
work and not mine, but I have had the privilege of pulling the
handle, so to speak, and starting the machinery which you
arranged. . . ." Selected by the Republican hierarchy to be
McKinley's vice presidential running mate primarily to get
him out of businessmen's hair—the vice presidency was a
notorious graveyard for aspiring politicians during the nineteenth century—Roosevelt moved somewhat reluctantly back

to the nation's capital.

Prior to 1900 Riis had not been a very perceptive observer of national affairs, except in relation to urban problems. His attitudes on federal powers followed the mugwump tradition of desiring an honest, independent, and neutral chief executive. He admired the courage of Grover Cleveland, the one national Democrat he voted for, and he distrusted William Jennings Bryan. Nevertheless, on the state and local levels he had advocated vigorous executive leadership, regulation of monopolistic corporations, and social programs to combat environmental decay. As the new century began, the fifty-one-year-old Riis had eyes on Washington as much as Albany, and after Leon Czolgosz fired a fateful bullet into William McKinley at the Buffalo, New York, fairgrounds, he began to extrapolate his beliefs into an enthusiastic support of the Square Deal and Roosevelt's brand of progressivism.[33]

9

SENTIMENTAL NATIONALIST

During the first four years of the twentieth century, Jacob Riis's deep feelings of nationalism became dominant in his personality and encompassed his entire life style. In his autobiography *The Making of an American,* and in an adulatory book about Theodore Roosevelt, he attempted to delineate the ingredients of good citizenship. Each year he toured the country, lecturing on the slums and charging his audience to work to give ghetto residents an opportunity for the fruits of American life. As an advocate of the creative play movement, Riis espoused character traits such as physical fitness and manliness that fostered national strength. He attempted to model his personal life on these ideals in his activities as an author, elder statesman for reform, father, and sportsman. And finally there was Roosevelt, whose expansionistic foreign policy and moralistic pronouncements did much to buttress Riis's nationalism, give clarity to his political beliefs, and buoy up his spirit.

Riis had long demonstrated the qualities of a patriot. He maintained from childhood a reverence for Denmark's Viking and monarchical traditions and an idealistic image of the unique spirit of America. Contained within his moralistic personality were desperate needs to love and to do honor to intangible ideals and national symbols. In *How the Other Half Lives* he had bemoaned the lack of a truly American community or a national consciousness among the ghetto neighborhoods of New York. He liked to tell audiences about two children whom he saw scribbling "Keep off the Grass" on a wall because it was the only English that they knew. During the depression of 1893–97 he retained his confidence in America's fundamental institutions and worked with zeal to save the traditional bonds of the family and the neighborhood. Riis saw his reform activities as moral crusades and wrote about them in the rhetoric of combat. In 1898 when the United States entered a shooting war, he became an unabashed jingoist for his country's cause. He was proud when his eleven-year-old daughter objected vehemently in school to inferences that the Spanish did not blow up the battleship *Maine*. After Roosevelt learned of the incident, he wrote to Riis on 26 January 1899: "Tell your daughter that she is the stuff out of which we make the truest and best Americans." Later that year the Riis family appropriately sent toy soldiers to Roosevelt's son Quentin on his birthday.[1]

Riis's nationalism lent force to his reform programs but also narrowed the scope of his proposed solutions to remedy unjust conditions. Social justice, he felt, was necessary to avert calamitous disorder and to preserve existing institutions against anarchists and revolutionaries. Patriotism became a justification for converting Washington, D.C., into a model city and making the public schools into laboratories for useful citizenship. Nevertheless, while Riis's nationalism did not blind him to the suffering and degradation, it blunted the edge of his outrage. He had done much to usher in an era of introspection and muckraking, but after 1902 younger and angrier men took the center of the stage. With middle age he had found security and status within the system, and he told Roosevelt that he was "too old to wish for change." Furthermore, his idolization of Roosevelt caused him at times to worship the cult of personality at the expense of a closer examination of the fundamental flaws in American society.[2]

After Riis's severe illness in 1900, his pattern of living became less hectic and more fixed than had been the case during the 1890s. Semiretired from newspaper work, he made a lecture tour each winter, then rested, wrote, and engaged in philanthropic activities through the spring and early summer. In August he went off to Canada with friends to hunt and fish. Returning home in the late fall, he filled his schedule with short lecture tours and flurries of writing until his winter tour again resumed. Visits with Roosevelt in Washington, election campaigns, and participation in many reform groups provided additional variety to his life. He told a friend that his heart condition prevented him from looking too far into the future, however, as he was "prepared for an ambush in that quarter, always."[3]

Riis missed the excitement of news reporting and lamented the time his body needed to mend after his lecture tours. After one lengthy vacation he confided to Richard W. Gilder that he longed for work. "It is, after all, the great comforter," he said. He told Bliss Perry that "I must ever be content to fill the little role of stirring up others to do the work I shall soon be too old to do. . . ." Reminding him of his own precarious health were the deaths of his mother on 22 February 1903 and of his close friend John R. Proctor, who succumbed ten months later to angina pectoris, the same ailment that afflicted Riis. Nevertheless, he declared that his faith in immortality overcame any fears of death and joked about his body's weakness. During a brief stay at a hospital, he told settlement worker Jane E. Robbins that on "All Fools Day perhaps I will come out with the other dunces." A year later he said to Endicott Peabody, ". . . Let us praise God for the turmoil, the fun, the glory of living."[4]

Speaking to crowds during his lecture tours in a diminutive and raspy voice that still contained a Danish accent, Riis's demeanor was less than magnetic; but he held his audience's attention with a wealth of anecdotes that in turn pleased, surprised, and shocked. In December 1900 he delivered a ninety-minute talk and stereopticon display at the Davenport, Iowa, Y.M.C.A. on the topic, "The Battle with the Slum." The next day a local reporter provided a perceptive insight into Riis's popularity and success. He wrote that "There is in each human breast an insatiable desire to go slumming. The lecture was an opportunity to go with a man of experience to visit the holes in the great American city . . . and at the same time to be free from contamination. . . ."[5]

Jacob A. Riis Settlement

On 5 March 1901 the King's Daughters honored Riis on his silver wedding anniversary by renaming their neighborhood settlement at 50 Henry Street after him. Theodore Roosevelt, Endicott Peabody, Jane Addams, and many other close friends sent congratulatory messages. Civic and reform leaders gathered with immigrant families to witness the dedication of the Jacob A. Riis House. Settlement officers Margaret Bottome and Mrs. Julian Heath and humanitarian reformers Felix Adler and Josephine S. Lowell gave brief addresses. Riis's good friend Bishop Henry Potter, in eulogizing Riis, said, "To think of a modern reporter as a philanthropist rather taxes the imagination. But he has touched, as only one in his profession can, the most distressing forms of human life and yet kept his optimism. . . . Mr. Riis has the mother heart as well as the father heart." Riis accepted his honor, according to the 6 March issue of the *New York Times,* by replying, "The world is not bad. It is good. You simply have to touch it right."

Later in the day Riis held a party in his home. Attending it were former Danish neighbors from Brooklyn, business associate Paul Dana, editors William McCloy of the *Evening Sun,* Richard W. Gilder of the *Century,* and Silas McBee of the *Churchman,* wealthy philanthropist-lawyer-banker Jacob Schiff, who impressed Riis more than any man except Roosevelt, he once told Lillian D. Wald, and a host of charity, housing, and settlement reformers. Riis described the festivities to Jane Addams, whom he called "my dear spinster." He wrote:" Old feuds, little feuds that had made hearts sore, were healed . . . and men that had turned their backs to one another shook hands and made a new start." Summing up his life with Elisabeth, Riis told his sister Emma: "Think of the long time; but for me it is like a breath of air, so short; and the time left is even shorter."[6]

The Making of an American

During the summer of 1901, Riis completed work on his autobiography *The Making of an American*. The book reflected the author's sentimental and exuberant personality, which was in turn both guileless and shrewd, idealistic and realistic, egotistical and disarmingly candid. He paid little heed to dates or chronology and freely roamed from personal anecdotes to descriptions of slum tenements and then to flashbacks about his youth. He emphasized his love for Elisabeth as a dominant force in his life. He took most pride in his Americanism and his skill as a reporter. "I would love my fellow man," he declared. "For the rest I am a reporter of facts" (p. 424).

In his autobiography Riis was quite critical of his own shortcomings. Recalling that two of his friends committed suicide, he blamed himself for drifting apart from them and not giving them advice and comfort. He disliked cant in others and often deflated his own self-importance. Coming from beautiful Denmark, he noted that it took little wisdom to see the harm in rat-infested tenements and schools and blocks of buildings so crowded that fresh air and sunlight never entered. Riis concluded: "For hating the slum what credit belongs to me? Who could love it?" He added that "Perhaps it was the open, the woods, the freedom of my Danish fields I loved, the contrast that was hateful" (p. 423). Admitting to a love of prestige and victory, he said that personal status gave him more power to accomplish his goals and that what mattered in a fight was the justness of the cause. Believing that his experiences served as a bridge between the two Americas which he had described in *How the Other Half Lives,* he wrote that rich and poor, employer and employee, Jew and Christian "only need to understand each other and their common interest to see the folly of quarreling" (p. 188).

Riis wanted his autobiography to provide a lesson in how a poor immigrant could find a useful place in American society if he had a strong will, proper values, steadfast purpose, and an abundance of faith. Strong moral purpose could help the rootless newcomer conquer the certain failures which he would face. With perhaps some exaggeration he dramatized his own low ebb as a shabby, penniless vagabond sleeping in doorways and without blanket or overcoat during one cold October storm. Walking to the North River, he had contemplated suicide. He wrote that "An overpowering sense of desolation came upon me. I hitched a little nearer the edge. . . . What was the use of keeping it up any longer with, God help us, everything against and nothing to back a lonely lad?" (p. 70). In the nick of time, he continued, a shivering mongrel dog pressed up against him, and he recovered his courage and senses. From then on he never wasted time on self-pity or pessimism. As he recorded his odyssey to success, he subtly contrasted his own perseverance and grit with other Danes who had abdicated all responsibility once they landed in America. All of Riis's early ventures failed—finding a job, editing a newspaper, giving a lecture, writing a police story; even his fights to tear down Mulberry Bend and outlaw police lodging houses took a decade. When things stalled, Riis said, he thought of the stonecutter who hit his rock a hundred times to no apparent effect, but then with the next blow the stone split into two (p. 253).

Riis took great pride in his Danish heritage and believed that it deepened his Americanism. His writing revealed his intense dislike for Germany, the country which stripped his homeland of Schleswig and Holstein. He justified his dual loyalty by asking, "What sort of a husband is the man going to make who begins by pitching his old mother out of the door to make room for his wife? And what sort of a wife would she be to ask or to stand it?" (p. 8). He wrote: "Happy he who has

a flag to love. Twice blest he who has two, and such two"
(p. 396). Each Sunday Riis proudly flew the American flag at
his home, but he still thought of King Christian as his monarch.
His most cherished possessions were the Cross of Dannebrog,
which the king awarded to him in September 1900, and a pass-
port which Theodore Roosevelt gave him. Thus, in his call for
the Americanization of the immigrant he did not wish to blot
out cultural traditions and loyalties but only to teach values and
tools that would enable people to become productive citizens.[7]

In his autobiography Riis equated his usefulness as a
citizen with his urban reform work. He claimed that a blighted
environment imperiled the institutions of democracy, that corruption in politics sprang from unstable homes and poor
schools and foul air, that the slum would dig the grave of the
republic. "A man cannot live like a pig and vote like a man,"
Riis said. "With no home to cherish, how long before love of
country would be an empty sound?" (p. 319). Revealing his
nationalism, he called for an annual federal census or enroll-
ment to give each citizen a sense of identity with his country
and to facilitate vaccination procedures and selections for jury
duty and military service.

Riis refused to put labels on his reform philosophy other
than to endorse practical experimentation to help the dispos-
sessed. The Golden Rule best synthesized his religious ideal,
whereas the neighborhood settlement, where all classes met as
friends and learned from each other, best represented his social
ideal. On a political and economic level, he favored governmental action to expand opportunity and reconstruct the urban
environment. He called the precepts of social Darwinism cold
and obsolete and rejected socialist doctrines as impractical.
He wrote: "I don't care two pins for all the social theories that
were ever made unless they help to make better men and
women by bettering their lot" (p. 68). "Isms" only confused
the issue; what people needed was common sense and a keen
eye of observation. "I had no stomach for abstract discussions
of social wrongs. I wanted to right those of them that I could
reach," he wrote. Responding to a reviewer who labeled *A*

Ten Years' War maudlin and abortive, Riis angrily replied: "Those are the fellows for whom Roosevelt is not a good enough reformer; who chill the enthusiasm of mankind with a deadly chill, and miscall it method—science" (pp. 67–68). He did not carry his eclectic style to extremes, however. Admitting that his methods were often clumsy, he praised reformers such as Jane Addams, Jane Robbins, and Felix Adler who combined professionalism with love.

The climax of *The Making of an American* was Riis's overwhelming realization, while on a trip to Denmark in 1899, that he was a loyal American. His visit to Ribe was almost like reliving his childhood, since so few things had changed. Girls now attended the Latin school, but at the Domkirke there still were separate pews for each sex.[8] During a meeting with King Christian, the old monarch asked how his fellow Danes fared in the New World. Riis replied that they made good American citizens and "better for not forgetting their motherland" and their king. While at the city of Elsinore, Riis fell ill with malaria. After the fever left him, he rested listlessly in a bed facing the sea across to Sweden. Suddenly he caught sight of a ship flying the American flag. "Gone were illness, discouragement, and gloom!" Riis wrote; he shouted and laughed and waved his handkerchief. His book concluded: "I knew then that it was my flag; that my children's home was mine, indeed; that I also had become an American in truth. And I thanked God, and, like unto the man sick of the palsy, arose from my bed and went home, healed" (p. 443).

The Making of an American enjoyed great popular acclaim. Translations appeared in several foreign languages, and high schools and colleges used it as a textbook. Reviews were favorable, although one writer regretted Riis's clumsy phraseology and forwardness in discussing his romantic affairs. Hutchins Hapgood remarked that "There is a constant touch of sentimentality which in a less vigorous man would be displeasing," but he praised the book as a remarkable achievement. Felix Adler recognized that the book's primary importance was in giving "the human touch to matters hitherto almost monopolized by the theorist and the scientific student of abstract conditions and colorless statistics." Riis himself expressed satisfaction with his accomplishment but told Bliss Perry that his "pet" book would always be *A Ten Years' War*.[9]

The success of *The Making of an American* brought renewed demands for Riis to address interested groups about urban reform. A year after its release, he received six hundred dollars for a series of lectures at the Philadelphia Divinity School on the subject of the "Peril and Preservation of the Home." On 22 January 1903 a reviewer for the Philadelphia *North American* named Leigh Mitchell Hodges, in an article entitled "The Optimist," described Riis's message as paradoxical, at once sentimental and blunt, angry and hopeful. Describing old battles with slum landlords, Riis exclaimed: "We took their idol, money, put our foot on its necks, and trod hard." A Philadelphia publisher printing the addresses in book form attempted to delete its "radical" rhetoric, but Riis objected vociferously and successfully. But he later claimed that the publisher was "out of his head" for advertising *The Peril and Preservation of the Home* falsely by not mentioning that it was a collection of speeches.[10]

Creative Play and Gotham City Politics

One manifestation of Riis's optimistic nationalism was his advocacy of creative play. He viewed physical fitness as a necessary attribute of individual well-being and national strength, but he decried regimentation of children's play as autocratic and unnecessary since youngsters had the imagination and good sense to know what was best for them to do. When lecturing on "The Bad Boy," he would wax indignant at people who "classed and organized into team play and group play and heaven knows what, and to what grave scholastic ends." In 1902 Charles M. Schwab, a wealthy steel magnate, asked him to organize a beach front play area for slum children. When he met with

Schwab's advisers, Riis had to fight down a plan to order the youngsters' time with educational and character-building activities. He turned down the job and told Schwab to "give the children a rousing good time for once, and just let them occupy themselves for the few hours they are there."[11]

Believing that children became criminals for the want of recreational areas, Riis in 1903 revived a plan, which he had drawn up in 1897 as secretary of Mayor Strong's Small Parks Committee, to convert Randall's Island, located in the East River of Manhattan, into a network of playgrounds, parks, pavilions, and gymnasiums. Such facilities were the rights of all citizens, not merely the beneficent favors of politicians, he declared. Obstructing his plans was the fact that on the proposed site was a private, state-supported reformatory, the House of Refuge, which leased the land from the city. Riis criticized the dismal, century-old prison as inadequate for the needs of reforming delinquents. In order to open the way for his recreational center, he advocated new and separate institutions away from the city and modeled after a farm and cottage plan.[12]

On an inspection tour of the House of Refuge, he found scandalous conditions, which he exposed in several articles. The 850 boys and girls received only one change of underwear every two weeks; and their food, what little there was, tasted foul. Hardened criminals shared quarters with first offenders, and the atmosphere resembled an adult prison. Bureaucratic and legislative snarls stalled his plan in 1903, but Riis retained hope that Randall's Island would eventually serve the people rather than just detain them.[13]

Riis's increasing preoccupation with national affairs and his frequent departures from New York City on lecture tours and vacations reduced his contact with the administration of Mayor Seth Low. Nevertheless, he still held strong opinions about the slowness of municipal reform. In November 1902 he depaired that the mayor, although personally honest and compassionate, had neither ended corruption nor inaugurated programs to provide for the poor. His tightfistedness stood in the way of new parks and schools.[14] The police department was as bad as ever, he told Roosevelt on 7 November 1902, and he sometimes wished that General Leonard Wood, the overseer of Cuba after the Spanish-American War, could reign in Mulberry Street for a year.

During the mayoralty campaign of 1903, Riis accepted a special assignment for the New York *World* to interview the two candidates, the incumbent Seth Low and Democrat George B. McClellan, the personable and able son of the Civil War general. According to the reporter, the mayor was deliberate and somewhat cautious, "nothing to enthuse over, perhaps, but safe to tie to. . . ." Of McClellan Riis wrote: "I met a courteous, clean-shaven gentleman, exceedingly well dressed, who bade me sit down beside him. We sat. He was altogether so pleasant that it exasperated me a bit." The one rough moment came when McClellan mentioned Republican posters which quoted Riis as having said that "Tammany fed the pauper on dry crusts and sea water." The reporter replied that he disapproved of the posters and had been misquoted, since the phrase he used was "tea water." His sketch of McClellan was friendly but expressed doubt that the man could operate free from Tammany.[15]

This fear of Tammany, more than his satisfaction with the direction of municipal reform, caused Riis to support Seth Low for a second term. In October he made several speeches on behalf of the mayor. On the day after the election, when McClellan's victory over Low became certain, Elisabeth Riis wrote to the defeated candidate that her family was so "thoroughly disappointed, disgusted and ashamed, we hoisted our flag on half mast this morning."[16]

Emulating Roosevelt

During the late summer of 1901, Riis went to Lake Wahwaskesh in Canada for a ten-week vacation, beginning a ritualistic custom that he was to repeat on several other occasions.

Although Riis enjoyed comfortable quarters in a log cabin with a guide, a cook, and other male companions, he searched out wilderness areas which he named "Happy Valley" and "Silent Forest" and took long canoe trips which left him exhausted but regenerated. He felt that the uninhabited surroundings gave him all the spiritual nurture which the slum denied to its victims. The fields and foliage reminded him of Denmark. The forest became a fantasy world where he could act out the manly virtues which Roosevelt so often evoked in his glorification of the strenuous life. Roosevelt gave him a copy of *Wilderness Hunter* and wrote on its jacket: "May you enjoy the north woods as much as I enjoyed the great plains and the Rockies." Hunting became for Riis almost a mystical experience. Once he told his wife that he had tracked a bear for a week. When Elisabeth expressed relief that he never encountered it, he answered, "I would rather be eaten by a bear in a big fight for its skin than die in my bed." Once after watching a deer slowly die before his eyes, he told Roger Tracy that he felt like a murderer and would never shoot a deer again. He enjoyed shooting partridges, however, and bragged that, despite their being out of season, he shot six of them in "self defense."[17]

During the 1901 hunting trip, Riis received reports that a deranged assassin had mortally wounded President William McKinley. The news sorrowed him, but he sensed that destiny had called Roosevelt to rule over the American people. He asked the new president for permission to write his biography. The idea "delighted" Roosevelt, who invited him on 9 October to visit the White House.

Throughout Roosevelt's first term in office, his friendship with Riis remained intimate even though the nature of the presidency and the physical distance between the two men precluded frequent personal meetings. The long periods of separation caused Riis to tell Roosevelt on 20 October 1902: "Sometimes I wish I were a Secret Service man and could be where you are, always." Beyond their ties of friendship, Riis became important to the president as a publicist, an adviser, and an apologist and link to humanitarian reformers.

In 1902 Roosevelt's bold assertions of presidential power in the Northern Securities Company antitrust case won Riis's enthusiastic praise. He wrote Roosevelt that "Vested interests are rightly sacred until they injure the commonwealth which created them to serve its interests." He favored a constitutional amendment to allow governmental action against private corporations when their activities threatened the national interest. "Did the fathers know it all? Was history completed and bound in covers a hundred years ago?" Riis asked. When the New York *Sun* criticized Roosevelt, Riis charged that his old paper was "so conscienceless in its advocacy of capital, these days, that I distrust anything it says or does."[18]

In October 1902 Riis defended Roosevelt's actions in the anthracite coal strike as being in the best national interests of all classes. He feared that without a strong executive "the arrogance of the money powers will bring on a revolution." The refusal of the coal owners to arbitrate their dispute with the United Mine Workers was an act of colossal stupidity that "brought us, to my mind, with one long stride nearer to the state-socialist's scheme than fifty years of dreaming and arguing have done." Ten months later Riis opposed compulsory arbitration of a local strike in Pennsylvania because the dispute did not do harm to the nation's strength. Purely humanitarian arguments did not justify presidential action, he wrote Lyman Powell, but he suggested that a state board or interested private citizens should attempt to mediate the grievances.[19]

Roosevelt feared that his actions in the coal strike would allow the Democrats to win the New York gubernatorial election of 1902. Riis disagreed but confided on 11 October that he would not "regret if Odell is beaten, for I don't like him." Benjamin Odell was a consummate politician, but Riis saw the Republican governor as a selfish egotist. Shortly after his reelection Odell met with Riis for an hour. The reformer told Roosevelt on 12 November that he "came away as far from what I wanted as when I went in."

Presidential Adviser on Immigration and Cities

In most areas of national policy, Riis formed his views after Roosevelt had acted, but in the fields of immigration control and urban reform for Washington, D.C., the president sought out his advice. He convinced Roosevelt that making the nation's capital into a model city and instituting a policy of planned immigration were desirable goals.

Riis wanted the federal government to rationalize its immigration policy by directing people to areas where they could find employment. He recommended a national labor bureau to screen applicants in their native country. If federal officials coordinated the needs of the nation with the skills of the newcomers, then there would be relief from the flood-tide of people coming into Ellis Island, which glutted New York City's labor supply and housing facilities. He believed, perhaps mistakenly, that rural areas were in need of "men of strong arms and strong courage," while the "shoe pinches" only in the cities. Disagreeing with nativists who feared for American institutions, he had confidence that the immigrants were "all right if we only give them half a chance." Riis put this conclusion in quotes as the "unvarying report of the early Tenement House Committees."[20]

Riis believed that the overpopulation crisis originated not in the ignorance of immigrants but from the greed of rapacious employers, fraudulent steamship lines, and slum landlords. In 1900 and 1902 he opposed legislation in Congress to set up literacy requirements but approved of the 1882 law which barred paupers, criminals, and the insane, and the Foran Act of 1885 against contract labor. Those who came to America, Riis believed, had hope and ambition, whereas the weak and despondent stayed in their native land. He had "small sympathy with the cry to 'shut the door.' . . ." He said: "We cannot have too much of the right kind: and we don't want the wrong kind." [21]

Roosevelt followed his friend's counsel in a feud that flared within the Bureau of Immigration between Commissioner-

General Terence V. Powderly and federal officials at Ellis Island. In 1900 Powderly, the former General Master Workman of the Knights of Labor, had carried out an investigation into graft and inefficiency at the New York port of entry which cost eleven immigration agents their jobs. Two years later Powderly's enemies charged the former labor leader with having put political pressure on one of his assistants, Edward F. McSweeney. Powderly's argumentative and impolitic personality heightened the controversy. After Riis called Powderly "a wart that should be removed," the president asked him to resign.[22]

Ironically, five years later Powderly was back in the Immigration Bureau, advocating immigration control procedures similar to Riis's proposals. Roosevelt, who like Powderly was more of a restrictionist than Riis, endorsed the plan, although he harbored legitimate doubts as to its practicality. Other matters seemed more urgent and less politically dangerous, and so the president did not work actively for its implementation.

Riis's interest in Washington's tenement problem was the outgrowth of a speech he delivered on 15 December 1903 at the annual meeting of the Associated Charities of Washington, D.C., Charles F. Weller, the Secretary of Associated Charities, had long been an active advocate of housing reform in the capital city, and so he enlisted Riis's aid in publicizing the need for dramatic governmental action. On the day of Riis's lecture, Weller took him through back alleys and past decaying tenements and presented him with grim statistics of infant mortality. Hours later Riis told an overflow audience that "I am not easily discouraged, but I confess I was surprised at the sights I saw in the national capital. You people of Washington have alley after alley filled with people that you do not know." In three hundred blind alleys, rotten core areas containing rear tenements and jerrybuilt shanties buried in the center of outwardly pleasant blocks, 457 out of 1000 black babies died before their first birthday. And yet there was no existing machinery to end the evil. On the following day

Riis repeated his sentiments at a hearing before the Joint Committee of the District of Columbia. He later claimed that he roused one senator from his boredom when he described a disease-infested area where the Senate barber shop sent its towels. Soon afterwards the District government established a committee for sanitary housing, but Congress refused to grant it any substantive powers.[23]

Washington's tenement house conditions distressed Riis deeply. They offended his sense of national pride, blighting the luminous accomplishments of the Roosevelt administration. Yet Washington was one of his favorite cities, and he wrote that he felt young again when he visited there.

On 8 October 1904 Roosevelt asked Riis for suggestions on how to make Washington "a model city of the United States." In reply Riis sent him a model bill for a housing code and statistics on tenements, sweatshops, and child labor. He told Roosevelt that the most urgent problem was the existence of blind alleys but also advocated such programs as public kindergartens for the poor. The previous spring Riis had introduced the president to thirty-four-year-old Denver Judge Ben B. Lindsey in order to consider adoption of a progressive juvenile court system for Washington, D.C. In his annual message to Congress, Roosevelt incorporated all of these suggestions, but again legislative inaction frustrated the plans.[24]

Congress expressed interest in tearing down unsanitary buildings but turned its back on positive measures to help the poor. Meanwhile slum landlords were making from 20 to 60 percent profits on their tenements. In 1904 the Sanitary Housing Company, a private philanthropic organization, began building some model housing units, but the program languished without public funds. In 1906 Congress created a Board of Condemnations, which razed more than two hundred tenements before the Supreme Court in 1907 stripped it of much of its power. Roosevelt appointed a Homes Commission to study the slum problem, and in 1908 this group recommended a wide range of responses to the distressed conditions, including playgrounds, a labor bureau, workmen's accident insurance, minimum wage laws, and government loans to philanthropic housing corporations.

Roosevelt incorporated these provisions into another model city bill and pushed actively for its passage, but Congress refused to act on the programs or even grant a loan to the Sanitary Housing Company. After Congress turned down a request to pay supervisors at playgrounds, Riis angrily charged that reactionary politicians were making the nation's capital a city of shame.[25]

Defending and Pestering the President

Frequently Riis had to answer the pointed questions of reformers who believed that the president was closer in spirit to mossback Senators such as Nelson W. Aldrich of Rhode Island and John C. Spooner of Wisconsin than to their cause. The interests of the president and reformers were one, Riis told Roosevelt on 20 October 1902, "so that you may get backing and we gumption." He defended Roosevelt's police action in the Philippines and his arrogant expansionism in Panama as morally correct, even though these actions distressed many of his friends. "I confess that the half-hearted criticism I hear of the way of the administration with Panama provokes in me a desire to laugh," he declared after Roosevelt provoked a "revolution" in order to wrest the Central American Canal Zone away from a reluctant but supposedly sovereign Colombia. He added: "I am not a jingo; but when some things happen I just have to get up and cheer. The way our modern American diplomacy goes about things is one of them."[26]

In the midst of the Filipino insurrection, Riis discovered that the army had ceased sending the names of enlisted men who died in combat, causing a six-week delay in communicating the messages to the victims' families. The army thought that the twenty-five dollar fee justified only sending the names of officers. Riis, in response to a parental plea, went to Roosevelt, who had been ignorant of the procedure. The president immediately countermanded the order. By 1906 he still thought that the critics of the Filipino war policy were wasting "their foul breath," but he wished "we could sell those wretched islands to Japan and let them do the civilizing." He admired the Japanese greatly and hoped for their victory over Russia in the war of 1904–05.[27]

Soon after Roosevelt became president, he asked Riis to become governor of the Danish West Indies in the event that the United States successfully completed negotiations for the purchase of the islands. Responding on 17 March 1902, Riis recommended another person, saying, "What *I* might do as the little pooh-bah of three islands there is absolutely no telling." Yet the idea intrigued him, and he hinted to Endicott Peabody that he was open to persuasion. In October 1902, however, Denmark's upper legislative body, the Landsthing, failed by one vote to ratify the treaty of acquisition, thereby quashing Roosevelt's ambitious plan. The United States did not gain sovereignty to the islands until 1917.[28]

In 1903 a woman asked Riis whether he would support the United States in the event of a war with Denmark. Riis replied that it would break his heart, but he would fight for America. He added that the two countries could never be enemies, however.[29]

On several occasions Riis requested Roosevelt and his advisers to intercede on behalf of one of his former countrymen. He asked William Loeb, the president's secretary, to help a Danish worker keep his job at the Charlestown Navy Yard. When Loeb told him that the man was unworthy, Riis confessed that the Dane had lied to him. "Tell the President not to lay it up against me, though I *was* a chump. I will not soon bother him again with a Danish case," he said. A year later he asked the State Department to investigate the value of Mexican land in which a Danish banker wanted to invest. The government forwarded the request to their embassy in

Mexico City. The owner of the land wanted to borrow money from the Danish banker, but the Mexican consul discovered that the owner had misrepresented the land's value, thereby saving Riis's acquaintance from going through with the deal.[30]

Following the pattern of Roosevelt's governorship, Riis asked his friend for numerous favors. Most were for minor matters, such as passing on the request of a sculptor for the president to model for a statue. Roosevelt declined that honor, but in 1903 he visited the summer home of the children of the Jacob A. Riis Settlement at Pelham Bay Park. He declined to appear at several charity benefits, however, explaining that if he did so, he would have to accept too many similar favors. On three occasions Riis consulted the president in regard to political appointments of postmasters, and he won a pardon for a man who deserted from the navy to join the army.[31]

To Know Him Is to Love Him

In 1903 Riis's labor of love was the writing of a biography of Roosevelt, his hero, and the agent, he believed, of a new era of progress and national purpose. Entitling his book *Theodore Roosevelt the Citizen,* he wrote that the president stood for "a broad Americanism that cares nothing for color, creed, or the wherefrom of the citizen, so that, now he is here, he be an American in heart and soul; an Americanism that reaches down to hard-pan" (p. 256). He dedicated his work to the young men of America "whose splendid knight" Roosevelt was and who modeled their lives from his example of manliness, morality, and honesty.

Riis meant his book to be the impressions of a friend rather than a "life" or public biography. In it he chronicled anecdotes about his intimate memories, the walks through the slums, the horseback rides, the expressions of love which Roosevelt had honored him with. He mentioned the sending by the president and his wife of a telegram to his mother shortly before her death, wishing her their loving sympathy and telling her that "Your son is breakfasting with us."[32] He also told of his wearing the Cross of Dannebrog at a White House dinner and his embarrassment in the midst of the other dignitaries. The president noticed his discomfort and told him "I am so much honored and touched by your putting it on for me" (pp. 281–82).

To Riis, Roosevelt's life represented the triumph of will, morality, and service, the highest qualities of citizenship. As he rose to the apex of political life, Roosevelt confounded the cynics and fatalists who threw up their hands at injustice rather than work for its abolition. He retained his faith in progress, thus demonstrating that "The man who believes in the world growing better helps make it better, and so, in the end, is bound to win. . . ."[33] He searched for the ideal, while setting aside the empty husk, Riis declared, and added that material things pass away but "The moral remain to bear witness that the high hopes of youth are not mere phantasms" (pp. 402–3). He cleansed the political processes and party machinery and gave them moral purpose. Riis contrasted Roosevelt's life of public service with the curdled spirits of men such as John Jacob Astor, who left the country in anger or disgust. In fact, he hoped that his friend would run for mayor of New York City after he left the presidency in order to demonstrate the primacy of urban problems.[34]

In public life, Riis wrote, Roosevelt transformed his code of morality into responsible principles of government. He combined a Jeffersonian faith in democracy with a Hamiltonian belief in positive government. He was a second Lincoln, guiding the American people through the hazardous problems of the Industrial Revolution and bringing all social classes together in harmony. For he realized, Riis claimed, that "Whether for good or ill, up we go or down, poor and rich, white or black, all of us together in the end, in the things that make for real manhood" (p. 373).

Critics panned *Theodore Roosevelt the Citizen* as syrupy

hero worship which bore little resemblance to reality, but Riis was more concerned with the president's reaction. At first he thought he had failed him. "I feel like crawling into a mouse-hole—a rat-hole would be too big, . . ." he wrote Silas McBee. His spirits picked up when he heard that teachers in Baltimore and Kansas were reading it aloud to their students. Finally came the president's verdict. It humbled him that Riis should love and honor him so much; "You have not painted me as I am, but as I would like to be, . . ." Roosevelt said.[35]

Riis hoped that his book would help in the 1904 presidential campaign. In May he and his family visited the White House before embarking for Denmark. In July he wrote from Ribe that "I don't see how we can help winning." Back in America in time to campaign for the president during his autumn lecture tour of the Middle West, he greeted Roosevelt's landslide victory in November with prayers of thanks. Buoyed up with optimism that anything was possible, he wrote Lyman Powell that Roosevelt now "will go South and all opposition there will cease. To know him is to love him. . . ."[36]

Riis was not alone in revering the president. Already the most popular chief executive since Abraham Lincoln, Roosevelt championed the preindustrial virtues of rugged individualism, hard work, and the strenuous life at the same time that he was attempting to expand opportunity in an industrial setting and to make government more responsive to twentieth-century needs. Although Roosevelt was in many respects a conservative in his infatuation with order and security, in popular esteem he was a liberating hero of the common people doing battle against bullies and malefactors.[37]

10

MINISTERING TO THE CHILDREN

In the later years of his life, the central focus of Riis's philanthropic activities was the building of tangible, practical institutions for children, such as social settlements, hospitals, clubs, and schools. Like that of his fellow progressives Jane Addams, Endicott Peabody, and Ben Lindsey, his work with unfortunate children was intimately related to his desire to bring to them some of the blessings of family life and community that otherwise were missing from their lives. Riis was very much a family man. In fact, he was a possessive parent who involved himself deeply in the affairs of his offspring, even as they began to drift apart from him.

An Elder Stateman's Grand Tour

For seven months beginning in October 1904, Riis set out on the most extensive lecture tour of his life, traveling to all sections of the country. He spoke on the need for a crusade to save the children of the tenements and to reconstruct the urban environment. His strenuous schedule required him often to speak five nights a week in different towns; but he hoped that he could earn enough money to sustain him in retirement. His goal, already two-thirds complete, was to have savings totaling thirty thousand dollars. When he left Elisabeth, who was bedridden with lumbago and other ailments, he said that this would be his last grand tour. He promised to write her regularly about the things he saw and the people whom he met, especially their sons John in Denver and Ed in Sacramento.[1]

From all parts of the country, Riis wrote loving letters to "Lammet," which he hoped would bind them together in spirit. Signing them "mulluvkat," he sometimes compressed flowers and leaves for her, and he described for her vicarious pleasure the natural beauty of his adopted country. Whether writing about the hills of Utah or the wet and green pastures surrounding Mt. Rushmore, he mixed his glorification of nature with statements of religious faith. He told Elisabeth that "the Lord is here in the mountains and on the plains, as he is on Long Island, and we are all in His keeping; not even a sparrow falls to the earth without His will. . . . "[2]

Riis searched out new experiences and insights that might make more understandable the variety of cultural habits among people in his country. In Salt Lake City he listened intently to the earnest conversation of his Mormon hosts, impressed with their vigor and faith. "It is exciting and interesting to get their side of the story we all know, and it is by no means a one-sided story," he wrote. The Mormon practice of polygamy both fascinated and repelled him, and he explored its effect on family life. Later he wrote that he "detected a coarse strain" in the children, which he attributed to the materialistic origins of polygamy.[3] Moving on to Idaho, he wanted to visit an Indian reservation, but a governmental agent replied that it was inadvisable because a white man had recently killed two braves. Two months later he visited Juarez, Mexico, and inspected the adobe "mud-houses" of the poor. The living conditions were squalid and disheartening, he reported on 11 February 1905, but the people had "a certain pose that is graceful."

When Riis came upon groups of people whose habits conflicted with his sense of propriety and civic purpose, he was quick to criticize their shortcomings. He found the town of Pocatello, Idaho, to be a railroad village of "dog-fights and dives" whose people were more interested in violence than in reform. On the eve of his appearance in Pocatello, he discovered that a prizefight threatened to cut down attendance at his lecture. The promoters mollified him somewhat by canceling the boxing match in return for free tickets to his speech. He had "no use" for Reno, Nevada, which he labeled a frontier haven for vice, and in his lecture there he said that "a community of gamblers was devoid of conscience and no good."[4] In Walla Walla, Washington, he saw advertisements for white laborers only. At first he thought that the employers were discriminating against Negroes but learned that they were turning away Chinese. Riis complained on 27 November 1904 that cynical employers were exploiting the orientals as a source of cheap labor on the West Coast, just as their counterparts in New York were enslaving immigrants from southern and eastern Europe.

The dynamic mood of the Far West, its material growth and vigor, impressed Riis greatly. It seemed a perfect environment for a sober and industrious man to make his fortune in. But it amazed him to discover "The majestic unconcern about pennies [that] people show here—nothing goes, less than a nickel. I saw a man throw a penny away yesterday in the street." Proud of his own frugality, he told Elisabeth that he had planned "to buy a new hat, but today a man took mine in the barbershop and as his is much better, I can get along awhile yet."[5]

Riis did not have confident hopes for his oldest son, Ed, however, who worked for a newspaper in San Francisco. Ed wanted to become an independent writer, but his father doubted that he had the talent or stamina to make it on his own. He told Ed that security was more important than idle dreams of fame and great wealth.[6]

A conservative and somewhat domineering parent, Riis

tried hard to curb or at least channel the restless spirits that his sons possessed. In rearing his children he had mixed corporal punishment and strictness with exuberant bursts of affection and love. When they were young, he loved to make up intricate animal stories with which to amuse them at bedtime. Now that they were scattered about the country, the lecture tours were a way to see them, as well as educational and messianic experiences for himself. Riis was like a slightly pompous shepherd ministering to his flock. He expected his offspring to be the model or the evidence which bore out his optimistic faith in the family as the cornerstone of civilization. It was their duty, he said, to demonstrate "that in our family we practice as we preach, or try to." He told John, his second son, that unless he was resolute he would "disgrace me" and himself.[7]

John, who resembled his father as a youth, had long been a problem for Riis. Since 1898 when the sixteen-year-old youth attempted to enlist into the navy to fight in the Spanish-American war, John had run away from home almost every year. In the fall of 1898, Jacob sent him to a military academy, but during Easter vacation John disappeared. Four days later Jacob found him in Atlantic City, New Jersey, attempting to set sail on a cruiser. A succession of similar incidents led Riis to believe that John was ungovernable, and so he sent him to live on a New England farm with a minister. When John fled from there, his father reluctantly found work for him on a ranch in Colorado. From 1902 until the winter of 1904, John wandered around the plains states, taking odd jobs as his father had done three decades previously.[8]

In frequent letters Jacob advised, criticized, prejudged, and warned John about matters of finance, morality, and the danger of idleness. He said that when he was young he scoffed at his elders but had been stupid and selfish for doing so. Everything depended on hard work and character, he wrote. On 4 March 1904 he expressed anxiety "to hear that you have got a steady job—at anything, John?" A month later he told John that "a fellow is apt to rust if he stays *always* in the same place. But you are ahead on that count."[9]

After he visited with John in Denver, Riis told Elisabeth on 13 November 1904 that the rigorous life in the West had steadied John's eyes, filled him out, and made him into a man. He confided to John on 22 December that his own life was "full of regrets and failures," and he hoped that "my boys and girls will do better than I did, and help the kingdom come in their day. . . . " Becoming satisfied with John's progress, he began to see the image of himself in his son. Six months later, on 17 June 1905, he admitted that he had been harsh and out of patience because he had been smothering subconsciously the "misgivings of my own yearning heart."

In Sacramento, California, in December, Riis heard about a Danish woman with four children who was in dire need of help. For several years she had been ill with rheumatism but could not afford to pay for hospital care. Riis arranged for a meeting with some wealthy acquaintances and received pledges for enough money to pay for the woman's hospital care and to buy her children Christmas presents. Proud of his deed, he told Elisabeth on 19 December that it cost him only twenty-five dollars, which was a third of his earnings for the speech he delivered that day. "Isn't it bully?" he concluded. He included in the letter to his wife, who also had rheumatism, a check for fifty dollars as his Christmas present to her.

Riis loved the cheers of greeting from audiences, their sighs of grief when he told a compelling story, their laughter at his jokes, their applause at the end of his address. And even though the constant flattery of well-wishers made him slightly uncomfortable, it reenforced his optimism and his sense of worth. He told Elisabeth in December that the people of Tacoma, Washington, would not allow him to leave until he had answered many questions. He won over the group when he told a hostile clergyman that the man must have been a descendant of the ass which Jesus rode to Jerusalem. Three weeks later, on New Year's Eve, he said that he was leaving San Jose "amid great applause—I spoke to the California

Teachers' Association, and they hailed me with long acclaim as a fellow teacher."

In an indirect and self-deprecating manner, Riis sought recognition for his accomplishments. All during the trip he kept resisting efforts by Lyman Powell to secure him an honorary degree from Smith College. He did not want it or deserve it, he said, and argued that he could do his "remaining work better as Jacob Riis than as Dr. Riis." Yet he had brought up the subject in the first place by asking Powell to work for a degree for the Reverend Joshua Kimber, the secretary of the Board of Foreign Missions at Riis's church, so that the man could have the acclaim which he deserved in the twilight of his life. The adamant tone and repetition of Riis's disclaimers belied a desire, perhaps unconscious, for learned men to accept him as their peer.[10]

In January 1905 Riis reluctantly rested for two weeks at a sanitarium in California before beginning the southern leg of his tour. His heart needed mending, but his restless spirit rebelled at the inactivity. "Having made up my mind to idle, I am idling with all my might," he announced. Near the hospital lived a cloister of monks whose daily routine seemed purposeless to the reformer. He ridiculed their "silly Latin" speech and the idea of "a *young* monk forever singing and pacing back and forth behind the garden wall. Ugh!"[11]

During a two-day visit in February to Tuskegee Institute in Alabama, Riis endorsed the gradualist philosophy of his host Booker T. Washington as holding out the best hope for the social and economic advancement of black people. The Negro principal and the Danish-American reformer had met earlier through their mutual friendship with President Roosevelt. In September 1904 Riis had taken Washington and the Archbishop of Canterbury to the tenement districts of New York's East Side, an experience which confirmed the educator's long-held belief that the city was inimical to the welfare of his people.[12]

Riis's support of Washington reflected in part an attempt to salve his idealistic conscience against his less than total commitment to full social and political equality for black people. In this action he was following the lead of Roosevelt, who had invited the black educator to dine at the White House and used him as a Southern political adviser. He was torn between a belief in the inherent equality of all people and a naive tendency to view Negroes as culturally childlike.[13] Likewise, he equivocated between a hatred of Southern bigotry, lynching, the brutalization and economic enslavement of black people, and a simplistic opinion that injustices by Northerners during Reconstruction had caused these regrettable but understandable reactions from white Southerners. He told Roosevelt that Southerners were "waking up, but the awakening is beset by black and ugly dreams. Yet they are hearty, good people, and we have got to allow for—especially—the reconstruction period. The carpet-baggers were worse than Sherman." In his biography of the president, which was marred by racist expressions such as "nigger in the woodpile," Riis eulogized Booker T. Washington as representing the best effort and hope of "our black-skinned fellow-citizens . . ." (p. 369). In December 1903, upon the death of his close friend John R. Proctor, a Confederate veteran and Civil Service commissioner, he told Silas McBee that Proctor's life dignified "the whole cause of your beloved South . . . and gives it a right to be as it were."[14]

Describing his impressions of Tuskegee, Riis praised its emphasis on preparing students for practical trades while not neglecting the virtues of cleanliness, character, and manliness which, in short, were the ingredients of citizenship. "Everybody is anxious to learn and is learning," Riis wrote. He somewhat patronizingly declared that the students would become good farmers, carpenters, cobblers, painters, and wagonmakers. On the day of his speech, the Tuskegee choir serenaded him with spirituals. He told Elisabeth on 20 February that the moving songs contained "all the sorrow and suffering and patient endurance of the slavery days. . . ." He added that "such a people, with such hope, can never perish. The future is theirs, surely, and I told them so. Impulsive, childlike, generous, they appealed tremendously to me." Finally forsaking his condescension for a moment, he contrasted the progress at Tuskegee with the shallow bigotry which pervaded the South. He wrote, "I feel as if I had at last viewed the real South, coming as I do from the white men's South where the one conscious, desperate effort seems to be never to learn and never to unlearn anything."

Family Tragedy

Arriving home a week later, Riis took his ailing wife to Roosevelt's inauguration. Close to his monetary goal of thirty thousand dollars in savings, he set out again for the Middle West. With feeling of regret and guilt, he left Elisabeth and his two children Billy and Kate. The latter had left school to take care of her mother. He also sensed with dismay that his mind was atrophying and growing sterile from repeating the same speeches so often. Complaining that his nomadic life took him far from the subject of his lectures, he wrote Endicott Peabody that "I haven't grown a bit myself, or had a chance, so I fear I am becoming an old fogy."[15]

In early May Riis cut short his trip when he learned that Elisabeth had caught bronchial pneumonia. "Without her I cannot live," he told a friend. For two weeks he watched his wife's health deteriorate. When the doctors gave up all hope, he telegraphed the grim news to Peabody, and added, "God is mighty. His will be done." That night he wrote in his diary, "Lammet died, God help us all."[16]

The kindness of friends and the hopeful promises of his religious teaching helped to cushion Riis's grief. Of the many messages of condolence, a letter from Roosevelt touched him most profoundly. The president said that they were growing old and were "in the range of the rifle pits," but that God held out to them a better life after death. Riis told Lincoln Steffens that his tears of sorrow were not bitter, because Elisa-

beth's soul was "just over the river." To Richard W. Gilder
he said that the storm had ended. "I would not call her back
if I could. She was so tired," he wrote.[17]

The loss of Elisabeth left a great void in his life, for she
had been the object of his vast outpourings of affection, the
anchor to his family, and a cause for his religious beliefs. Six
months previously he had declared his independence from
his "heart's damnation." Now he felt more and more like an
old man and talked at times as if he would not live out the
year. In moments of depression her death seemed to be a
punishment for his desertion during his long tour. Within a
month he threw himself into fund-raising projects for a hospital for tuberculosis victims and for the Jacob A. Riis Settlement. The stings of sorrow were with him each hour, he
told John on 6 August, but God had use for him yet in the
world. It was "easy to die for your country," he philosophized,
"but not always so easy to live for it." Yet at times he had
nagging doubts about the legitimacy of his social programs
and even his religious faith. He told Lyman Powell that "I *do*
believe, but often it is, I fear, only to escape condemnation."[18]

Never again did Riis argue theology with abandon, as
he had done with friends and aquaintances such as the Mormon elders. Criticizing speculation into questions such as
immortality, he preferred "the old fiery Methodist preaching.
It had no note of doubt in it and it satisfies me. . . ." He disliked unitarianism, he confided to his sister Emma in 1907,
because it was "a cold and barren religion" which "denies
the divinity of Christ." To honor Elisabeth and perhaps buttress his faith, he donated money for memorial windows at
the old family church in Brooklyn and at the Domkirke in
Ribe. The arrangements in Denmark for the latter, which
were to include a display of his books and a picture in his
honor of the Prodigal Son, fell through.

Fund Raiser: Sea Breeze Hospital

Interspersing his charity work with vacations in the Adirondack Mountains and the Canadian woods, Riis was able to revive his spirits. Offering to write an article for *Century* about Sea Breeze Hospital, he told editor Richard W. Gilder on 22 July that "incidentally life is worth living to me again. I have not been so happy in months." Several newspapers mentioned him as a possible candidate for mayor of New York City. Uninterested, Riis told his son John on 20 August 1905 that the populace "will not make this child a candidate if it knows itself, and I think it does."[19]

During the autumn of 1905, Riis surprised many of his friends in patrician reform circles by supporting the reelection of Mayor George B. McClellan despite his connection with New York's Democratic machine. Mayor McClellan had endorsed the Sea Breeze Hospital project, and he sought out the advice of housing experts in overseeing the Tenement House Department. After Lawrence Veiller and Robert DeForest charged the department's commissioner Thomas C. T. Crain with negligence and dishonesty, McClellan forced him to resign. These deeds spoke louder than campaign rhetoric, Riis told Jane Robbins, and he was thankful that the mayor won election to a second term.[20]

Riis's efforts to raise money for Sea Breeze Hospital grew out of an experimental clinic for slum children with bone and gland tuberculosis which the Association for Improving the Condition of the Poor had established in 1904. The hospital patterned its outdoor treatment after successful experiments along European seacoasts. Unfortunately, the existing facilities could provide for only forty-five patients or 1 percent of New York's tuberculosis victims. Realizing the need for a larger hospital, William H. Allen, the general agent for the AICP, pledged that his organization would build and furnish equipment for a new medical center if the city would maintain its operating costs and purchase the necessary property at Rockaway Beach. Allen, estimating the private

17. Greek Children in Gotham Court.

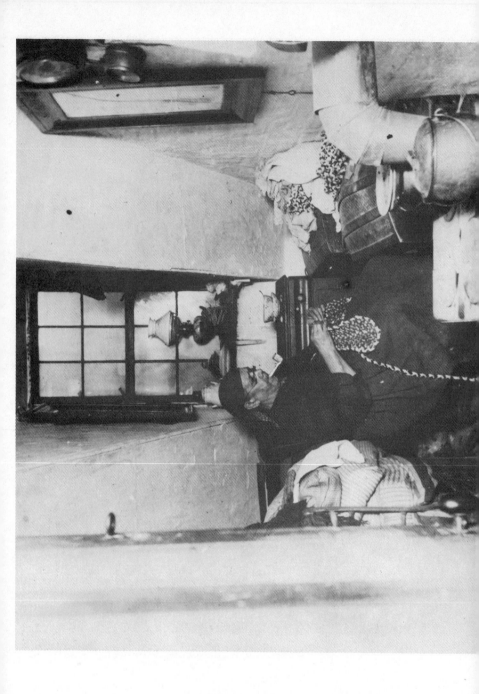

18. Old Mrs. Benoir, an American Indian, in her Hudson Street attic.

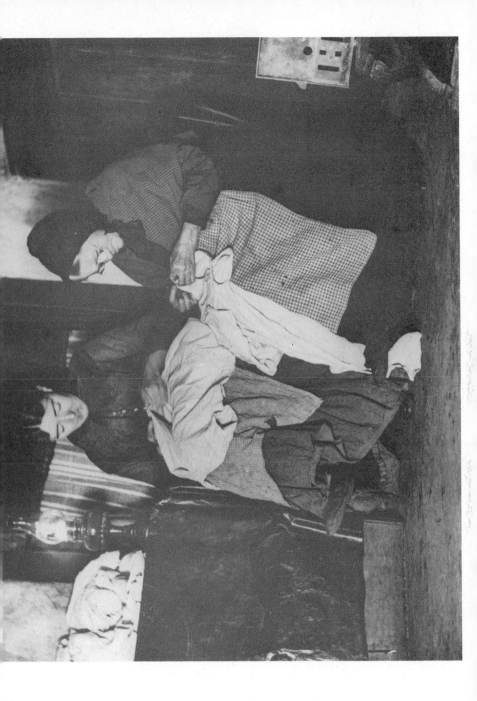

19. Two sewing women in Elizabeth Street attic.

20. Blind Beggar.

21. Bandit's Roost, about 1888.

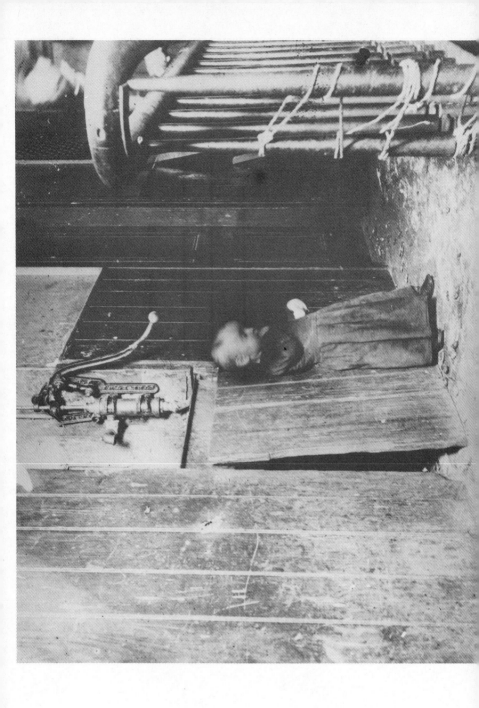

22. Tenement child near a stairway.

23. Rear tenement in Roosevelt Street.

24. Baxter Street Alley.

cost at $250,000, persuaded John D. Rockefeller to donate half of the amount on the condition that others matched his gift.[21]

The tuberculosis hospital project had tremendous appeal to Riis. Six of his brothers had died of the dread disease; moreover, the primary benefactors would be helpless slum children. Using the donation drive as a tonic for his personal loneliness, he mobilized his pen and his network of wealthy friends on its behalf. He persuaded Roosevelt to visit the Sea Breeze clinic in July in order to dramatize and publicize the project. After the president and the reformer talked with the crippled children, Riis told Mrs. Roosevelt on 22 July 1905 that he was filled with joy and gratitude because the patients seemed "the happiest little mortals on Earth." Two weeks later he asked Roosevelt to make another public gesture of support; but the president, arguing that his appearance had precipitated a flood of requests for similar favors, said on 19 August that this was "the kind of thing that can be done once, and not again without impairment of influence." In magazine articles Riis appealed to the goodness of the comfortable classes to build an institution whose tangible merit no one could rationally doubt. He wrote that such a practical expression of Christian brotherhood was the keystone of his "message to my people and day." Henry K. McHarg pledged $25,000 for the new hospital; the Carnegie family gave $10,000. Other donations large and small brought the deficit to less than $25,000 by June 1906. That month an anonymous philanthropist promised to pay the remaining amount.[22]

It proved much easier to raise the money for the hospital than to prod the city into acquiring the site on Rockaway Beach. At public hearings critics raised the specter of graft, and questioned the costliness of the land purchase and the uncertainty of maintenance costs. Some uninformed complainants feared that the crippled children would pollute the water. In March 1907 the Board of Estimate and Apportionment approved the project, but the advocates of the hospital had to wait more than four years for any further positive action.

Mayor George McClellan favored prompt purchase of the land but met adamant resistance from Tammany officials, especially the city comptroller, who had split with him over other matters. When McClellan's successor remarked that a seashore hospital would be too damp for its patients and likely fail, Riis called his attention to the French and English institutions and asked him to talk to the hundred children whom the small Sea Breeze clinic had cured during its seven years in existence.[23]

By 1911 Riis had become chairman of the Seaside Park Committee, a division of the New York Parks and Playgrounds Association, and had expanded his goal to include a public recreational park at Rockaway Beach in addition to the hospital. On 19 October 1911 condemnation proceedings finally began at the seashore site, and Riis told members of his committee that "we may now disperse." Five days later John A. Kingsbury, who had succeeded William H. Allen as the general agent for the AICP, thanked Riis for his "endless enthusiasm and tireless endeavor," on behalf of "the many little sufferers."[24]

Not until 1914 did municipal authorities begin construction of the hospital, and in the meantime Riis began to get impatient "to swing my hat the day the dirt begins to fly." In the fall of 1913, the Tammany candidate for mayor, Edward E. McCall, blasted the project as extravagant. Fearing yet another delay, Riis angrily rebuked McCall in a letter to the *New York Times*. Fortunately for the fate of the hospital, McCall lost the election to John Purroy Mitchel, a young lawyer and former member of the McClellan administration who had allied himself with municipal reformers, charity officials, and settlement workers. Mitchel named John Kingsbury of the AICP as his top charities commissioner; and on 27 January 1914 groundbreaking ceremonies took place for the new Sea Breeze hospital and an adjacent park.[25]

Riis's interest in Sea Breeze had led him in 1906 to study and publicize the selling of Christmas stamps as a tactic for fund raising. Two years previously he had become aware of

European methods when he received a package from Denmark with eight stamps on it. On investigation he learned that in one year the Danish people raised over a million dollars for a tuberculosis center. Writing for *Outlook,* he declared that Christmas stamps had proved themselves both popular and successful and that it was better for millions of citizens to build a hospital than for one millionaire to do it by himself. During the winter of 1907, the Red Cross and the National Tuberculosis Association applied his suggestion on an experimental basis in Delaware. When it worked, they expanded it into a national program. In December 1907 Riis told Dr. Jane Robbins that "The Red Cross had not entered my mind. I thought of the government taking it up, as in Denmark, but this is better, much better."[26]

One Man's Family

A year after Elisabeth's death the fifty-seven year-old Riis fell in love with his secretary Mary Phillips, an attractive and intelligent woman twenty-eight years his junior. His warm nature required companionship, a home, and an object for his love. He had met Mary before Elisabeth died, and in December 1905 wrote her that he would "be glad to see you again, you darling. . . . So long, sweet—your old Jake." Coming from one whose letters to his children were usually signed "Affectionately your father, Jacob A. Riis," the note signified a feeling much deeper than mere cordiality. Mary took care of his settlement and hospital work and his financial affairs while he was away from New York, and she was a close companion for his young son Billy. In the summer of 1906, Riis wrote her warm letters while he vacationed in Canada with his son. Before he left for his winter lecture tour, he evidently asked her to be his wife.[27]

All during 1906 Riis was in poor health. He suffered two mild heart attacks which forced him to curtail his lecturing. During the summer he told Steffens, "My body is stricken with boils and weakness and my head feels vacant when the strain comes on." Yet he needed the podium and his reform activities to convince himself of his usefulness. After delivering a speech in Boston in March, he wrote Richard W. Gilder that he was "better for it, much better. What the dickens— let us wear out, if we must, [but] never rust." Just one more cross-country junket, he told Gilder, and then he would retire.[28]

In October 1906 Riis became embroiled in New York's gubernatorial election, primarily because the Democratic candidate, editor William Randolph Hearst, made comments which impugned the character of his close friend Gilder. Hearst called *Century*'s editor a zephyr, and his newspaper labeled him "a pathetic imitation of a young girl" with "little mouse eyes, and . . . [a] thin body shivering in his black cape, gliding into a room among men." Riis called Hearst a heartless demagogue who appealed to class hatred, and asked President Roosevelt to endorse his Republican opponent Charles Evans Hughes. The reformer feared that the aristocratic Hughes would otherwise run poorly in the tenement districts. Earlier Roosevelt had appeared publicly with Hughes and had appointed Oscar S. Straus to his cabinet in order to win Jewish voters to the Republican cause. He refused to take a public position on the 1906 election but allowed Secretary of State Elihu Root to blast Hearst's methods. In November Hughes won the election, which Roosevelt pronounced afterward to be "a victory for civilization."[29]

Traveling around the country during the winter, sleeping on trains and in cold hotel rooms and living out of a suitcase, Riis intensified his love for Mary. On 30 January 1907 he promised to be faithful in marriage to his "Mariettabean" but warned that "if you grow *fat,* I shall certainly spank you . . . otherwise I will be gentle, very. I am not a Turk." He worried about the reaction of his children to his plans, however, and finally told them that their mother had sent Mary to them and that she would hold the family together. His daughter

Kate, who wedded a medical student in June, was for a short time resentful of the plans. Nevertheless, on 29 July 1907 Jacob and Mary were married at Ipswich, Massachusetts, a vacation spot that reminded Riis of Ribe. Soon afterward they reopened his house at Richmond Hill. The pictures of Elisabeth remained in their home, but thereafter Jacob always referred to her as mother.[30]

Mary and Jacob Riis had a rewarding marriage. She made him feel young and proud and useful. Unlike Elisabeth, she often accompanied him on trips. She took great satisfaction in helping him research and proofread manuscripts, and she became active in settlement work and New York politics. Three months after their wedding, Jacob poured out his affections to her. He wrote, "I myself long for your soft arms, dear, and your soft bosom to lay my head on. . . . Beloved one, I think of you early and late, and in the night watches when I wake, and thank God who sent you to comfort me when the world was dark. I know *she* loves you too. . . ." Two years later, when Mary's first and only baby was born dead, Riis told Endicott Peabody that "I cannot grieve for the child while I may keep her, for without her I should be bereft indeed."[31]

In 1907 Riis told his wife that "my set notions of order, of neatness . . . have become a big part of me, perhaps too big. . . ." His married children and their mates probably would have agreed, for he intruded into their lives with frequent advice concerning their manners and habits and, above all, their handling of money. In his love and concern for their welfare, he betrayed somewhat his confident generalizations about the wisdom of youth. He was still the critical father even after they married and moved away from Richmond Hill. In 1908, for example, he reproved Kate for wearing improper underwear. Soon after Elisabeth died, he had arranged for his son John to live with Judge Ben B. Lindsey in Denver. The judge arranged for him to work in a school for delinquent boys until he was able to join the Forest Service as a ranger. Fearing that John gambled, Riis scolded him for not repaying him a debt of forty-five dollars. "Until a man saves money to make him independent, he is not a man in the full sense," Jacob said. He disliked John's wife Charlotte and told her that she did not deserve the name Riis after she disclaimed any desire to have children. In 1910 Charlotte left John and returned east. Jacob called her a jade and advised his son to stop supporting her and to divorce her. John and Charlotte were divorced in 1912.[32]

Riis's most serious domestic quarrel involved his oldest daughter Clara and her husband, a doctor named Fiske. In 1908 they moved to California, and for six months Dr. Fiske was unemployed. Complaining that he suffered from a disease of the nerves, he appealed to his father-in-law for financial help for Clara and their children. Riis called him an idler, a drunkard, and a parasite; he would send money only if Fiske agreed to leave his family, go to another town and get a job. Fiske protested, "Shame on you. And you posing as a high-minded doer of good." But he accepted the offer and left his family. Jacob then aided Clara but had one of her neighbors carefully scrutinize her habits. His daughter endured the forced separation for a year and then secretly moved to Los Angeles to be with her husband. When Riis found out, he wrote Kate that "I should have known it from her letter, 'tis so flippant and cynical and full of digs into everybody."[33]

Clubs for Boys

Between 1906 and 1911 Riis was in the vanguard of efforts to establish boys' clubs in order to provide outlets for the creative energies of youths and to channel their boisterous habits into constructive ends. Working with the Federated Boys Clubs, the Boy Scouts, and the Big Brother movement, he hoped that these groups would add to the variety of slum life and substitute in a small way for the squalid environs and inadequate family life that hampered the maturation process of so many children of the tenements. The clubs, therefore, were for him an extension and supplement to his settlement work and his advocacy of parks and playgrounds. In 1906 he was a founder of the Federated Boys Clubs, a nonsectarian organization that enlisted the services of adolescents, primarily in large cities, for projects to improve their neighborhoods. By 1911 the clubs had over a hundred thousand members.[34]

The Boy Scouts, which Riis also helped to organize, was slower to attract ghetto members, but he believed that potentially it held great promise for bringing slum children into closer contact with nature. Realizing that young people in the tenements had little respect for authority, he saw hope in the fact that the highest values of the "tough," courage and resoluteness, were potential qualities for good. In *The Battle with the Slum* he had written that "the boy who flings mud and stones is entering his protest in his own way against . . . jails for schools and the gutter for a playground. . . . [against] dummies for laws and the tenement for a home. He is demanding his rights, of which he has been cheated—the right to his childhood, the right to know the true dignity of labor that makes a self-respecting manhood" (p. 246). Therefore he wanted scoutmasters to guide the slum child along desirable paths, while being careful to allow him to have fun and freedom from needless regimentation so he would not rebel against the program. "For the American boy is just a little steam boiler with his steam always up," he said. "His play is his safety valve. Sit on it, and the boiler blows up."[35]

In 1910 the founders of the Boy Scouts of America asked Riis to speak at their first organizational meeting on the subject of children. The Boy Scouts were in miniature a personification of the Progressive era's faith in national vitality and morality. What better synthesis of the Progressive credo than the scouting motto "Be prepared" or the admonition to be "brave, clean, and reverent." The sixty-one-year-old Riis told his sympathetic audience that each child was in part a savage, in part an altruist, but most of all an opportunist who takes things as he finds them in his environment. Each child has the goodness of God within him, he con-

cluded, and the mission of scouting—indeed, the duty of
civilization—should be to allow that spark to flower, to
channel it unobtrusively so as not to destroy the boy's freedom.[36]

In urging Americans to support boys' clubs and scouting,
Riis appealed to their patriotism and termed the groups vital
for both order and justice. He wrote that the Boy Scout movement was conducive to good citizenship because it "breathes
loyalty to authority, to law, a lesson our boys need to learn,
East and West, North and South." He hoped that the groups
would reenforce the traditional values of American society,
help unify neighborhoods, and bring children of all classes
together as equals.[37]

In 1911 Riis worried about the rising crime rate and the
revival of New York gangs. In an article entitled "What Ails
Our Boys?" published in the October issue of Craftsman, he
claimed that parents and policemen were too lenient on delinquents. To make his point, he told about a reign of terror in
New York thirty years previously that was a consequence of
a regulation forbidding policemen to carry clubs. The lawlessness subsided, he said, when Chief Thomas Byrnes countermanded the order and told his men to "take no prisoners,
unless they bring them in on a shutter" (pp. 3–4). The anecdote was uncharacteristic of Riis's public statements but
in line with his strict practices of rearing his own children.

Riis's tendency, more pronounced later in life, to roman-
ticize the past led him into inconsistencies. Never forgetting
the poverty of Mulberry Street, nonetheless he usually told
anecdotes about its most colorful aspects. For example, he
tended to view newsboys within the rising-entrepreneur stereotype fostered by self-interested publishers. In How the Other
Half Lives he called them independent spirits "as bright and
sharp as the weasel." In the December 1912 issue of Century
he expressed disappointment that "the newsboy of old . . .
[has been] shorn of his lawless privilege of sleeping out . . .
[and] has surrendered some of his picturesqueness." Although
Riis praised Newsboy Protective Associations, his partial ac-

ceptance of the rags-to-riches, Horatio Alger newsboy myth prevented him from discovering fully the sordid reality about one of the most exploited groups of child laborers.[38]

Fund Raiser: Riis Settlement

Of all Riis's private charity commitments, the social settlement which bore his name was most important to him. In 1905 when he began a campaign to raise enough money to pay off its thirty-thousand-dollar debt, the Riis Settlement provided services for more than a thousand children and half as many adults. Located in two adjacent buildings in the Lower East Side, the center emphasized recreational and educational activities, including kindergartens, athletics, sewing, plays, lectures, piano and dancing classes, and clubs for mothers, fathers, boys, and girls. During the summer there were excursions to private schools such as Groton and to a summer cabin on Long Island. Unlike many settlements, this one had no resident staff except the custodian. With more than fifty volunteers to supplement the paid staff of ten, the yearly operating budget was only about two thousand dollars, although operating and maintenance costs were somewhat higher. The most famous "graduate" of the Riis Settlement was singer Eddie Cantor.[39]

The settlement movement had grown rapidly since the days during the late 1880s when Riis had helped to found the King's Daughters settlement. A variety of compelling reasons —religious, humanitarian, utopian, educational, and economic —pulled people into the movement; and the amorphous and flexible nature of its goals allowed room for individualism and nonconformity. Most settlement workers, no matter how divergent their social philosophy, agreed upon the urgency of action to combat the slum environment and had a sincere desire to open the way for its residents to enjoy a better life. Jane Addams expressed her vision of the settlement ideal in social and democratic terms. The vision of Stanton Coit, founder of Neighborhood Guild, the first settlement in the United States, was utopian and economic. Felix Adler stressed the ethical and esthetic possibilities of settlement work, while C. P. Henderson espoused spiritual and missionary purposes. Most of these leaders hoped that on a political level the settlements would serve as spearheads for reform.[40]

The settlements had their critics, however, especially from radicals who advocated fundamental economic change rather than meliorative efforts to make an inhumane system somehow bearable. The economist and social critic Thorstein Veblen believed that settlement workers were teaching "the inculcation, by precept and example, of certain punctilios of upper-class propriety in manner and customs." Jack London, a romantic and naturalist writer whose contact with the slums filled him with revolutionary outrage, wrote that settlement workers were the agents of "a race of successful and predatory bipeds who stand between the worker and his wages, and they try to tell the worker what he shall do with the pitiful balance left to him." His book *The People of the Abyss* (1903) concluded that settlement workers "do everything for the poor except get off their backs."[41]

Following the personal and practical bent of its founder, the workers at the Jacob A. Riis Settlement attempted to establish programs that would bring neighbors together, provide necessary services, and brighten the lives of the participants. The only philosophy Riis insisted upon was the ideal of brotherhood; otherwise the functions should simply serve the people. He told Jane Robbins, a resident at the College Settlement, that his motives were spiritual, and hers democratic, but that "they are the same thing."[42]

Riis's involvement in settlement activities extended far beyond his intimate connection with the institution which bore his name. Occasionally he did volunteer work for the University and College settlements, and in 1901 he was a founder of Greenwich House which Mary Simkhovitch turned into a model for the nation. A close friend of Lillian Wald, he made many visits to her house on Henry Street. In 1904 he worked under Miss Wald on the Social Halls Association which raised a hundred thousand dollars to build a community center. The building contained restaurants, meeting rooms, a dance hall, bowling and billiard facilities, and as a concession to the male residents, a solitary bar. Riis viewed the community center as a benign substitute for the saloon and the street, previously the only places where young people in the slums could congregate socially.[43]

As president of the Jacob A. Riis Settlement, Riis's most important task for many years had been soliciting financial contributions. He had seen that the board of directors included several millionaires such as Mrs. Andrew Carnegie, whom he admired, and John D. Rockefeller, whom he secretly detested for his materialism. To obtain funds, he had given innumerable lectures. On potential patrons he used a mixed assortment of arguments, cajolery, flattery, appeals to sympathy, and promises of such favors as a ride in the presidential yacht. Therefore, in 1905 he was treading a familiar path when he went to his friends and acquaintances to raise the thirty thousand dollars to pay off the debt.[44]

Within a year Riis had collected enough money to pay off the settlement's mortgages and to finance a new gymnasium and an extensive renovation project. The recent death of his wife prompted many people to be generous. He donated a thousand dollars himself and received pledges from Andrew Carnegie, John D. Rockefeller, and other reliable patrons such as Miss Helen Gould, Henry McHarg, and Jacob Schiff. To maintain the gymnasium, he arranged for a half-dozen private academies, including Groton and St. Paul, to pay $1,200 yearly. In return he promised to speak at each school once a year, and he honored the students with plaques so that "my boys and girls may always know them for friends." He hoped that the contact between the academy-trained boys and the slum children would expand into mutual visits and volunteer work. "I want so to bring the young together, those of the slum and those of wealth and fairer chance, on the same natural level," he wrote.[45]

By October 1906 the refurbished quarters were ready for use. They included a carpentry shop, two playrooms, a salesroom for secondhand clothing, a domestic science room, and sleeping quarters for guests. Most dear to Riis's heart was the gymnasium, located in the back of the lot where a playground had been. To save the play area, Riis had the contractor put another playground on the roof of the new building. At the dedication ceremonies for the gymnasium, which he had named for Roosevelt, he expressed the wish that the users of the facilities would develop "the sturdy ideals of manhood and citizenship" which the president personified. Reading a personal message from Roosevelt that made use of the "new spelling" of words such as "thru" and "thoroly," he jocularly told the crowd that his answer to his friend in the White House was that he "thought his letter fine and his spelling vile."[46]

In 1907 Riis told his wealthy benefactors that they had made possible great accomplishments, but that more money was necessary. One never could rest on past deeds; the slate was clean, he said, "but the crowds are all the time increasing. Each year brings heavier demands." Four months later he told a woman who wanted to begin a settlement house to combine the methods of organization with public appeals to the heart. He told her to use his book and pictures of impoverished "waifs" and to have faith, because, in the final analysis, "it is all a question of faith. Everything is."[47]

Riis compared the role of religion in settlement work to yeast in the making of bread; it was indispensable but no good if people could taste it. Dogma had no place, he thought, but the Christian ideal of brotherhood was essential to rekindle the spark of God that was in each person and to keep materialism within bounds. Even though the Riis House was supposedly nonsectarian, he wrote that settlement work was "profoundly *religious* work, the great revival of our faith that goes out searching for the lost brother, and that if we cut that out we cut off our own power." He and the others did not preach disunion or any creed, he claimed, but they tried "to live the

Christian life among our neighbors. . . ."[48]

In 1908 a religious controversy flared up around Riis because he had given inspirational talks to the settlement children during Christmas and Easter. He believed that these holidays were exceptions to his proscription against mixing religious teaching with settlement work. Earlier when Jewish groups in New York City attempted to end Christmas celebrations in the public schools, Riis complained vehemently and told Jacob Schiff that bigots would retaliate by questioning the large number of Jewish teachers in the school system. On 24 April he told his daughter Kate that the "Catholic priest and Jewish rabbi in our neighborhood have jumped on me with all their eight feet, all through Holy Week, declaring me a proselytic and a grafter." He placated his critics somewhat in a magazine article entitled "What Settlements Stand For," but in December he decided to hold a Maccabean festival to balance the settlement's Christmas program. Calling on Rabbi Stephen S. Wise, a friend and fellow-participant in several reform activities, Riis asked for help in ending the false impression that he was seeking converts to the Christian faith. "I want them to be good Jews; I want them to be the best of Jews; and I want you to come down to the Riis Settlement and tell them so," he told the rabbi.[49]

Both Riis and Rabbi Wise spoke at the December Maccabean festival at the Roosevelt gymnasium. The president sent a message telling the children to be true to their heritage. Riis later remarked that the audience learned lessons of courage and patriotism from the rabbi's account of the religious origins of the Biblical story, and he hoped that the Jewish youths gained an insight into the spirit of Christian brotherhood. Rabbi Wise later related that in Riis's remarks concerning the bravery of the Hebrew people, "He could not have spoken with deeper admiration if he had been thinking and telling of his own fearless Danish forebears."[50]

Three years later, in making out his will, Riis provided for an advisory board to meet once a year to see that the Riis Neighborhood Settlement did not fall "into narrow sectarian

ways. . . ." He asked, however, that the settlement always be
faithful "to the zeal and spirit of our Christian faith. . . ."
Among the members of the board were his wife Mary, Roosevelt, Dr. Jane E. Robbins, Felix Adler, Robert W. DeForest,
Endicott Peabody, Alfred T. White, Lyman Abbott, and Mrs.
Grace Dodge. Good friends all, the group constituted a
veritable *Who's Who* in patrician reform circles.[51]

Riis believed that the benefits of social settlements out-
weighed the minor failings of human error and that their popularity in the tenement districts proved their worth. For him the
settlement was a spiritual bridge between the rich and the poor,
a two-way path among equals that knew no condescension.
"Forget the gap! It isn't there—it's a ghost," he once told an
audience at University Settlement.[52] Holding out hope for an
organic unity in society, he believed that harmony would
begin when the wealthy dropped their pretensions and when
immigrants became proud of themselves and their heritage.

11

EVANGELICAL PROGRESSIVE

On the night of 1 October 1912, Jacob Riis stepped to the podium of the stage at a high school auditorium in Springfield, Massachusetts, to tell twelve hundred people about Theodore Roosevelt and his Progressive crusade. The scene had the air of a revival meeting. For more than an hour the crowd had sung martial hymns, both religious and patriotic, and had listened to declarations of faith in their righteous cause and warnings of impending doom if the forces of reaction defeated it. As the crowd waited for the main speech of the evening to begin, their mood was taut and passionate. On the stage Riis looked small and older than sixty-three years. Then suddenly he pulled from his pocket a huge red bandanna, symbolic of the Rough Rider charge up San Juan Hill and thus an icon of the third party movement, and he waved it about his head. Tumultuous shouts and cheers engulfed the room, and he and his audience were one.[1]

Bull Moose Progressive

The roots of Riis's personal loyalty to the Progressive

Party's standard-bearer went back to the days of Mulberry Street during the 1890s; but his commitment to a strong central government was more recent. During Roosevelt's second term in office, he had come to champion an active assertion of presidential authority, or as Roosevelt stated, a "sane and courageous radicalism," as a necessary middle way between the destructive agents of revolution and the selfish defenders of the status quo. Supporting, for instance, the president's delicate balancing of factions in guiding the Hepburn Act through Congress and thereby strengthening governmental control over railroad rates, he said that "It is just as well the process is slow—the surer it is." He challenged the "heartless" corporations and the apathetic members of Congress to become receptive to moral issues even if only because of their practical necessity. He ridiculed the "mugwump attitude" of "the man who is so determined to hold the scales even in a moral issue between God and the devil that he cannot take sides." Also irksome to him were the actions of the Supreme Court, which in large part nullified progressive measures that aimed at redressing on a state and local level the most intolerable grievances of the poor. Realizing that the corporations and the courts were the bedrocks of a system which he was anxious to preserve, albeit to reform, he became increasingly disenchanted with their shortsightedness and absence of social purpose.[2]

Riis's agreement with Roosevelt's denunciation of destructive journalism in his "muckrake" speech of 1906 demonstrated the distinction he made between tearing down the roots of society and improving upon their inadequacies. In fact, his writings, especially *How the Other Half Lives,* had set the trend for the investigative and propagandistic methods of exposure that blossomed forth during the Progressive era. Muckrakers such as Lincoln Steffens looked to him as their master and consciously emulated his techniques of reporting. Riis continued to write incisive invectives against the exploitation of laborers and the mistreatment of immigrants, but he believed that the tactic of exposure was efficacious only when it was a vehicle to a legitimate and desirable end. Thus, he feared that the stridency of such muckraking articles as David Graham Phillips's *Treason of the Senate* would set class against class. While his realistic and passionate style and his commitment to social betterment made him a kindred spirit with his younger colleagues, he was more optimistic than most of them. And he preferred to submit his work to staid journals such as *Survey, Outlook,* and *Century* rather than the mass circulation muckraking periodicals which to him were somewhat too sensationalistic and excessive in their criticisms of the American system.[3]

As long as Roosevelt was in office, Riis had faith that the enemies of the public interest would be in rout. In 1907 he had told Endicott Peabody that "More and more Roosevelt seems to me a man of destiny, chosen of God to do a work no one else that I can see could have done." The following year he hoped that his friend would seek a third term but accepted his handpicked successor, William Howard Taft, despite lingering doubts about Taft's energy and commitment to change. After the 1908 election he wrote his daughter Kate: "Hurrah for Taft and for Governor Hughes! Also for [California] Governor [Hiram] Johnson. The world is all right." But during the next four years, as the inept Taft alienated himself from Roosevelt and most urban reformers, Riis's disillusionment with the Republican Party regulars increased.[4]

For Riis, whose values were traditional and whose personal habits were conservative, there was no dichotomy between democracy and orderly process, between wanting stability and advocating social and economic reforms to blunt class conflict. A religious man, his views were almost identical to Social Gospel ministers Washington Gladden and Walter Rauschenbusch. Calling himself a practical Christian whose bywords were brotherhood and the Golden Rule, he told audiences during his 1911 lecture tour that service to the poor was "the kernel of our Christianity and our democracy both." Always on the lookout for innovative experiments being tried in other parts of the country and the world, he praised Danish welfare experiments with old age pensions and unemployment insurance, and New Zealand's compulsory arbitration laws which abated dangers of boycotts and strikes without crushing unions. Likewise, he lauded the movements among civic groups in Western cities both to outlaw gambling and to prohibit child labor. The New West was synonymous with efficiency, he wrote, and "has no time to shoot up towns; its bad men languish decorously in jail, or are heading straight for it."[5]

Riis opposed violent tactics to effect change. In 1911 when strikers in New Jersey allegedly dynamited a steel plant and killed several people, the deed outraged him. He said that he would fight syndicalist labor leaders such as the McNamara brothers and William D. Haywood "to the last drop of blood that is in me." He rued that during a period of progress, "cheap assassins with their hideous pretense of 'principle' " were giving comfort to reactionary groups. "We can and will right our wrongs in an orderly way or the republic is a mockery, . . ." he told Jane Robbins.[6]

People often asked Riis his opinion of socialism. His response was that there were two types of socialism, moral and materialistic. The former, which he labeled "What is Mine is Thine," was a just and democratic ideal and a Christian gospel. The selfish creed "What is Thine is Mine" reduced the individual to a cog in an impersonal machine. He said that "Men will not be better citizens of the socialistic state than they were in the old unsocial setting and they cannot be made over by law. You must change their hearts." Yet he warned that the opponents of a socialistic economic order could justify their position only be eschewing greed and preserving opportunity for all people.[7]

Rejecting the extremes of laissez-faire capitalism and socialism, Riis advocated social control by regulatory and service agencies of government when it was in the public interest. He argued that "We can prevent our children becoming senseless automatons in the industrial grind. . . . If we do not, we shall be paying too much for our prosperity." Action was necessary to wipe out undeserved poverty, which he defined as the absence of enough money to maintain a secure and decent home. He blamed poverty on ignorance, exploitation, industrial inefficiency, and government's failure to protect its citizenry. Poverty bred a culture of errant and cancerous habits, and their manifestations in gangs of toughs and drunken derelicts were warnings to civilization. Thus, issues affecting the welfare of all people, such as housing, education, wages, working conditions, social insurance, and workmen's compensation, were legitimate areas for governmental regulation. The Supreme Court had nullified legislation which established many of these functions, and Riis warned that if judges clung to an obsolete code of law, the people would lose respect for the judicial system. Unless the law expressed the "wisdom of the commonwealth in its day," it was meaningless, he declared.[8]

Riis's call for an equitable reordering of the environment made him a part of an amorphous Progressive movement, composed of disparate groups and individuals who advocated governmental intervention to deal with the atavistic and revolutionary consequences of industrialization. The spokesmen for Progressive reform reached no consensus as to solving their grievances, but most of them sought to create institutions and promulgate laws that would make workable the traditional ideals of democracy and opportunity. Riis's primary concern was individual and moral, and the most fundamental institutions were the home and the community. Others concerned themselves more with scientific method and legal and material objectives. Middle class reformers were united not by a blueprint or program but by their hatred of certain prevalent injustices and by their impatient but hopeful mood.

Riis and the Professional Altruists

The struggle for tenement house reform exemplified the points of agreement and difference between individualistic, moralistic progressives such as Riis and Felix Adler and professional altruists such as Robert DeForest and Lawrence Veiller. Both groups had worked for the passage of the New York Tenement House Code and were in agreement that New York City's housing problems remained critical throughout the first decade of the twentieth century.

Many factors contributed to New York City's housing crisis. For one thing, legislators in Albany continually refused to supply adequate funds for the Tenement House Department, and therefore inspection procedures were at best infrequent and usually haphazard. Each year lobbyists for tenement landlords attempted to mutilate its powers. Riis wrote that "Its friends have to sit up nights with it [like a sick baby] all through every session of the legislature, repelling attacks upon it by greedy self-interest." In one session sixteen bills were submitted that would have weakened the department. Lawmakers compromised by cutting its budget. Even if the inspection system had been completely effective, the overcrowding and high rent rates would have remained. Riis complained in 1904 that "The Other Half will soon live in the streets, from present reports of landlord rapacity." He favored governmental rent and price controls and public acquisition of land for resale to limited-bond corporations in order to halt land speculation and encourage model tenements.[9]

In order to further the cause of urban reconstruction, Riis in 1905 had joined the Charities Publications Committee, whose task it was to plan large-scale investigative and publication projects for special issues of a crusading, scholarly magazine *Charities and the Commons*. Editing *Charities and the Commons* and dominating its publication committee were two of his close friends, Edward T. Devine and Paul U. Kellogg. They hoped to unify the scientific, factual thrust of housing experts and the Charity Organization Society with the humanitarian, pragmatic, and socially conscious spirit of the settlement movement. The magazine represented a merging of the Charity Organization Society's rather traditional organ *Charities* and settlement worker Graham Taylor's innovative journal

The Commons. The new masthead of *Charities and the Commons* proclaimed the espousal of "Philanthropy and Social Advance." Riis wrote frequent articles of exposure for the magazine, and he interested Devine and Kellogg in devoting one issue entirely to the problems of Washington, D.C.[10]

The most ambitious project which the Charities Publications Committee planned was an exhaustive survey of the municipal problems of Pittsburgh, Pennsylvania. The able twenty-eight-year-old Kellogg organized the Pittsburgh survey along lines similar to the New York Tenement House Exhibition of 1900. Taking the advice of Riis and Jane Addams, he decided to blend statistical method with astute publicity gimmicks. Kellogg gathered around him experts in city planning, labor problems, and social work, including John R. Commons, Florence Kelley, and Robert A. Woods. Riis had high praise for the results of the Pittsburgh survey and called for a similar study of the New York housing crisis.[11]

Despite his close rapport with the editors of *Charities and the Commons,* which aptly changed its name to *Survey,* Riis believed that there was a trend toward the overemphasis on method which was destructive to the goals of urban reconstruction. Admitting that his temperament was unsuited to the new techniques of analysis, he feared that too often reformers were turning these legitimate means into ends, and thereby neglecting practical achievement. Poignant stories of human suffering and personal interrelation with the victims of poverty were more useful, he said, than tables of statistics which separated men into fractions. "My day was the day of the bludgeon," he told Steffens. "The day of scientific method has come, and I am neither able to grasp its ways, nor am I wholly in sympathy with them. Two or three times a week I am compelled to denounce the 'sociological' notions of the day—and cry out for common sense." It irked him that social workers were earning large salaries and were becoming so professional and so imbedded with data that the individual became lost. "And right there I part company," he told Jane Robbins in 1911; "I cannot like a crowd. I like the person."[12]

In 1910 when Robert DeForest and Lawrence Veiller formed the National Housing Association, Riis welcomed the new organization. Although he disliked Veiller somewhat, he had confidence in DeForest, calling him "so cool and withal so wondrous good." He suggested that the housing experts work closely with people such as Felix Adler who had long regarded tenement house reform as just one aspect of urban reconstruction. Veiller thanked Riis for his support and hoped that he would be the agency's foremost publicist. "You have been a national housing association yourself for a great many years past," Veiller told him.[13]

In a letter to Robert DeForest, Riis advocated that the National Housing Association sponsor a fact-finding survey of American and European cities in order to plan for future growth; but the new group reacted to his proposal with coolness. Riis recognized that model tenements, restrictive legislation, playgrounds and parks, and bridges and rapid transit to the suburbs had not alleviated the housing crisis. Quick action in New York was vital, he said, in order to relieve the distress in Manhattan and to prevent the slums from flowing into other boroughs. He offered to look into German methods of city planning while on a summer trip there. The cautious and somewhat conservative Veiller opined that governmental regulations were not the solution to overcrowding in the suburbs. He wanted "enlightened builders [to] lead the way and influence others." A month later, in April 1910, DeForest dashed Riis's hopes that his organization would concentrate on New York City, saying that problems there were only a part of the housing question and "what is done in New York does not affect our national effort."[14]

Riis came to believe that the National Housing Association had removed itself too much from local battles to be able to effect tangible results for New York. In June 1911 he addressed the National Conference of Charities and Correction in Boston on the subject of "What Bad Housing Means to the Community." Holding up two pamphlets of the National Housing Association, he noted that they "say it all" on the latest methods and goals of slum control. He added that "To me they summon up, incongruously enough, the days when we labored in the underpinnings as it were—incongruously because our methods in the new scientific light are supposed to have been very crude and ineffective. Crude they certainly were; I am not so sure as to the other." Then, lest anyone had missed his point he shouted out: "We weren't quite as filled up with statistics as the present day is, and we didn't seem to need them then."[15]

Riis's criticism of Lawrence Veiller and the new urban professionals in 1911 was an accentuation of a lifelong tendency to deemphasize doctrine in favor of practical action. Yet it marked quite a deviation from his support during the 1880s of the Charity Organization Society. Then he viewed the methods of scientific philanthropy as sound and necessary complements to his eclectic, untutored views about poverty. In the depression-ridden 1890s, he focused more on preventing poverty and treating its causes rather than just its consequences. When the COS's young professionals became interested in tenement house reform and other programs of urban reconstruction, Riis worked in tandem with them. But just when the formalized methodology and bureaucratic structure of the COS began to infatuate progressives, Riis began rebelling against these precepts as cold, impersonal, and elitist. He was skeptical about the curing wonders of legislation and the gospel of efficiency. He had seen good laws become moribund and count for nothing in New York, even when William L. Strong and Seth Low were mayor. And he ruefully remembered how Congress buried Roosevelt's model city program for Washington, D.C.

The immediate future belonged to the Lowells and Veillers who built social work and urban planning into permanent professions. Yet they did not end poverty, and after a time they served their own bureaucratic imperatives as much as the poor. In his twilight years Riis appeared backward-looking, an anachronistic romantic; but his emphasis on neighborhood organization and the democratization of urban planning have enjoyed a renaissance in recent years, perhaps because the professionals sacrificed community for expertise and perhaps because the only palatable interest group for the poor are the poor people themselves.

Americanization of a Reformer

Riis's cross-country lecture tours in 1909 and 1910 kept his idealistic tenets of progressive reform in the public eye. During this time almost all his addresses were variations of three speeches, the autobiographical "Making of an American," the inspirational "My Neighbor," and the urban-oriented "Battle with the Slum." Each of them stressed the themes of citizenship, service, social justice, and brotherhood. He admonished his audience that "The first, the all-important [task] is *to find your neighbor. . . . Go, find him.*"[16] Experience had perfected his personal, anecdotal delivery and taught him the nuances of crowd reaction. Once, for instance, while telling about the death of his dog at a police lodging house, he saw a small puppy come up to the stage. He petted it for a few moments silently and resumed his story while the animal lay at his feet. He still used photographs to expose the dark side of American life but blended his descriptions of poverty with confident predictions of improvement. He portrayed the people of the tenements, the Jewish laborer, the Italian waif, the gang member with a pure heart, the Bohemian cigar maker, as having the potential to move into the mainstream of American life. "Our country has grown great—our cities wealthy," Riis declared, but he warned that "In their slums lurk poverty and bitterness—bitterness because the promise has not been kept that every man should have an even chance to start with."[17]

One of Riis's most touching stories concerned Skippy of Scrabble Alley, a boy who grew up to be a gang leader and · a murderer. He told of Skippy's execution, his final thoughts as the executioner pulled the black cap over his eyes. There was "Scrabble Alley with its dripping hydrant, and the puddle in which the children splashed with dirty, bare feet; the dark basement room with its mouldy wall; the notice in the yard, 'No ball-playing allowed here,' the policeman who stamped him as one of a bad lot, and the sullen man who thought it had been better for him, the time he was run over, if he had died."[18]

In discussing urban decay and reconstruction, Riis interposed slides and anecdotes with a series of blunt epigrams. "You cannot, friends, build the republic on a crust and expect it to be robust," he often said. Emphasizing the priority of housing reform, he stated that "Where home goes, go family, manhood, citizenship, patriotism." Corruption hurt the cities, he declared, but "Municipal hook-worm, the citizen indifference of the past, has been ten times as costly to us as Tweed was." He personally visited the slum districts of cities where he spoke in order to make his comments more germane. Paraphrasing a report by the St. Louis Tenement House Association, he said that the rats there were so large that they ate cats. In Los Angeles he was angry because newspapers did not print any of his references to the slum sections of their city.[19]

Proud of his Danish ancestry and convinced that the cultural variety of ethnic groups enriched his country, Riis praised equally the objectives of cultural pluralism and Americanization. Jokingly he said that immigrants like himself made the best citizens because they entered their new home laughing while native-born babies entered it crying. He hoped that public schools would teach children about non-American heroes such as Kossuth, Garibaldi, Moses, and Kosciusko, in order to instill pride into the sons and daughters of immigrants and to teach the young to respect other cultures. He asked his audiences to accept hyphenated Americans as brothers and to work to create conditions that would cause them to become loyal citizens. He was a member of the Society for the Protection of Italian Immigrants, which gave out legal aid, publicized employment opportunities, and furnished loans to the needy; and he also joined the North American Civic League for Immigrants, whose goals were the assimilation, naturalization, education, and protection of the newcomer. Conservative businessmen founded the organization in Boston in 1907, but in New York Frances Kellor and others used the Civic League as a pressure group for welfare legislation.[20]

Riis frequently referred to Danish statesmen who personified the ideals of bravery, patriotism, charity, and service. One of his favorite stories concerned Peder Tordensjold, an admiral who refused to surrender his ship even after he had exhausted his supply of cannon balls. Enrico Dalgas, whom Riis called "the Gifford Pinchot of Denmark," founded the Heath Society which converted barren moorland into arable fields by adopting scientific farming methods and cooperative planning. Another hero was Nikolai Grundtvig, a bishop who led Denmark out of its sterile, preindustrial conditions by fighting for tuition-free public education, land redistribution, and religious and political equality. Finally Dr. Niels Finsen invented a process of curing dread diseases by reflecting the rays of the sun onto patients.[21]

Riis meant his speeches to appeal to the nationalism of his audience. After almost every lecture, he asked the people to join him in the singing of "My Country 'Tis of Thee." Speaking in 1910 at Culver Military School in Indiana, he received an elaborate escort to the campus. Then to his delight the commandant allowed him to inspect and review the cadets. His speech later that day mentioned the heroism of American soldiers such as the Rough Riders, and he told also about a pilgrimage which he had recently made to the battlefields of Gettysburg. Three years later while in San Antonio, Texas, he went to a simulation of the Battle of the Alamo. When he saw no sign of an American flag, even though it was George Washington's birthday, he argued vociferously with the officials until they raised one on the fort.[22]

During his lecture trips Riis sensed a dissatisfaction with President William Howard Taft and an impatient yet confident sentiment for change among his middle class audiences. This mood he had done much to create with his poignant slides and compassionate rhetoric about the "other half." He had mirrored his praise of America with the warning that disorder and suffering would multiply if the people did not grasp power away from the plutocrats, whom he defined as the impersonal agents of big business and the corrupt political bosses.

The Last Campaign for Roosevelt

Thus, in 1910 when Roosevelt returned to the United States from an African safari and European grand tour, Riis already believed that the Taft administration was in an unholy alliance with Wall Street. Philosophically he was in agreement with Roosevelt's New Nationalism speech in late August which attacked the executive and judicial branches of government for abandoning human rights in their zealous protection of property. The former president began to ally himself with Taft's political enemies, the insurgents, during the Congressional campaign of 1910. For different reasons the election results in November disappointed both Taft and Roosevelt, but Riis was "rather glad" that the Democrats gained control of the House of Representatives because it "wiped the slate clean."[23]

Although Roosevelt denied interest in running for president again, Riis began to hope that events and the will of the people would change his mind. In October 1911 the final rupture between Roosevelt and Taft occurred when Attorney General George W. Wickersham brought an antitrust suit against United States Steel Corporation. During the Panic of 1907, Roosevelt and his advisers had approved the purchase by J. P. Morgan's U.S. Steel Corporation of Tennessee Coal and Iron Company. By challenging the legality of his "gentlemen's agreement," Taft seemed to be casting doubts upon the integrity of his predecessor. In Cleveland at the time, Riis labeled Taft "worse than a fool" after learning from James R. Garfield, a former cabinet member and participant in the Morgan agreement, that Taft had been present and seemingly approved the consolidation. As Roosevelt began to amend his position of noncandidacy, Riis used his lectures to drum up popular support for the former president. In Michigan on 1 December 1911, a Norwegian minister introduced him by saying that "Mr. Riis is a friend of our President—not the big man who sits in that office now, but the great man who sat there before him." Riis and his audience then roared their assent.[24]

In February 1912 Roosevelt threw his hat into the ring for the Republican nomination and announced that he would enter a dozen primaries. Viewing the campaign as a righteous crusade, Riis declared that Roosevelt's enemies were villains who deserved no quarter. He longed to see Nicholas Murray Butler, the president of Columbia University, "dragged in the road, beaten." Roosevelt was the Lord's agent, he wrote, doing battle to end special privilege and to confirm "the eternal justice and goodness of the world, and the fitness of the people to rule themselves. . . ." Roosevelt swept to a succession of smashing victories in California, Minnesota, Nebraska, Maryland, South Dakota, New Jersey, and finally Ohio, the president's home state. Taft's political lieutenants controlled the party machinery, however, and in a stormy series of sessions they denied Roosevelt the Republican nomination. The former Rough Rider and his partisans walked out and held a rump convention. Afterwards they announced the formation of a Progressive Party that would continue the battle for social justice.[25]

For more than a decade, Riis had hoped for the emergence of a viable political party that would clearly represent the principles of democracy and social reform. Never a party regular, he had allied himself with nonpartisan political agencies in New York, such as the Committee of Seventy and the Citizens' Union, in reaction to the machine methods of Tammany Hall and Boss Platt. He believed that the success of independent reformers such as Judge Ben Lindsey in Denver augured well for a national Progressive Party. Shortly before the Republicans assembled to nominate Taft, he told Lindsey that "The people will not be defrauded again. If they don't nominate him, he will be [a candidate] anyhow. And then we shall be truly on the homestretch." The verdict of the Chicago convention shattered his hope that Roosevelt could transform the Republican Party into an agency for reform. In its wake he had confidence that Roosevelt still could win the presidency if the Democrats nominated a "fossil" such as their 1904 candidate Alton B. Parker. He suggested that the Progressives would do well in that event to pick William Jennings Bryan or Governor Woodrow Wilson as their vice-presidential candidate. When the Democrats nominated Wilson, who had carried out a modest program of progressive reform in New Jersey, Riis's optimism diminished; but he still believed that Roosevelt would win out, in 1916 if not in 1912. In any event, he told his sister, the profession of faith was more important than victory at the polls. This glorification of principle over practical outcome was as uncharacteristic of him as party irregularity was of the Rough Rider.[26]

When the Progressive Party convention met formally in August to nominate Roosevelt and Governor Hiram Johnson of California as their standard-bearers, Riis followed the accounts of the proceedings at his home as he rested from his heart trouble. Fellow humanitarian Progressives massed at the convention, organized a "Jane Addams Chorus," and sang "The Battle Hymn of the Republic." Jane Addams and Ben Lindsey received thunderous applause as they seconded Roosevelt's candidacy, following a nominating speech by Albert J. Beveridge of Indiana. A day later the crowd greeted the Rough Rider with a fifty-two minute ovation, waving red bandannas and singing "Thou wilt not cower in the dust, Roosevelt, O Roosevelt! Thy gleaming sword shall never rust, Roosevelt, O Roosevelt." The former president then delivered a "Confession of Faith," and proclaimed that "We stand at Armageddon, and we battle for the Lord."[27]

Many Progressives looked upon their party platform, which Riis endorsed without reservation, as the most impressive achievement of the convention. Urban reformers active in settlement work had inserted planks advocating the prohibition of child labor and tenement sweatshops, federal standards on wages, hours, and safety standards for businesses engaged in interstate commerce, unemployment, and old age insurance, and workmen's compensation. The platform also favored women's suffrage, popular review of judicial decisions regarding the constitutionality of legislation, and the establishment of farm schools to encourage agricultural education. The social planks, which viewed urban and industrial dislocations as national in scope, advocated using the federal government in bold new ventures as "an agency of human welfare."[28]

Some reformers, but not Riis, distrusted aspects of the Progressive crusade that smacked of militarism, racism, and the acceptance of monopolistic practices. The party advocated preparedness and the building of two battleships a year. The delegates rejected a proposal to affirm the principle of racial equality. And Roosevelt's adviser and chief financier George W. Perkins expunged from the platform a statement that attacked monopolistic corporations. Riis's hatred of Germany and pride in American strength squared with the preparedness plank, in contrast to the repugnance of Jane Addams who "found it very difficult to swallow those two battleships."

Largely unaware of black impatience with discrimination, Riis did not assign high priority to racial equality. For example, in 1911 he observed a chain gang of black convicts working on a highway in Columbia, South Carolina. The practice of hiring out convicts as contract laborers repelled him, but he thought that the prisoners looked quite happy because they were singing as they worked. Finally Riis welcomed big business representatives into Roosevelt's camp since he was more interested in policing corporations strictly than in breaking them up.[29]

In the autumn Riis took to the stump and delivered a score of speeches on Roosevelt as spokesman for the common man. The newspapers called his anecdotal and personal campaign delivery unique and effective. His vitality returned as he made his way through New England, Ohio, Michigan, Missouri, and Illinois. On 23 October the Detroit *Free Press* commented that he looked physically stronger and younger than he had in some years. He complained about the disorganization of the new party, but the crowds he attracted caused him to dare hope for victory. For example, on 24 October he told Kate: "It is almost a miracle if we win this year, but I believe we will."

In his talks Riis refuted a charge by President Charles W. Eliot of Harvard College that the Progressive candidate was a dangerous man and a militarist, and he then turned around the accusation at the Taft administration and the Supreme Court. "Who now is the dangerous man," he asked, "the one whose face is set forward toward the new day with its hope, or these, facing backward toward the old despair?" Responding to Taft's charge that the Progressive Party had no principles, he concluded that five words could define its purpose: "Human rights before property rights."[30]

Post-Election Wounds

Riis interpreted Roosevelt's defeat in November as the successful launching of a movement rather than a signal of its demise, and he agreed to become a publicist and investigator for the new party to the extent that his health allowed. He told Emma that Roosevelt had triumphantly carried his message to the people, won 4,500,000 votes, and routed the forces of reaction. Nevertheless, the result was a disappointment. Speaking in Rugby, North Dakota, in mid-November, he lashed out angrily at an audience which did not applaud sufficiently when he showed a stereopticon picture of Roosevelt. In December he agreed to serve on the Immigration Committee of the National Progressive Service, an investigative and lobby group for the new party. The committee chairmen hoped to be sort of a government-in-exile and included Gifford Pinchot (Conservation), George Record (Popular Government), Jane Addams (Social and Industrial Justice), Paul Kellogg (Social Insurance), and Frances Kellor (Coordinator). Poor health curbed Riis's active participation in 1913, and he declined to get involved with state affairs, although his son John helped organize a Progressive Club in Utah.[31]

A month after the 1912 election, Riis covered the annual conference of the National Housing Association for the New York *Sun*. He had sought out the assignment so that he might gain facts about tenement house conditions for articles and lectures. In his dispatch he emphasized the unity of housing reformers in their espousal of national standards of safety and decency and strict government regulation of the practices of landlords. Amplifying upon this point in an article for *Century*, he endorsed the principles of the Progressive Party's social and industrial plank. Also he called for governmental commissions to plan for urban growth, map out elaborate zoning regulations for the future, and recommended the public acquisition of unused land.[32]

In 1913 Riis made a final public declaration of faith in Roosevelt. Shortly after the 1912 election the defeated candidate asked him to testify in a libel suit against a newspaper editor who had written that Roosevelt "lies and curses in a most disgusting way; he gets drunk too, and that not infrequently. . . ." For years Riis had answered false rumors about his famous friend, such as that he was an epileptic, or that he invented a spiked club to use on labor agitators while he was a police commissioner. In 1910, after some newspapers spread the rumor that Roosevelt shot his neighbor's pet bird while drunk, Riis blamed Wall Street interests for the "damnable" lie, and declared that the perpetrators were "slimy, crawling things" who deserved the "brimstone pit." When the rumors of alcoholism broke out again in 1912, Riis advocated jail sentences for the people who planted the stories. "It is shocking to be so powerless against such a vicious lie," he said.[33]

On 27 May Riis took the stand in court as a character witness regarding Roosevelt's sobriety. Roosevelt drank only at public dinners and then only light wines and champagne, he said. Over the objections of defense counsel, he went on at great length about his friend's exemplary character. Roosevelt's lawyer asked whether he ever saw the former president under the influence of alcohol. "Lord, no," Riis replied. "Is he a blasphemous or foul-mouthed man?" the attorney queried. Riis answered that "He is a gentleman, and during all his life I never heard him say anything more profane than 'by Godfrey.'" The jury exonerated Roosevelt, who asked for damages of six cents.[34]

For Riis the Bull Moose campaign had been the climactic expression of his reform sentiments, his nationalism, and his fervent love of Roosevelt. Finally, he felt, there was a national political party which committed itself fully to social reforms which he had been advocating for two decades. But in the wake of Roosevelt's defeat, which turned out to be a quixotic, personal, one-shot affair, Riis had neither energy nor heart to commence being, for the first time in his life, a party regular.

12

THE CITY AND THE FARM

In 1913 Jacob Riis moved permanently to a farm in Barre, Massachusetts. He had bought the property at his wife's suggestion on the condition, he told his daughter Kate on 1 August 1911, "that she raise the crops—I do the Rip Van Winkle act, anyway, the loafing and hunting and fishing." The two hundred acres were rocky, and the century-old mansion and farm buildings were badly in need of repair; but the scenic beauty of the pine woods and brook and huckleberry bushes was an irresistable attraction to the proud new owner, who told Kate that it was in an area "undefiled by the smoke of factory chimneys." And the size and shrouded dignity of the old house, with its "noble lines and sound timbers," reminded him of his native country's manors. He thought also that it would be a good investment, but refurbishing the property and cultivating six acres of earth for potatoes took all his savings. When he moved away from Richmond Hill, reporters asked him if he was abandoning the city. Riis responded that he would always be a New Yorker and an urban reformer.[1]

New Year's Eve Festival

Before Riis left New York City, he organized a New

Year's Eve festival so that citizens could rededicate their lives
to their God and country rather than revel, as he put it, in
cynicism and vulgar debauchery. In 1912 civic leaders asked
for his help in arranging for a municipal Christmas tree to
adorn Madison Square. Remembering a Danish tradition of
ceremoniously blowing in the New Year with bugles, he
expanded their plans to include a series of neighborhood
New Year's pageants. They would be joyous but orderly, he
told reporters, so that the city might get rid of "the damnable
tin horn and . . . all the worse wickedness" that characterized
past celebrations. To aid him he formed a Citizens' Committee
of Thirteen, which included ministers, businessmen, and settlement workers. Handling the musical arrangements for the
Madison Square festivities, he had church choirs and settlement
children lead the crowd in singing religious hymns and patriotic
songs. One of them, entitled "The U.S.A. Forever" and sung
to the tune of "Dixie," included the proclamation that "the
United States and hearts and hands/Will make the greatest of
all lands/Work away, work away, for the land of the free."
Thousands of people gathered at the outdoor locations, but the
New York Times reported that "the mighty clamor" of heck-
lers, hornblowers, and other unruly elements disrupted and
submerged plans for a sane welcoming in of the New Year.
Riis thought it was a hopeful and auspicious beginning for
the festival becoming a permanent tradition, symbolic of
brotherhood, that would be his final legacy to the city.[2]

Ambivalence toward the Old Town and the Empire City

As Riis became older, he tended both to glorify his birthplace and to become disillusioned with the spirit of modern
Denmark. The myths of his memories conflicted with the
realities of the present. He was eager for his countrymen to
recognize his success and was sensitive to real or imagined
slights at their hands. For ten years he brooded over an inci-

dent that occurred in 1904 during his last visit with Elisabeth to Ribe. At an honorary dinner for him, someone interrupted the speaker's compliments by sarcastically calling out that he knew enough about Jacob Riis and wanted to hear something else. Afterward his wife said, that "We do not belong here any more." When she died a year later, church officials at the Domkirke turned down his offer to dedicate a memorial window in her honor. In 1909 he wrote a warm and idyllic account of life in Ribe but privately acknowledged that the old town of his youth no longer existed and perhaps never had been as idyllic as he remembered. In 1913 when the Danish government refused to improve military fortifications around Copenhagen, Riis charged that a craven spirit had engulfed his people. They had fallen into evil ways, "into a vulgar prosperity to which they are apparently willing to sacrifice country and all," he told Kate on 9 September 1913.[3]

Riis continued to aid needy Danish immigrants, but he thought that most young men who were coming to America were lazy and too restless. They would be wise to follow his former example and not expect favors, he told Emma. He regretted his softheartedness in loaning money to a young Dane named Viggs and asked Emma to keep silent about it. The shibboleths of the COS against indiscriminate almsgiving were still to some degree with him. In 1912 Viggs quit a job which Riis had found for him and asked his patron for traveling money to California. The reformer called him a "rolling stone" and angrily denied the request.[4]

Riis's personal move to Pine Brook Farm and his continuing interest in urban reform represented in microcosm his ambivalence about the city. Instinctively he still equated rural life with beauty and the urban scene as unnatural and potentially inimical to society's necessary bonds of family and community. Yet he distinguished between the metropolitan setting and the slum environment. He hated the slum but as early as 1890 had asked people to accept the metropolis as permanent and beneficial so that they would accept their duty to make life there palatable. His repugnance at certain aspects of urban life served as fuel to spark his efforts to create new institutions to hold together the home and the neighborhood. In February 1912 Riis spoke to civic leaders in Chicago on "The City and Its Duty to Its People." He tied the future destiny of the nation with the city and affirmed that man could make the urban environment as perfect as he desired if he worked at it.[5]

All his life he wanted to merge the efficiency of the city with the beauty and moral virtue of nature. He hoped that corporations would move away from the large cities, and he publicized experiments in planning new cities within a rural setting, such as a Jewish settlement in Woodbine, New Jersey. Woodbine floundered until its leaders attracted industrial firms into their town, but afterward the community seemed to offer the best of both environments.[6]

On occasion Riis's sentiments in favor of rural life became truly dominant in his rhetoric. In an article which compared German cities with the country, he wrote that the further he went from the cynical veneer and materialistic grip of the cities, the more zest for life he found among the peasant citizenry. In 1911 he told members of the National Farm School Association that economic independence, ethical growth, and democratic principles could best flourish in a rural setting. On 28 June 1912, in a letter to Emma, he equated personal freedom and security, much like Thomas Jefferson a century earlier, as owning a piece of land and knowing how to till it.[7]

When he moved to Pine Brook Farm, the sixty-four-year-old reformer had the surface appearance of an old man, but he retained his vitality, his perceptive mind, and his combatant spirit. His weak heart required long periods of rest, his hair had whitened, and he walked with a cane. He told Emma that on several occasions he had offended aged men on street cars by offering them his seat. " 'Keep it' they tell me very curtly, 'I am younger than you.' And I guess they are right. But I do catch myself so often in believing that I am still a young man," he said. The deaths in quick succession of his friends Josephine Shaw Lowell, Richard W. Gilder, and John B.

Devins seemed harbingers of his own fate. Honoring Devins, the former COS agent who with Riis had mobilized emergency relief projects during the depression of the 1890s, he wrote: "They drop out, the old fighters, one by one, and it grows lonesome in the gap they leave, till we pull ourselves together, close up ranks, and catch our step again."[8]

With Jacob and Mary at Pine Brook Farm were his son Billy and his mother-in-law. In the fall of 1913, Billy became a freshman at Williams College. Riis thought that the intimate, traditional school was a good choice and preferred it over Columbia, whose president was Nicholas Murray Butler, a Taft Republican and, according to the reformer, an "egregious ass." John, Kate, and Clara still lived far away from him, but Ed had returned east to work on the staff of the Brooklyn *Eagle*. Still pessimistic over Ed's ability, on 25 January 1914 Jacob told his wife with wry humor, "Surely I can not afford to die. What would *he* do without me?"

The Pine Brook Farm brought Riis comfort and happiness but also problems and insecurity. It cost him $20,000 to improve his property into a profitable enterprise. In addition to the repairs to the house, he had to build barns and sheds, a henhouse, and tenant quarters. There were more bills for a new well and tools, wagons, animals, fertilizer, and seed. Mary handled the financial arrangements with shrewdness, but in 1912 and 1913 they barely broke even on their potato crop. Jacob told a friend: "Whereas I struggled all these years with bosses and politics, I am now fighting the blight and the potato bug, and winning out. If only we can have some rain." He chafed at the apathy of his workers and compiled a long questionnaire for hiring a foreman for them. His queries were practical and personal, concerning both their experience and skills and whether they smoked, drank, or swore, and if so, how much. The form ended with a warning that "Unless you are a very industrious, hard working man don't answer." Throughout all the hardships, however, he still believed that rural living "beat the city fifty times. . . ."[9]

In the autumn of 1913, Riis once again assembled his

slides and lecture notes in preparation for another winter tour. In his engagement book he wrote this verse: "Do all the good you can /To all the people you can/As long as ever you can." He told his wife that they needed the money for Billy's tuition and for twelve new cows and that the Progressive Party had implored him to become a spokesman for their reform programs. His ambitious plans did not surprise Mary, but she worried about his health. Fearing that the exhausting travel would kill him, she nevertheless realized that he needed the therapy of work and the cheers of an audience as much as relaxation on the farm. She wrote Roosevelt about his deteriorating health and asked if he could visit them and perhaps dissuade her husband from taking on a heavy schedule. The former president could not come but wrote that Riis's condition saddened him. "Jake has been the staunchest of friends to me, he is the most lovable of men, and, as you know, I think him the very best and most useful citizen in all this wide land."[10]

Embarking on a trip through the Middle West, Riis was fatalistic about his future. He asked Kate on 2 October to remember that God governed all events and "Whatever happens to us in His world can only be for the best because it *is* His world. . . ." In one of his daily love letters to Mary, he said that he sometimes wished that he had been a teacher so he would have gotten a pension upon his retirement. In December he rested for a month at Battle Creek Sanitarium and then traveled south. After his mother-in-law died in January 1914, Riis told his daughter Kate that he would prefer a quick death to becoming an invalid.[11]

During his addresses many people questioned him about politics. In Detroit on 13 January he praised President Woodrow Wilson as a courageous and wonderful man but predicted Roosevelt's election in 1916, as either a Progressive or a Republican. The Grand Old Party without him was dead, he believed.[12]

Great Dane's Demise

On 23 April in New Orleans, Riis collapsed from a heart seizure. He went back to Battle Creek, but in May he told Mary that he wanted to return to his farm. She, Billy, and a nurse went with him by train to Barre. During the final automobile ride to their farm, he collapsed again. He never regained his strength and died on 26 May 1914. Three days later Endicott Peabody presided over the funeral services. "I have been very happy," Riis had written in his autobiography. "No man ever had so good a time" (p. 441).

On this sad occasion for the family, Riis's young grandson Jacob Riis Owre arrived at the farm with Jake's favorite daughter Kate. Forty-five years later he recollected the scene as best he could:

Vaguely I remember sitting with my mother in the dingy railroad station in Springfield; I remember a clattering, sooty little railroad car. And I remember well, strangely, the two things at Pine Brook Farm that my grandfather mentioned most in his letters: the pair of maples in front of the old house—I lay under them in the tall grass and looked up to the sky through their branches—and the swift-running brook, where my "uncle Billy" showed me the clear, cold pool in which the fish hung almost motionless just below the surface. But my grandfather, I do not remember from that occasion at all. Perhaps when my mother and I arrived, he was already buried, as he had specified, under an unmarked granite boulder in the cemetery situated down the hill from the farm.[13]

Many people paid tribute to Riis and mourned his death. Roosevelt said it was "as if I had lost my own brother." Roger Tracy, his oldest ally in the Mulberry Street tenement house crusades, said he would not attend the funeral because he did not want to see the man who was the embodiment of life lying still in a coffin. Children of the Jacob Riis Settlement and working class members of the Society for Italian Immigrants sent their condolences. John A. Kingsbury began a movement to rename after him the public park adjacent to the Sea Breeze Hospital on Rockaway Beach. Perhaps fittingly, Riis's last published article was about the children's hospital, and he was working on one about the creative play movement when he died. At a conference of settlement workers, Jane Robbins told how he had caused a generation of young idealists to become reformers, and how he had given them confidence that they could effect change. His greatest disappointment, she said, was the lack of progress in housing conditions.[14]

Nine months after Riis's death, Paul U. Kellogg wrote that his most substantial contribution to reform was his ability "to make Good captivating, adventurous, stirring to the pulses."[15] The slums remained; many people forgot or never digested his warning that two Americas separate and unequal could not endure. But Kellogg and other humanitarians hoped that Riis's books and example would allow his spirit to live on.

Riis died on the eve of World War I and in the autumn of the Progressive movement, at a time when few humanitarian reformers enjoyed his eminence but at a juncture when young college students found his moderation less stimulating than the iconoclastic ideas of antirationalists, anarchists, and revolutionaries. The war would soon cause two of his idols, Theodore Roosevelt and Jane Addams, to part paths, and the postwar disillusionment would leave the welfare goals of the Bull Moose Party moribund for a generation. Perhaps fate was kind in sparing him the agony of the war because his patriotism, loyalty to Roosevelt, and hatred of Germany would have sorely tempted him to follow paths of intolerance and chauvinism that marred the Rough Rider's place in history. Though Riis loved Roosevelt more, his ideals were more in harmony with those of Miss Addams, who like him believed that a healthy environment could redeem man's goodness and provide a communality of interests among all people. Both settlement house founders worked to temper individualism and materialism with a pluralistic social ethic. They were links between nineteenth and twentieth-century liberalism, as they called on decent citizens to hold in abeyance their fear of the state and use government to reform the urban environment.[16]

Few people ever looked upon misery as did Riis, and few people retained such optimism over a lifetime. His own life bridged the gap between the two Americas that he confronted as an immigrant. He walked with the rich and powerful while retaining his bond with the slum resident. "I have lived in the best of times," he wrote, "when you do not have to dream things good, but can make them so."[17]

Conservative critics feared that Riis's optimism raised the expectations of the poor to unrealistic heights, causing disillusionment and discord when their hopes were not met. Radicals thought it simplistic to imagine that social democracy could be achieved and the slums eradicated under corporate capitalism. Some of his reform colleagues thought his maxims unscientific and ill-suited to a twentieth-century world. Whatever his limitations, Riis kept injustice in the public eye and his instincts were a boon for the creative play, neighborhood revitalization, and social settlement movements. Fond of telling skeptics that optimism and reform by humane touch were crucial ingredients for progress, in this regard, in the final analysis, he was essentially correct.

NOTES AND REFERENCES

Notes are grouped by text paragraph; a single superscript will often cover several references within the paragraph, and the note will be a composite.

Chapter 1

1. Waldemar C. Westergaard, *Denmark and Slesvig, 1848–1864* (London, 1946), p. 19; Jacob A. Riis, "Niels Juel's Chair," *Outlook*, 100 (20 February 1912), 325; John Danstrup, *A History of Denmark* (Copenhagen, 1949), pp. 120–21; Jacob A. Riis, *The Old Town* (New York, 1909), pp. 27–30, 78.

2. Riis, *Old Town*, pp. 7–14, 24. On Riis's background in Ribe, see also Jacob A. Riis, *The Making of an American* (New York, 1901); Louis E. Ware, *Jacob A. Riis: Police Reporter, Reformer, Useful Citizen* (New York, 1939); Roy Lubove, *The Progressives and the Slums: Tenement House Reform in New York City, 1890–1917* (Pittsburgh, 1962).

3. Regarding the Riis family, see Jacob Riis Owre, "Genealogy," Jacob A. Riis MSS, Library of Congress, Washington, D.C. (hereafter LC); Niels E. Riis, "Books of Poetry," Jacob A. Riis MSS, New York Public Library, New York (hereafter NYPL); Jacob A. Riis to Endicott Peabody, 15 September 1900, Endicott Peabody MSS, University of Harvard Library, Cambridge, Mass. (hereafter Harvard); Jacob A. Riis to Lyman Powell, 17 March 1904, Riis MSS, NYPL.

4. Riis, *Making of an American*, pp. 14–16; William D. P. Bliss, *The Encyclopedia of Social Reform* (New York, 1897), p. 490; Riis, *Old Town*, pp. 13–15, 123.

5. Riis, *Old Town*, pp. 137–38; Riis to Emma Reinsholm, 28 June 1909, Riis MSS, LC.

6. Riis, *Making of an American,* pp. 4, 399; Margaret E. Burton, *Comrades in Service* (New York, 1915), p. 1; Jacob A. Riis, "Boys' Fun in the Old Town," *Outlook,* 83 (2 June 1906), 278–81.

7. Niels E. to Jacob A. Riis, 28 March 1873, Riis MSS, LC; Jacob A. Riis, "My Boyhood's Black Friend," *Outlook,* 85 (19 January 1907), 129.

8. Riis, *Old Town,* p. 192; Aksel H. Nellemann, *Schools and Education in Denmark,* trans. John B. Powell (Copenhagen, 1964), pp. 9, 11.

9. Latin School Records, Ribe, Denmark. Quoted in Ware, *Jacob Riis,* p. 7.

10. Jacob A. Riis, *Theodore Roosevelt the Citizen* (Washington, D.C., 1904), pp. 18–19; Jacob A. Riis, *Children of the Tenements* (New York, 1903), pp. 150–51; Jacob A. Riis, "Midwinter in New York," *Century,* 59 (February 1900), 520.

11. Riis to Reinsholm, 1 April 1907, Riis MSS, LC; Jacob A. Riis, "Christmas in Denmark," *Churchman,* 15 (21 December 1907), 956.

12. Riis, *Making of an American,* pp. 22–32; Danstrup, *History of Denmark,* pp. 122–23.

13. Riis to "Friends," 4 May 1870, Riis MSS, LC.

14. Jacob A. Riis, "In the Gateway of Nations," *Century,* 65 (March 1903), 674–75; Riis, *Making of an American,* pp. 33–35; New York *Tribune,* 6 June 1870; Ware, *Jacob Riis,* pp. 14–16.

Chapter 2

1. Arthur M. Schlesinger, *The Rise of the City, 1878–1898* (New York, 1933), p. 75; Bayrd Still, *Mirror for Gotham: New York as Seen by Contemporaries from Dutch Days to the Present* (New York, 1956). p. 205; Robert U. Johnson, *Remembered Yesterdays* (Boston 1923), pp. 161–62; Allon Schoener (ed.), *The Lower East Side: Portal to American Life (1870–1924)* (New York, 1967), p. 11; the last sentence paraphrases Van Wyck Brooks in *The Confident Years: 1885–1915* (London, 1953), p. 1.

2. Riis, "In the Gateway of Nations," 674; Mary R. Parkman, "A Modern Viking: Jacob A. Riis," *St. Nicholas,* 44 (January 1917), 210–11. For biographical information on Riis during the years between 1870 and 1877, see Riis, *Making of an American,* pp. 38–199.

3. Riis, *Making of an American,* pp. 66–74; New York *Tribune,* 31 January 1892; Joseph Husband, *Americans by Adoption* (Boston, 1920), pp. 150–51.

4. Riis, *Making of an American,* pp. 78–81, 86; New York *Herald,* 15 August 1897.

5. Niels E. to Jacob A. Riis, 26 March 1873, Riis MSS, LC.

6. Jacob A. Riis, diary, 1872–1874, Riis MSS, NYPL.

7. David M. Schneider and Albert Deutsch, *The History of Public Welfare in New York State, 1867–1940* (Montclair, N.J., Patterson Smith edition, 1967), pp. 13–39; *New York Times,* 14 January 1874; Leah H. Feder, *Unemployment Relief in Periods of Depression* (New York, 1936), p. 43; Roy Lubove, *The Professional Altruist: The Emergence of Social Work as a Profession* (Cambridge, Mass., 1965), pp. 2–30.

8. Riis, diary, 27 June 1873, Riis MSS, NYPL; Riis, *Making of an American,* pp. 116–18, 122–28.

9. Riis, *Making of an American,* pp. 129–32; Riis, diary, 16 August 1875, Riis MSS, NYPL.

10. Ware, *Jacob Riis,* pp. 33–34; South Brooklyn *News,* 4 March 1876, Riis MSS, LC.

11. Riis, *Making of an American,* pp. 186–91; Jacob Riis Owre, memorandum, 1958, Riis MSS, LC; Riis, *Theodore Roosevelt,* pp. 25–26.

12. South Brooklyn *News,* n.d., 1877, Riis MSS, LC.

13. Stephan Thernstrom, "Urbanization, Migration, and Social Mobility in Late Nineteenth-Century America," in Barton J. Bernstein (ed.), *Towards a New Past: Dissenting Essays in American History* (New York, 1968), pp. 159–73.

Chapter 3

1. Larzer Ziff, *The American 1890s: Life and Times of a Lost Generation* (New York, 1966), pp. 146–47; Joseph I. C. Clarke, *My Life and Memories* (New York, 1925), pp. 211–12; Edwin Emery, *The Press and America* (Englewood Cliffs, N.J., 1962), pp. 374–411; James Creelman, "Joseph Pulitzer—Master Journalist," *Pearson's,* 21 (March 1909), 246; James F. Muirhead, *America the Land of Contrasts* (New York, 1898), pp. 143–54.

2. Lecture notes, n.d., box 5, Riis MSS, LC.

3. Roger S. Tracy, untitled manuscript, box 4, Riis MSS, LC.

4. New York *World,* 25 June, 8 and 15 July 1883; New York *Morning Journal,* 4 and 15 April 1883. For other articles, see Riis MSS, LC.

5. New York *Mail and Express,* 19 September 1885.

6. Cincinnati *Enquirer,* 30 August 1885; Green Bay, Wisconsin, *Advance,* 14 February and 5 March 1884, Riis MSS, LC.

7. Jacob to Mary Phillips Riis, 11 January 1914; Tracy, untitled manuscript, Riis MSS, LC. Concerning the dominant values of the Progressive Era, see Henry F. May, *The End of American Innocence* (Chicago, 1964); Daniel Aaron, *Men of Good Hope* (New York, 1951).

8. Joseph Lee, *Constructive and Preventive Philanthropy* (New York, 1906), p. 56; Gordon Atkins, *Health, Housing and Poverty in New York City, 1865–1898* (Ann Arbor, Mich., 1947), pp. 167–68;

John A. Garraty, *The New Commonwealth, 1877–1890* (New York, 1968), pp. 192–94.

9. Robert H. Bremner, *From the Depths: The Discovery of Poverty in the United States* (New York, 1967), p. 38; Charles N. Glaab and A. Theodore Brown, *A History of Urban America* (New York, 1967), p. 235.

10. Frank D. Watson, *The Charity Organization Movement in the United States* (New York, 1922), pp. 275–76; Robert H. Bremner, *American Philanthropy* (Chicago, 1960), pp. 98–101; J. S. Lowell to Riis, 7 March 1907, Riis MSS, LC; Edward T. Devine, *When Social Work Was Young* (New York, 1939), pp. 21–23.

11. Josephine S. Lowell to Jacob A. Riis, 27 February 1893, Riis MSS, City College of New York (hereafter CCNY); Jacob A. Riis, "The Special Needs of the Poor in New York," *Forum*, 14 (December 1892), 494; Jacob A. Riis, "Homeless Waifs of the City," *Harper's Young People*, 22 January 1889, Riis MSS, LC.

12. Jacob A. Riis, "A Modern St. George," *Scribner's*, 50 (October 1911), 390–91; Lincoln Steffens, "Jacob A. Riis, Reporter, Reformer, American Citizen," *McClure's*, 21 (August 1903), 420-21; Josephine S. Lowell, "The Economic and Moral Effects of Public Out-Door Relief," National Conference of Charities and Correction, *Proceedings* (1890), p. 82; Helen S. Campbell, Thomas W. Knox, and Thomas Byrnes, *Darkness and Daylight in New York* (Hartford, Conn., 1897), p. 352; Charity Organization Society of New York, Fifth Annual Report (New York, 1887), p. 38.

13. William H. Harbaugh, *The Life and Times of Theodore Roosevelt* (New York, 1963), pp. 36–37; New York *Mercury*, 23 March 1884; New York *Tribune*, 3 and 4 May 1884. The quote is from John Dos Passos, *Nineteen Nineteen* (Boston, Sentry edition, 1963), p. 126.

14. Clifford W. Patton, *The Battle for Municipal Reform: Mobilization and Attack, 1875-1900* (Washington, 1940), pp. 14–15; Edward R. Ellis, *The Epic of New York City* (New York, 1966), pp. 327-28; Seymour J. Mandelbaum, *Boss Tweed's New York* (New York, 1965), pp. 1–6, 282–85.

15. Alexander B. Callow, Jr., *The Tweed Ring* (New York, 1966); George T. McJimsey, *Genteel Partisan: Manton Marble, 1834–1917* (Ames, Iowa, 1971), pp. 134–52.

16. New York *Tribune*, 7 October and 28 December 1884; Henry Neumann, *Spokesmen for Ethical Religion* (Boston, 1951); Riis, *Making of an American*, pp. 246–47.

17. New York *Tribune*, 7 October 1884; Robert A. Woods and Albert J. Kennedy, *The Settlement Horizon* (New York, 1922), p. 238; Lubove, *Progressives and the Slums*, pp. 26–33.

18. Henry F. Pringle, *Theodore Roosevelt: A Biography* (New York, 1931), p. 55; Henry S. Commager (ed.), *Documents of American History*, II (New York, 1949), pp. 116–18; Francesco Cordasco (ed.), *Jacob Riis Revisited* (Garden City, New York, 1968), pp. 339–59, 400–16.

19. The *Standard*, 5 February 1887, and other clippings, box 9, Riis MSS, LC.

20. Owre, memorandum, Riis MSS, LC; C. T. Christensen to New York Life Insurance Company, 5 June 1885, Riis MSS, LC; Ware, *Jacob Riis,* pp. 61–65.

21. New York *Tribune,* 1 June 1886; Woods and Kennedy, *Settlement Horizon,* p. 114; Jacob A. Riis, "The Passing of Cat Alley," *Century,* 57 (December 1898), 167.

22. New York *Sun,* 10 April 1896; *The Silver Cross,* August 1889, and January 1890, box 9, Riis MSS, LC. See also Allen F. Davis, *Spearheads for Reform: The Social Settlements and the Progressive Movement, 1890–1914* (New York, 1967).

Chapter 4

1. Riis, *Making of an American,* pp. 267, 298; New York *Tribune,* 26 January 1888.

2. Riis, *Making of an American,* p. 298; Charles H. Parkhurst, *My Forty Years in New York* (New York, 1923), pp. 106–7; A. F. Schauffler to Riis, 29 February and 3 March 1888, Riis MSS, LC.

3. George N. Thomssen to Riis, 27 April 1888, Riis MSS, LC.

4. New Bedford *Mercury,* 30 May 1888, Riis MSS, LC; New York *Tribune,* 30 December 1888.

5. Jacob A. Riis, "Homeless Waifs of the City," *Harper's Young People,* 22 January 1889; Jacob A. Riis, "The Tenement-House Problem," parts I and II, *Christian Union* (1889), Riis MSS, LC.

6. Charles Scribner's Sons to Riis, 24 May 1889, Riis MSS, LC; Jacob A. Riis, *How the Other Half Lives,* (Cambridge, Mass., edition, 1970), p. 3; Riis, *Making of an American,* pp. 300–3. Drawings were made of his photographs for publication purposes.

7. Jacob A. Riis, "The Poor of New York City," *Catholic World,* February 1891, Riis MSS, LC; Jacob to Mary Riis, 11 January 1914, Riis MSS, LC. *Hard Times,* which described the imaginary factory world of Coketown and dealt with the impact of industrialization on humanity and the environment, was perhaps the most controversial of Dickens's novels. Acclaimed as a masterpiece by some critics, it was dismissed by others as a maudlin fable. Sylvere Monod, *Dickens the Novelist* (Norman, Oklahoma, 1968).

8. Riis to [Mr.] Johsolf, n.d., Riis MSS, LC; Riis, *Making of an American,* pp. 304–6, 420–21; Riis to Agnes W. Bartlett, 20 March 1906, Willard Bartlett MSS, Columbia University, New York (hereafter Columbia).

9. J. O. S. Huntington, "Tenement-House Morality," *Forum,* 3 (July 1887), 516; Lubove, *Progressives and the Slums,* pp. 45–46.

10. Quotes from *How the Other Half Lives* come from the Hill and Wang edition (New York, 1957).

11. The tenement-house problem was not restricted to New York City, as Riis well knew. Arthur Mann, describing the overcrowded, disease-ridden dwellings of Boston during the 1880s, wrote: "The very wretchedness of the area attracted gamblers, pimps, prostitutes, sailors

out on a spree, and human wrecks of one kind or another." Mann, *Yankee Reformers in the Urban Age* (Cambridge, Mass., 1954), p. 4.

12. Lubove, *Progressives and the Slums*, pp. 2, 4; Robert W. DeForest and Lawrence Veiller (eds.), *The Tenement House Problem*, I (New York, 1903), p. 71; Riis, *How the Other Half Lives*, pp. 6–8.

13. Riis, *How the Other Half Lives*, pp. 39–41; Jacob A. Riis, "Feast Days in Little Italy," *Century*, 57 (August 1899), 494. See also Oscar Handlin, *The Uprooted* (Boston, 1951); Rudolph J. Vecoli, "*Contadini* in Chicago: A Critique of *The Uprooted*," *Journal of American History*, 51 (December 1964), 404–17.

14. New York *Mail and Express*, 19 September 1885.

15. James Russell Lowell to Riis, 21 November 1890, Riis MSS, LC. He said that he "felt as Dante must when he looked over the edge of the abyss at the bottom of which Gorgon lay in ambush."

16. Bremner, *From the Depths*, p. 69; Brooklyn *Times*, 15 December 1890; *True Nationalist*, 29 November 1890, Riis MSS, LC.

17. Harry Barnard, *Eagle Forgotten: The Life of John Peter Altgeld* (New York, 1938), pp. 132, 144; "How the Other Half Lives," *Christian Union*, 27 November 1890; Brooklyn *Eagle*, 21 November 1890; "How the Other Half Lives," *Independent*, 1 January 1891; "How the Other Half Lives," *Critic*, 17 (27 December 1890), 332. Most of these reviews are in box 10, Riis MSS, LC.

18. John Higham, *Strangers in the Land: Patterns of American Nativism, 1860–1925* (New York, Atheneum ed., 1968), p. 40; Henry Cabot Lodge, "The Restriction of Immigration," *North American Review*, 152 (January 1891), 34; Charles N. Glaab, *The American City: A Documentary History* (Homewood, Illinois, 1963), p. 279. John A. Garraty has noted that Riis labeled ethnic groups in a derogatory manner, but Garraty himself added this egregious comment on immigrants: "Either in ignorance or in panic—like placid stockyard sheep trailing the Judas goat or like herring huddling to escape the savage barracuda— they clotted together, finding a measure of security, but surrendering the best hope of swiftly improving their lot." Garraty, *New Commonwealth*, pp. 202–3, 205.

19. Robert Muccigrosso, "The City Reform Club: A Study in Late Nineteenth-Century Reform," *New York History*, 109 (July 1968), 248; Louis H. Pink, "Reminiscences," Columbia Oral History Project, New York (hereafter COHP); Brooks, *Confident Years*, pp. 73–74; Truman F. Keefer, *Ernest Poole* (New York, 1966), p. 11, 25; Louise C. Wade, *Graham Taylor: Pioneer for Social Justice, 1851–1938* (Chicago, 1964), p. 96; Ziff, *American 1890s*, p. 155.

20. James Ford, *Slums and Housing, with Special Reference to New York City* (Cambridge, Mass., 1936), p. 197; Glaab and Brown, *History of Urban America*, p. 241; Warner (ed.), *How the Other Half Lives*, p. xix. While the impact of *How the Other Half Lives* is clear, it is more difficult to determine its immediate popularity in relation to other books. Until the *Bookman* began compiling best seller lists five years later, such information was obscure. See Alice Payne Hackett, *70 Years of Best Sellers, 1895–1965* (New York, 1967).

Chapter 5

1. Riis, *The Making of an American*, p.304; Ware, *Jacob Riis*, pp. 78–81.

2. Bernard A. Weisberger, *The American Newspaperman* (Chicago, 1961), pp. 127–28; Frank M. O'Brien, *The Story of the Sun* (New York, 1918), pp. 241, 360, 398; Emery, *The Press and America*, pp. 506–7.

3. Lincoln Steffens, *The Autobiography of Lincoln Steffens*, I (New York, 1931), pp. 198, 203–5; Ware, *Jacob Riis*, p. 82.

4. Harold U. Faulkner, *Politics, Reform and Expansion: 1890–1900* (New York, 1963), p. 31; Riis, *Making of an American*, pp. 228–30; Husband, *Americans by Adoption*, pp. 148–49.

5. Herbert Shapiro, "Lincoln Steffens: The Muckraker Revisited," *American Journal of Economics and Sociology*, 31 (October 1972), 427–38.

6. Boston *Globe*, 8 May 1891; "General Conference of Charities" file, Riis MSS, CCNY; Washington *Post*, 10 November 1891.

7. Woody Klein, *Let In the Sun* (New York, 1964), p. 65; Cordasco (ed.), *Jacob Riis Revisited*, pp. 284–85.

8. Ware, *Jacob Riis*, pp. 89–90; Riis, scrapbook, pp. 63–64, Riis MSS, LC.

9. Riis, scrapbook, pp. 65–66, Riis MSS, LC; Eric Goldman, *Rendezvous with Destiny* (New York, 1952), pp. 86–87, 183–84; Christopher Lasch (ed.), *The Social Thought of Jane Addams* (Indianapolis, 1965), pp. 28–61; Riis to Peabody, 1 April and 12 May 1893, Peabody MSS, Harvard.

10. Riis, *Making of an American*, pp. 391–401; New York *Evening Sun*, 30 June 1893; Ware, *Jacob Riis*, pp. 93–97.

11. New York *Evening Sun*, 15 September 1893; Ware, *Jacob Riis*, pp. 96, 101; Riis, *Making of an American*, pp. 427–28; Riis to Ida A. McAfee, 21 January 1894, Riis MSS, LC.

12. Danstrup, *History of Denmark*, pp. 128–35; Peter Manniche, *Denmark: A Social Laboratory* (London, 1939), pp. 157–58.

13. Josiah Kinsey to Riis, 24 June 1891 and Z. D. Smith to Riis, 15 June 1891, Riis MSS, CCNY; New York *Post*, 25 April 1891; New York *Sun*, 20 June 1891; New York *Tribune*, 31 January 1892; Riis, *Making of an American*, pp. 232, 254.

14. New York *Evening Sun*, 16 and 17 February 1892; Cordasco (ed.), *Jacob Riis Revisited*, p. 207.

15. Josephine Shaw Lowell to Riis, 27 February 1893, Riis MSS, CCNY; Atkins, *Health, Housing, and Poverty in New York City*, pp. 141–42.

16. William H. Tolman, "Half a Century of Improved Housing Effort," *Yale Review*, 5 (February 1897) pp. 394–95; Jacob A. Riis, "Police Lodging Houses: Are They Hotbeds for Typhus Fever?" *Christian Union*, 14 January 1893, Riis MSS, LC; Lowell to Riis, 27 February 1893, Riis MSS, CCNY.

17. New York *Tribune*, 2 March 1893; J. S. Lowell to Riis, 16

December 1893, Riis MSS, CCNY; Jacob A. Riis, "New York's Way-farers' Lodge," *Outlook,* 98 (2 December 1893), 994–99.

18. Steffens, "Jacob A. Riis," 420–21.

19. Jacob A. Riis, "An Unnecessary Story," *Century,* 62 (May 1901), 149; Jacob A. Riis, "The Heart of New York," *Independent,* 76 (4 December 1913), 449.

20. Ware, *Jacob Riis,* p. 189; Dexter Marshall, letter to the editor, Port Jervis *Evening Gazette,* 23 January 1900, Riis MSS, LC.

21. Jacob A. Riis, "The Last of the Mulberry Street Barons," *Century,* 58 (May 1899), 119–21.

22. See also Jacob A. Riis, "Paolo's Awakening," *Atlantic,* 76 (November 1896), 698–707; Jacob A. Riis, "Feast Days in Little Italy," *Century,* 57 (August 1899), 494.

23. Riis to R. W. Gilder, 19 June 1898, Riis MSS, LC; Riis to Bliss Perry, 14 July 1901, Bliss Perry MSS, Harvard U. Library, Cambridge, Mass.

Chapter 6

1. David P. Thelen, "Social Tensions and the Origins of Progressivism," *Journal of American History,* 56 (September 1969), 336–37; Howard L. Hurwitz, *Theodore Roosevelt and Labor in New York State, 1880–1900* (New York, 1943), pp. 12–13.

2. Samuel Rezneck, "Unemployment, Unrest and Relief in the United States during the Depression of 1893–97," *Journal of Political Economy,* 61 (August 1953), 327; New York Association for Improving the Condition of the Poor, Annual Report, 1893–94 (New York, 1894), p. 52.

3. Jacob A. Riis, "Relief of the Unemployed: Charity or Work," *Current Literature,* Riis MSS, LC; New York *Evening Sun,* 21 December 1893; New York AICP Bulletin, 20 February 1895, Riis MSS, CCNY.

4. E. Scott to Riis, 24 October 1895, Riis MSS, CCNY; Jacob A. Riis, "Children of the Tenements," lecture notes, Riis MSS, LC.

5. Schneider and Deutsch, *Public Welfare,* pp. 50–54; Atkins, *Health, Housing, and Poverty in New York City,* pp. 139–41; Jacob A. Riis, "John Bancroft Devins," *Survey,* 27 (21 October 1911), 1062; Charles O. Kellogg to Riis, 10 and 24 August 1894, Riis MSS, CCNY.

6. Frances G. Davenport to Riis, 16 October 1894, Riis MSS, LC; Jacob A. Riis, "One Way Out," *Century,* 51 (December 1895), 304; Steffens, "Jacob A. Riis," 420–21.

7. Jane Addams, "The Subtle Problems of Charity," *Atlantic Monthly,* 83 (February 1899), 163–78; Roy Lubove, *The Urban Community: Housing and Planning in the Progressive Era* (Englewood Cliffs, N.J., 1967), pp. 10–13; Watson, *Charity Organization Movement,* p. 332. In *Self-Reliance and Social Security, 1870–1917* (Port Washington, N.Y., 1971), pp. 55–57, Hace Sorel Tishler argued that, important though the depression was to social thought, ideas of rugged

individualism were being challenged well before the 1890s; and, furthermore, "the depression by no means swept away considerations of
personal fault. ..."

8. Jacob A. Riis, "Report to the Council of Confederated Good
Government Clubs," 1897, Riis MSS, LC; James B. Reynolds to Riis,
27 February 1897, Riis MSS, CCNY; *New York Times,* 16 December
1896.

9. Jacob A. Riis, "The Tenement the Real Problem of Civilization," *Forum,* 19 (March 1895), 94; *New York Times,* 18 April 1895.

10. New York *Mail and Express,* 20 June 1895; lecture notes,
box 3, Riis MSS, LC; Lubove, *Progressives and the Slums,* pp. 245–48;
Jacob A. Riis, "Speech," *Charities,* 7 (1901), Riis MSS, LC. For similar
views on neighborhood reconstruction see John Dewey, "The School
as a Social Center," *National Education Association Journal of Proceedings* (1902), 381; James K. Pauling, "Public Schools as a Center
of Community Life," *Educational Review,* 15 (February 1898), 147–
54.

11. H. W. Mabie to Riis, 7 December 1894, Riis MSS, LC; New
York *Sun,* 10 April 1896; Mary K. Simkhovitch, *Neighborhood: My
Story of Greenwich House* (New York, 1938), pp. 88–89; Walter
Rauschenbusch to Riis, 27 January 1896, Riis MSS, NYPL; Clarence
E. Rainwater, *The Play Movement in the United States* (Chicago,
1922), pp. 71–74.

12. E. R. L. Gould, *The Housing of the Working People* (Washington, 1895), pp. 27–34; Rezneck, "Unemployment, Unrest and Relief in the United States during the Depression of 1893–97," 330.

13. Jacob A. Riis, "The Making of Thieves in New York," *Century,* 49 (November 1894), 115–16; Theodore Roosevelt to Osborne
Hawes, 5 May 1892, in Elting E. Morison (ed.), *The Letters of
Theodore Roosevelt,* I (Cambridge, Mass., 1951), p. 278; Riis, *Battle
with the Slum,* p. 230.

14. *Evangelist,* 15 February 1894, Riis MSS, LC; Ware, *Jacob
Riis,* p. 102.

15. Charles H. Parkhurst, *Our Fight with Tammany* (New
York, 1895); Steffens, *Autobiography,* p. 215. Parkhurst's Society for
the Prevention of Crime obtained much of its information concerning
corruption and vice from the City Reform Club (founded by Theodore
Roosevelt in 1882), which had been studying municipal malfeasance for
several years prior to 1892. Muccigrosso, "City Reform Club," 239–46.

16. "Lexow Committee File," Chamber of Commerce, Archives
of the New York State Chamber of Commerce, New York City;
Parkhurst, *My Forty Years in New York,* p. 141; Ellis, *Epic of New
York City,* pp. 424–29.

17. Jacob A. Riis, "The Social Evil: Its Remedy," Wilson Press
Syndicate Service, 31 December 1893, Riis MSS, LC.

18. Thomas Beer, *The Mauve Decade* (New York, 1926), pp.
140–41; Muirhead, *Land of Contrasts,* p. 193; Alexander Irvine, *From
the Bottom Up* (New York, 1910), pp. 144–55; James E. McGee,
"'Teddy' and the New York Police," *Central,* 12 (12 November
1919), 63.

19. Steffens, "Jacob A. Riis," 421; New York *Herald*, 16 September 1894; Jacob A. Riis, "Will It Last?", *Outlook*, 64 (21 April 1900), 911.

20. Roy Lubove, "Lawrence Veiller and the New York State Tenement House Commission of 1900," *Mississippi Valley Historical Review*, 47 (March 1961), 659; Johnson, *Remembered Yesterdays*, p. 88; Beer, *Mauve Decade*, p. 216.

21. Riis to Gilder, 18 May 1894, Gilder to Riis, 20 October 1894, Richard W. Gilder MSS, NYPL; Ware, *Jacob Riis*, pp. 103–5; Sol Cohen, *Progressives and Urban School Reform: The Public Education Association of New York City, 1895–1954* (New York, 1964), p. 11.

22. Lubove, *Progressives and the Slums*, pp. 90–93; Lawrence Veiller, "Reminiscences," COHP, pp. 44–45; Jacob A. Riis, "The Tenement-House Problem," *Harper's Weekly*, 39 (12 January 1895), 42–43.

23. Lubove, *Progressives and the Slums*, pp. 100–1; Riis, *Battle with the Slum*, pp. 136–38.

24. John S. Kennedy to Charles S. Smith, 8 October 1894, Lexow file, New York State Chamber of Commerce Archives, New York; Lorin W. Peterson, *The Day of the Mugwump* (New York, 1961), pp. 49–51; Patton, *Battle for Municipal Reform*, p. 39.

25. Davis, *Spearheads for Reform*, pp. 180–81; Parkhurst, *Our Fight With Tammany*, p. 284.

26. Jack M. Holl, *Juvenile Reform in the Progressive Era: William R. George and the Junior Republic Movement* (Ithaca, N.Y., 1971), pp. 2–103; Douglas A. Bakken, "William R. George and George Junior Republic Papers," Collection of Regional History and University Archives, Cornell University, Ithaca, N.Y. (hereafter Cornell); Joseph M. Hawes, *Children in Urban Society: Juvenile Delinquency in Nineteenth-Century America* (New York, 1971), p. 153.

27. Holl, *Juvenile Reform*, pp. 19, 106–12; Hawes, *Juvenile Delinquency*, pp. 155–57; Lyman Abbott, "A Republic in a Republic," *Outlook*, 138 (15 February 1908), 351–54.

28. Washington Gladden, "The Junior Republic at Freeville," *Outlook*, 104 (31 October 1896), 780–82; Mary Gay Humphreys, "The Smallest Republic in the World," *McClure's*, 9 (July 1897), 735–46; Jacob A. Riis, "Introduction," typescript, George Junior Republic MSS, Cornell.

29. Riis, "Introduction," George MSS, Cornell.

30. Holl, *Juvenile Reform*, pp. 110–28; Thomas M. Osborne to Riis, 7 December 1897, Riis MSS, CCNY.

31. Board of Trustees of the George Junior Republic Association to the State Board of Charities, 17 December 1897, Riis MSS, CCNY; notebook, January 1900, Riis MSS, LC.

32. Riis to Reinsholm, 1 January 1895; Riis, account book, 1895, Riis MSS, LC.

33. Riis to Reinsholm, 10 July 1895, Riis MSS, LC; Ware, *Jacob Riis*, pp. 136–37.

34. Robert H. Wiebe, *The Search for Order: 1877–1920* (New

York, 1967), p. 88; Riis to Reinsholm, 1 January 1895, Riis MSS, LC; Jacob A. Riis, "A Christmas Reminder," *Forum*, 16 (January 1894), 633.

35. *New York Times*, 29 March 1895; Riis to Albert Shaw, 21 January 1896, Albert Shaw MSS, NYPL.

Chapter 7

1. Richard Hofstadter, *The American Political Tradition* (New York, 1948), p. 236.

2. Riis, *Theodore Roosevelt*, p. 131; Roosevelt to Riis, 4 December 1894, and 3 January 1895, Theodore Roosevelt MSS, LC. All correspondence between Riis and Roosevelt is in this collection unless stated otherwise.

3. Steffens, *Autobiography*, p. 257; Roosevelt to Charles H. Parkhurst, 23 April 1895, Roosevelt MSS, LC.

4. Steffens, *Autobiography*, pp. 258–59; Ellis, *Epic of New York City*, pp. 434–36; Henry H. Stein, "Theodore Roosevelt and the Press: Lincoln Steffens," *Mid-America*, 54 (April 1972), 95.

5. Allen F. Davis, " 'Theodore Roosevelt-Social Worker', A Note," *Mid-America*, 48 (January 1966), 58–62; Harbaugh, *Theodore Roosevelt*, p. 86.

6. Pringle, *Theodore Roosevelt*, p. 98; Riis, *Making of an American*, pp. 329–32.

7. New York *Evening Journal*, 27 February 1901; New York *Mail and Express*, 20 June 1895; Hurwitz, *Roosevelt and Labor*, pp. 149–50.

8. Lord Charnwood, *Theodore Roosevelt* (London, 1923), pp. 50–55; Harbaugh, *Theodore Roosevelt*, pp. 87–88; James F. Richardson, *The New York Police: Colonial Times to 1901* (New York, 1970), pp. 252–53. In 1902 Riis called for the abolition of the Sunday drinking laws because they were unenforceable. He said: "I see nothing wrong in a man's taking a glass of beer if he wants it. It is the abuse of the saloon, not the saloon itself, that is an evil." Minneapolis *Journal*, January 1902, Riis MSS, CCNY.

9. New York *Sun*, 24 July 1896.

10. Tracy, memorandum, and Riis, account book, 1895, Riis MSS, LC.

11. New York *World*, 1 December 1895; Riis, *Battle with the Slum*, pp. 43–44.

12. New York *Evening Sun*, 20 April 1895; Parkhurst to Riis, 18 May 1895, Riis MSS, LC; New York *Tribune*, 9 June 1895.

13. Jacob A. Riis, "Parks for the Poor," *Christian Union* (8 August 1891); *The Evangelist* (20 December 1894), Riis MSS, LC; Allan Nevins, *Abram S. Hewitt, with Some Account of Peter Cooper* (New York, 1935), pp. 504–5; George Clausen to William L. Strong, 1 January 1895, Early Mayors' Papers, Municipal Archives and Record Center, New York (hereafter New York Archives); New York *Evening*

Sun, 16 January 1896; John Devins to Riis, 24 October 1901, Riis MSS, LC.

14. Emmons Clark to Riis, 28 July 1896, Riis MSS, CCNY; Riis to Strong, 5 April 1897, Early Mayors' Papers, New York Archives; Riis, *Making of an American*, pp. 326, 363.

15. Reprinted in Riis, *Children of the Tenements*, p. 140. See also Riis, *Battle with the Slum*, pp. 16, 39–40.

16. Jacob A. Riis, "The Clearing of Mulberry Bend," *American Review of Reviews*, 12 (August 1895), 172–78; "Mulberry Bend Park," Department of Parks, 1888–97, Early Mayors' Papers, New York Archives; Riis, *Battle with the Slum*, pp. 275–76.

17. New York *Sun*, 16 June 1897; Riis, *Making of an American*, pp. 283–84.

18. Schoener (ed.), *Lower East Side*, p. 165; Hurwitz, *Roosevelt and Labor*, pp. 146, 163–64.

19. New York *Evening Sun*, 28 January 1897; Hurwitz, *Roosevelt and Labor*, pp. 166, 198.

20. Riis, *Making of an American*, pp. 257–59; Devine, *When Social Work Was Young*, pp. 52–53; Riis, *Battle with the Slum*, p. 50.

21. Homer Folks, "Reminiscences," COHP, pp. 16–17; Riis, *Battle with the Slum*, pp. 154–65, 170–71; Ware, *Jacob Riis*, p. 132.

22. John Morton Blum, *The Republican Roosevelt* (New York, 1967), p. 15; Roosevelt to Cecil Spring Rice, 5 August 1895, Roosevelt MSS, LC; Hurwitz, *Roosevelt and Labor*, pp. 147–48.

23. Pringle, *Theodore Roosevelt*, p. 105; Riis, *Making of an American*, pp. 331–38; Gregory Weinstein, *The Ardent Eighties and After: Reminiscences of a Busy Life* (New York, 1947), pp. 138–39.

24. Harbaugh, *Theodore Roosevelt*, p. 92; Lothrop Stoddard, *Master of Manhattan: The Life of Richard Croker* (New York, 1931), p. 154; Richardson, *New York Police*, pp. 266–67.

25. Riis to Gilder, 29 July 1896, Richard W. Gilder MSS, NYPL; Richard Skolnik, "Civic Group Progressivism in New York City," *New York History*, 51 (July 1970), 424; Ware, *Jacob Riis*, pp. 142–44.

26. Marshall B. Clark to Riis, 18 July 1896; Henry M. Carson to Riis, 20 July 1896, Riis MSS, NYPL.

27. James R. Sheffield to Riis, 13 October 1896; Charles P. Skinner to Riis, 14 August 1896, Riis MSS, CCNY; New York *Evening Post*, 3 August 1896; Riis, "Report to Good Government Clubs," Riis MSS, LC.

28. Gilder to Riis, 5 August 1896; Riis to Gilder, 9 August 1896, Gilder MSS, NYPL; Joseph Lee, *Constructive and Preventive Philanthropy* (New York, 1902), pp. 59–60; Riis, "Report to Good Government Clubs," Riis MSS, LC; Riis, *Battle with the Slum*, p. 286.

29. Cohen, *Progressives and Urban School Reform*, pp. 8–49; Jacob A. Riis, *A Ten Years' War* (New York, 1902), pp. 208, 228.

30. New York *Tribune*, 5 April 1897.

31. Glaab (ed.), *American City*, p. 382, in William L. Riordan, *Plunkitt of Tammany Hall* (New York, 1905).

32. Riis to Gilder, 3 December 1896, Gilder MSS, NYPL; Patton, *Battle for Municipal Reform*, p. 63.

33. Riis to Gilder, 12 January 1897, Century Collection, NYPL; Riis to Gilder, 30 July 1897, Riis MSS, LC.

34. Dorothy Rose Blumberg, *Florence Kelley: The Making of a Social Pioneer* (New York, 1966), pp. 59–60; New York *World*, 18 December 1887; William R. Stewart to Strong, 7 June 1897, and other letters, Early Mayors' Papers, New York Archives; Abram S. Hewitt to Riis, 3 June 1897, Riis MSS, LC.

35. New York *Evening Sun*, 10 June 1897; Riis to Strong, 18 July 1897, Early Mayors' Papers, New York Archives.

36. New York *Sun*, 9 November 1897; Report of the Committee on Small Parks, City of New York, 1897 (New York, 1897).

37. Riis to Nathan Strauss [sic], 24 November 1897; Straus to Riis, 29 November 1897, Riis MSS, LC.

38. New York *Evening Sun*, 24 January 1898; Riis, *Battle with the Slum*, p. 309; Petition to the Board of Commissioners of Public Parks, 29 November 1897, Riis MSS, CCNY. On another occasion Riis bristled at Van Wyck's characterization of him as impertinent. Riis to Robert A. Van Wyck, 28 April 1899, Robert A. Van Wyck MSS, New York Archives.

39. Rainwater, *Play Movement in the United States*, pp. 201–2; Cohen, *Progressives and Urban School Reform*, p. 51.

40. Mary J. Eastman to Riis, 14 November 1897, Riis MSS, CCNY; Roosevelt to Riis, 4 September, 25 October and 10 November 1897, Roosevelt MSS, LC.

Chapter 8

1. Ware, *Jacob Riis*, pp. 170–72; Roosevelt to Riis, 19 April and 5 May 1898, Roosevelt MSS, LC.

2. Elisabeth to Jacob Riis, 28 February 1898; Riis, *Making of an American*, pp. 377–79; William E. Leuchtenburg, "Progressivism and Imperialism: The Progressive Movement and American Foreign Policy, 1898–1916," in R. Jackson Wilson (ed.), *Reform, Crisis, and Confusion, 1900–1929* (New York, 1970), p. 107.

3. Toronto *Mail and Express*, 19 September 1898, Riis MSS, LC; Riis, *Theodore Roosevelt*, pp. 88–89.

4. G. Wallace Chessman, *Governor Theodore Roosevelt* (Cambridge, Mass., 1965), p. 26; Harbaugh, *Theodore Roosevelt*, p. 111; Walter I. Trattner, "Theodore Roosevelt, Social Workers, and the Election of 1912: A Note," *Mid-America*, 50 (January 1968), 69.

5. Riis, scrapbook, p. 114, Riis MSS, LC; Harbaugh, *Theodore Roosevelt*, p. 113; New York *Sun*, 1 November 1898; Riis, *Making of an American*, pp. 382–83.

6. Harold F. Gosnell, *Boss Platt and His New York Machine* (Chicago, 1924), p. 124.

7. Riis to Silas McBee, 12 January 1899, Silas McBee MSS, Southern Historical Collection, University of North Carolina Library, Chapel Hill, N.C. (hereafter North Carolina).

8. Robert L. Duffus, *Lillian Wald: Neighbor and Crusader* (New York, 1938), p. 61; Davis, *Spearheads for Reform*, pp. 111–12; Riis to Jane Robbins n.d., Riis MSS, LC.

9. Jacob A. Riis, "The People's Institute of New York," *Century*, 79 (April 1910), 851–61; F. R. Conant to Anna Garlin Spencer, 20 January 1908, Anna Garlin Spencer MSS, Swarthmore Peace Collection, Swarthmore, Pa.

10. Chessman, *Governor Roosevelt*, p. 201; *American Federationist*, September 1902, Riis MSS, LC.

11. Adna F. Weber, *Labor Legislation in New York* (Albany, 1904), pp. 10–11, 17; Chessman, *Governor Roosevelt*, pp. 202–3.

12. Blumberg, *Florence Kelley*, pp. 172–74. A copy of the Roosevelt letter is in the Lillian D. Wald MSS, Columbia University, New York, N.Y.

13. Ben Schweitzer and Louis Dintenfor to Roosevelt, 24 February 1899, Edwin R. A. Seligman MSS, Columbia; Hurwitz, *Roosevelt and Labor*, p. 197; Jacob A. Riis, "Findings in the Matter of Complaint of the Brotherhood of Tailors of New York City against Daniel O'Leary, State Factory Inspector," 21 March 1899, in Seligman MSS, Columbia; on this whole matter see Jeremy P. Felt, *Hostages of Fortune: Child Labor Reform in New York State* (Syracuse, N.Y., 1965), pp. 30–95.

14. Riis, pamphlet, Seligman MSS, Columbia; New York *Sun*, 22 March 1899.

15. Hurwitz, *Roosevelt and Labor*, pp. 209–14; New York *Sun*, 1 June 1899; Henry White to Riis, 11 January 1900, Riis MSS, CCNY.

16. New York *World*, 1 October 1898; Hurwitz, *Roosevelt and Labor*, pp. 206-7.

17. New York *World*, 21 May 1899; Roosevelt to Riis, 23 October 1899, 18 December 1899, and 21 March 1900, Roosevelt MSS, LC.

18. Roosevelt to John D. Long, 27 April 1899; Roosevelt to Riis, 28 October 1899, Roosevelt MSS, LC.

19. Edward Devine to Riis, 3 August 1899, and 14 June 1900, Riis MSS, CCNY.

20. DeForest and Veiller (eds.), *Tenement House Problem*, I, pp. 110–11; Chessman, *Governor Roosevelt*, pp. 231–33; Lubove, "Veiller and the New York State Tenement House Commission," 668.

21. Riis to Gilder, March n.d., 1899, Riis MSS, LC; Chessman, *Governor Roosevelt*, pp. 231-33.

22. Veiller, "Reminiscences," COHP, pp. 12, 19; Riis, *Battle with the Slum*, p. 143; "A Ten Years' War," *Literary Digest*, 20 (14 April 1900), 449–50; *New York Times*, 12 February 1900.

23. George E. Mowry, *The Era of Theodore Roosevelt and the Birth of Modern America, 1900–1912* (New York, 1958), p. 66;

Jacob A. Riis, "Tammany, the People's Enemy," *Outlook,* 69 (26 October 1901), 487; Lubove, "Veiller and the New York State Tenement House Commission," 670–74; Veiller, "Reminiscences," COHP, pp. 25–26.

24. Veiller to Riis, 22 May 1900, Riis MSS, CCNY.

25. Lubove, *Professional Altruist,* p. 159; Lubove, "Veiller and the New York State Tenement House Commission," 663–64; Ware, *Jacob Riis,* p. 174; Riis, *Battle with the Slum,* p. 431.

26. Ware, *Jacob Riis,* p. 200.

27. Lubove, *Progressives and the Slums,* p. 181; Riis to Gilder, 10 October 1901 and 19 December 1903, Gilder MSS, NYPL.

28. Bremner, *From the Depths,* pp. 209–10; Robert DeForest to the Board of Estimate and Apportionment, 1 September 1903, Low MSS, New York Archives.

29. Riis to McAfee, 15 January 1900; Riis to Reinsholm, 28 May 1900; Riis to Robbins, 23 June 1900, Riis MSS, LC.

30. Riis, *Theodore Roosevelt,* p. 433; Riis, *Children of the Tenements,* pp. 341–46; Riis to Peabody, 15 October 1900, Peabody MSS, Harvard.

31. Thomas A. Fulton to Everett P. Wheeler, 22 May 1901, and "Platform of the Citizens Union," Everett P. Wheeler MSS, NYPL; Riis, *Battle with the Slum,* p. 63.

32. Riis, *Making of an American,* pp. 232–33; New York *Sun,* 15 January 1897; Riis, scrapbook, p. 133, Riis MSS, LC.

33. Riis, *Theodore Roosevelt,* pp. 60, 93, 105–6; Walter T.K. Nugent, *Modern America* (Boston, 1973), pp. 156–57.

Chapter 9

1. Riis to Seth Low, 23 October 1906, Seth Low MSS, Columbia University, New York; Mrs. Theodore Roosevelt to "Willie," November n.d., 1899, Riis MSS, LC.

2. Riis to Roosevelt, 7 October 1902, Roosevelt MSS, LC; Louis Filler, *Crusaders for American Liberalism* (Yellow Springs, Ohio, 1961), p. 45.

3. Riis to Powell, 23 May 1903, Riis MSS, NYPL.

4. Riis to Gilder, 10 October 1901, Riis MSS, LC; Riis to Perry, 14 July 1901, Bliss Perry MSS, Harvard; Ware, *Jacob Riis,* p. 228; Riis to Robbins, February n.d., 1901, Riis MSS, LC; Riis to Peabody, 29 May 1902, Peabody MSS, Harvard.

5. Davenport *Times,* 13 December 1900, Riis MSS, LC.

6. Riis to Lillian D. Wald, 21 February 1901, Lillian D. Wald MSS, Columbia University, New York; Riis to Gifford Pinchot, 26 February 1911, Gifford Pinchot MSS, LC; Riis to Jane Addams, 9 March 1901, Jane Addams MSS, Swarthmore Peace Collection, Swarthmore, Pa.; Riis to Reinsholm, 21 February 1901, Riis MSS, LC.

7. Regarding the Cross of Dannebrog, on 15 October 1900 Riis wrote Endicott Peabody that he was pleased to be "Sir Jacob" and that the next time he spoke at Groton "you ought to receive me with a brass band." Peabody MSS, Harvard.

8. See also Jacob A. Riis, "Our Beautiful Summer," *Outlook,* 80 (6 May 1905), 52; Jacob A. Riis, "A Kindly Journey," *Outlook,* 96 (31 December 1910), 1020.

9. Heinrich Micholski to Riis, 30 May 1907, Riis MSS, NYPL; Joseph B. Gilder, "The Making of Jacob A. Riis," *Critic,* 46 (January 1902), 63–64; Hutchins Hapgood, "Jacob A. Riis's *The Making of an American,*" *Bookman,* 14 (January 1902), 498; Felix Adler, "Riis," biographical file, Felix Adler MSS, Ethical Culture Society Building, New York City, N.Y.; Riis to Perry, 14 July 1901, Perry MSS, Harvard.

10. Riis to Powell, 10 May and 3 December 1973, Riis MSS, NYPL.

11. Riis to Peabody, 29 May 1902, Peabody MSS, Harvard.

12. Ware, *Jacob Riis,* p. 224; New York *Sun,* 18 October 1903; "Formal Opening of William H. Seward Park," pamphlet, 17 October 1903, Riis MSS, NYPL.

13. Jacob A. Riis, "The Case of the House of Refuge," *Charities,* 11 (4 July 1903), 28–29; Jacob A. Riis, "The Island Playgrounds of the Future," *Charities,* 11 (5 September 1903), 205–7.

14. For similar views by historians, see Irwin Yellowitz, *Labor and the Progressive Movement in New York State, 1897–1916* (Ithaca, 1965), pp. 184–85; Steven C. Swett, "The Test of a Reformer: A Study of Seth Low, New York City Mayor 1902–1903," *New York Historical Society Quarterly,* 44 (January 1960), 5–41.

15. New York *World,* 11 and 18 October 1903.

16. Elisabeth Riis to Low, 4 November 1903, Seth Low MSS, Columbia.

17. Riis, *Theodore Roosevelt,* pp. 75–76; Riis to Roosevelt, 14 November 1902, Roosevelt MSS, LC; Roger Tracy, memorandum, Riis MSS, LC; Riis to R. W. Gilder, 19 August 1901, Gilder MSS, NYPL.

18. Riis to Roosevelt, 7 and 11 October 1902, Roosevelt MSS, LC.

19. *Ibid.;* Riis to Powell, 13 August 1903, Riis MSS, NYPL.

20. Riis to Robbins, n. d., Riis MSS, LC; Riis, *Battle with the Slum,* pp. 204–7, 217; Bremner, *From the Depths,* p. 10.

21. Jacob A. Riis, "The Golden Rule in Poverty Row," *Christian Herald* (27 September 1905), 797, Riis MSS, LC; Jacob A. Riis, "The Gateway of All Nations," 843. See also Jacob A. Riis, "The Man Who Is an Immigrant," *Survey,* 25 (18 February 1911), 868-69; Maldwyn A Jones, *American Immigration* (Chicago, 1960), pp. 250–60.

22. Terence V. Powderly, *The Path I Trod* (New York, 1940), pp. 301–2; Riis to Roosevelt, 17 March 1902; Roosevelt to Riis, 18 March 1902, Roosevelt MSS, LC; *New York Times,* 16 March and 18 April 1902.

23. Constance M. Green, *Washington: Capital City, 1879–1950* (Princeton, N.J., 1963), pp. 152–53; "Paragraphs in Philanthropy: Housing Reform in Washington," *Charities,* 12 (9 January 1904), 55–56; New York *Tribune,* 11 December 1903; Jacob A. Riis, "Playgrounds in Washington and Elsewhere," *Survey,* 20 (18 April 1908), 102–3.

24. Riis to Roosevelt, 10 October 1904; Roosevelt to Riis, 22 October 1904, Roosevelt MSS, LC; Charles E. Larsen, *The Good Fight: The Life and Times of Ben B. Lindsey* (Chicago, 1972), pp. 91–92.

25. Green, *Washington,* pp. 151–56; Lubove, *Urban Community,* pp. 15–16; Riis, "Playgrounds in Washington and Elsewhere," 102–3.

26. Riis to Wald, 4 June 1906, Wald MSS, Columbia; Riis, *Theodore Roosevelt,* pp. 384–85.

27. John Riis, *Ranger Trails* (Richmond, Va., 1937), pp. 18–19; Riis, *Theodore Roosevelt,* pp. 270–71;Riis to Roosevelt, 23 March 1906, Roosevelt MSS, LC; Riis to Reinsholm, 29 March 1905, Riis MSS, LC.

28. Riis to Peabody, 15 April 1902, Peabody MSS, Harvard; Charles C. Tansill, *The Purchase of the Danish West Indies* (Baltimore, 1932), pp. 350–51, 361.

29. Riis to [no name], 23 September 1903, Riis MSS, LC.

30. Riis to William Loeb, 11 February 1908, Roosevelt MSS, LC; Riis to Loeb, 6 February 1909, and Louis Hostetter to the Assistant Secretary of State, 3 March 1909, State Department File, 1906–1910, no. 18114, National Archives, Washington, D.C.

31. Jacob to John Riis, 15 August 1903, Riis MSS, LC; Riis, *Theodore Roosevelt,* pp. 356–57; Riis to Roosevelt, 1 December 1901, 10 March 1902, and 15 January 1903, Roosevelt MSS, LC.

32. See Theodore and Edith Roosevelt to Mrs. Riis, 20 December 1902, Roosevelt MSS, LC.

33. Riis, *Theodore Roosevelt,* p. 285.

34. McBee to Riis, 30 December 1903, Riis MSS, NYPL; Riis, *Theodore Roosevelt,* pp. 99, 102.

35. Riis to McBee, 30 December 1903, Riis MSS, NYPL; Riis to Roosevelt, 11 January 1904; Roosevelt to Riis, 17 February 1904, Roosevelt MSS, LC.

36. Jacob to Elisabeth Riis, 17 May 1904, Riis MSS, LC; Riis to Powell, 27 December 1904, Riis MSS, NYPL.

37. Roderick Nash (ed.), *The Call of the Wild: 1900–1916* (New York, 1970), pp. 1–15; David W. Noble, *The Progressive Mind, 1890–1917* (Chicago, 1970), pp. 152–64.

Chapter 10

1. Riis to Powell, 26 April 1904, Riis MSS, NYPL; Jacob to Elisabeth Riis, 13 and 26 November and 3 December 1904, Riis MSS,

LC. All correspondence between Riis and members of his family is located there, unless noted otherwise.

2. Jacob to Elisabeth Riis, 10 December 1904.

3. Jacob to Elisabeth Riis, 22 November 1904; Jacob to John Riis, 1 April 1907, Riis MSS, LC.

4. Jacob to Elisabeth Riis, Thanksgiving, 1904. Jacob A. Riis, "The Gambling Mania," Century, 73 (April 1907), 927.

5. Jacob to Elisabeth Riis, 8, 10 and 12 December 1904.

6. Jacob to Elisabeth Riis, 19 and 23 December 1904.

7. Jacob to John Riis, 28 February and 11 July 1904.

8. Riis to Peabody, 17 September 1898, Peabody MSS, Harvard; V. L. Meigs to Riis, 13 April 1899, Riis MSS, NYPL; Jacob to Elisabeth, 17 April 1899, and 10 November 1902; John Riis, Ranger Trails, p. 12.

9. Jacob to John Riis, 26 April 1904, Benjamin B. Lindsey MSS, LC.

10. Riis to Powell, 27 December 1904, and 2 and 7 March 1905, Riis MSS, LC; Riis to Powell, 26 April 1904, Riis MSS, NYPL.

11. Jacob to Elisabeth Riis, 18 and 24 January 1905.

12. New York Sun, 30 September 1904; August Meier and Elliott M. Rudwick, From Plantation to Ghetto (New York, 1966), p. 180.

13. During this time most so-called experts in education, science, and the humanities espoused now-discredited theories of racial inferiority of blacks. See Wilhelmena S. Robinson, "Changing the African-American Image through History," Negro History Bulletin, 33 (February 1970), 44–46; John S. Haller, Jr., Outcasts from Evolution: Scientific Attitudes of Racial Inferiority, 1859–1900 (Urbana, 1971).

14. Riis to Roosevelt, 12 May 1906, Roosevelt MSS, LC; Riis to McBee, 30 December 1903, McBee MSS, North Carolina.

15. Riis to Reinsholm, 4 and 29 March 1905, Riis MSS, LC; Riis to Peabody, 7 March 1905, Peabody MSS, Harvard.

16. Riis to Mrs. Waterbury, 7 May 1905, Riis MSS, LC; New York Times, 19 May 1905; Riis to Peabody, 18 May 1905, Peabody MSS, Harvard; Ware, Jacob Riis, pp. 233–35.

17. Riis to Steffens, 23 May 1905, Lincoln Steffens MSS. Columbia University, New York; Riis to R. W. Gilder, 20 May 1905, Gilder MSS, NYPL.

18. Riis to Powell, 27 December 1904; Riis to Reinsholm, 25 June 1905, Riis MSS, LC; Riis to Bartlett, 20 March 1906, Bartlett MSS, Columbia; Riis to Powell, 22 June 1905, Riis MSS, NYPL.

19. Riis to Robbins, 20 December 1905; Riis to Reinsholm, 13 February 1906 and 21 July 1907, Riis MSS, LC; Ware, Jacob Riis, p. 242.

20. New York Sun, 26 August 1905; New York World, 7 September 1905; Veiller to George B. McClellan, 11 February 1905; McClellan to T. C. T. Crain, 9 February 1905, George B. McClellan MSS, LC; Riis to Robbins, 23 November 1905, Riis MSS, LC.

21. Laura Winnington, "Sea Air for Tuberculosis," Outlook, 80

(8 July 1905), 645–46; Jacob A. Riis, "The Children's Plea," *Outlook,* 82 (31 March 1906), 753; John A. Kingsbury to the Board of Estimate and Apportionment, 5 April 1912, John A. Kingsbury MSS, LC; Jacob A. Riis, "A Gift of Health," *Outlook,* 83 (21 July 1906), 654.

22. Riis to Powell, 17 April 1906, Riis MSS, NYPL; Louise W. Carnegie to Riis, 9 April 1906, Riis MSS, LC.

23. Jacob A. Riis, "Preaching and Practice," *Charities and the Commons,* 21 (2 January 1909), 509; New York *World,* 7 September 1905; William J. Gaynor to Riis, 5 September 1911; Riis to Gaynor, 6 September 1911, Riis MSS, LC.

24. Riis to Wald, 21 June 1911, Wald MSS, Columbia; Kingsbury to Riis, 24 October 1911, Kingsbury MSS, LC.

25. Riis to Mr. Opdyke, 26 April 1912, Kingsbury MSS, LC; *New York Times,* 28 October 1913; Davis, *Spearheads for Reform,* pp. 186–87; Jacob A. Riis, "The Story of Sea Breeze," *Outlook,* 107 (9 May 1914), 87.

26. Jacob A. Riis, "The Christmas Stamp," *Outlook,* 86 (6 July 1907), 511–14; Ware, *Jacob Riis,* pp. 261–62; Riis to Robbins, 18 December 1907, Riis MSS, LC.

27. Jacob Riis Owre, *Epilogue to The Making of an American* (New York, 1970), p. 315; Riis to Mary Phillips, 23 July 1906 and 12 January 1907, Riis MSS, LC.

28. Riis to Low, 2 August 1906, Low MSS, Columbia; Riis to Steffens, 8 August 1906, Steffens MSS, Columbia; Riis to R. W. Gilder, 29 March 1906, Riis MSS, LC.

29. *New York Times,* 28 and 29 October 1906; Roosevelt to Riis, 28 October 1906, Riis MSS, LC; Harbaugh, *Theodore Roosevelt,* p. 332.

30. Owre, *Epilogue,* pp. 315–18; Ware, *Jacob Riis,* pp. 256–60.

31. Owre, *Epilogue,* p. 318; Riis to Peabody, 20 September 1909, Peabody MSS, Harvard.

32. Jacob to John Riis, 23 November and 17 December 1906, 11 and 18 December 1910, 28 July 1911, Riis MSS, LC.

33. Dr. Fiske to Riis, 12 and 13 August 1909, Riis MSS, NYPL; Riis to Mr. and Mrs. Oscar Owre, 11 May 1911, Riis MSS, LC.

34. Jacob A. Riis, Stephen S. Wise, E. K. Coulter, Victor F. Redder, and O. S. Marden to Felix M. Warburg, 22 November 1911, Felix M. Warburg MSS, American Jewish Archives, Cincinnati, Ohio.

35. New York *Tribune,* 25 June 1910; Ware, *Jacob Riis,* p. 273; Jacob A Riis, speech, Chicago, 29 April 1910; Riis to L. Pearl Boggs, 30 June 1909, Riis MSS, LC.

36. New York *Tribune,* 25 June 1910; Jacob A. Riis, "Boy Scout Movement," lecture notes, Riis MSS, LC; Ernest Thompson Seton, *Boy Scouts of America: A Handbook of Woodcraft, Scouting, and Life-Craft* (New York, 1910).

37. Jacob A. Riis, "The Boy Scouts," *Outlook,* 105 (25 October 1913), 421.

38. David E. Whisnant, "Selling the Gospel News, or: The Strange Career of Jimmy Brown the Newsboy," *Journal of Social History,* 5

(spring 1972), 269–309; Jane Whitbread, "What's a Leg to a Newsboy?" *Christian Century,* 54 (6 January 1937), 13.

39. Jacob A. Riis Settlement, Annual Report for 1905, Riis MSS, NYPL; Jacob A. Riis, "What Settlements Stand For," *Outlook,* 89 (9 May 1908), 69–70; *East Side Chamber News,* April 1938, Riss MSS, LC.

40. Davis, *Spearheads for Reform,* pp. 26–39; Felix Adler to Albert Kennedy, 21 August 1931, Felix Adler MSS, Ethical Culture Society Building Archives, New York; C. P. Henderson, *Social Settlements* (New York, 1899).

41. Thorstein Veblen, *Theory of the Leisure Class* (New York, Mentor ed., 1959), p. 224; Bremner, *From the Depths,* p. 65.

42. Robbins to R. W. Gilder, 2 July 1908, Gilder MSS, NYPL.

43. Lillian D. Wald, *House on Henry Street* (New York, 1915), pp. 216–18; "The Movement for Neighborhood Social Halls," *The Commons,* 9 (May 1904), 193–98; Jacob A. Riis, "Fighting the Gang with Athletics," *Colliers,* 46 (11 February 1911), 17.

44. Riis to Andrew Carnegie, 26 January and 22 December 1904, Andrew Carnegie MSS, NYPL; Riis to Robbins, 27 June 1909, Riis MSS, LC.

45. Riis to Peabody, 1 December 1905, and 11 and 22 May 1906, Peabody MSS, Harvard; Riis to Low, 23 October 1906, Low MSS, Columbia.

46. Paul U. Kellogg, "What Jacob A. Riis and a Thousand Boys Are Up To," *Charities and the Commons,* 17, (27 October 1906), 168–70; Riis to Low, 23 October 1906, Low MSS, Columbia; Riis to Charles Milice, 30 October 1906, Theodore Roosevelt MSS, Harvard University, Cambridge, Mass.; New York *Sun,* 28 October 1906; Ware, *Jacob Riis,* p. 253.

47. Riis to Mrs. Fred Goddord, 21 March 1907, Bryant-Godwin MSS, NYPL; Riis to Miss Nye, 17 July 1907, Riis MSS, LC.

48. Riis to Low, 23 October 1906, Low MSS, Columbia.

49. Riis to Robbins, 26 December 1906, Riis MSS, LC; Stephen S. Wise to Newell D. Hillis, 12 June 1914, Riis MSS, NYPL.

50. Jacob A. Riis, "The Jacob Riis Neighborhood Settlement," *Outlook,* 92 (29 May 1909), 294; Wise to Hillis, 12 June 1914, Riis MSS, NYPL.

51. Copy of will, 7 November 1911, Riis MSS, LC.

52. Jacob A. Riis, speech, 29 February 1908, Riis MSS, LC.

Chapter 11

1. Springfield, Mass., *Daily Republican,* 2 October 1912.

2. New York *World,* 21 April 1907; Riis to Roosevelt, 16 April 1906 and 12 January 1908; Roosevelt to Riis, 18 April 1906, Roosevelt MSS, LC.

3. Riis to Roosevelt, 22 May 1906, Roosevelt MSS, LC; David

M. Chalmers, *The Social and Political Ideas of the Muckrakers* (New York, 1964), pp. 13–14; Jacob to Mary Riis, November n.d., 1911, Riis MSS, LC.

4. Riis to Peabody, 8 September 1907, Peabody MSS, Harvard; Riis to Katherine Owre, 4 November 1908, Riis MSS, LC.

5. Jacob A. Riis, "What My Faith Means to Me," *Circle* (January 1910), Riis MSS, LC; David M. Noble, *The Paradox of Progressive Thought* (Minneapolis, 1958), pp. 23–45; Jacob A. Riis, "Heading Off the Slums in the West," *Charities and the Commons,* 19 (7 March 1908), 1704–6; Jacob A. Riis, "How Helena Became a Clean City," *Charities and the Commons,* 19 (28 March 1908), 1793–95.

6. Ware *Jacob Riis,* pp 277–78; Riis to Robbins, 21 December and 5 December 1911, Riis MSS, LC.

7. Riis, Chautauqua speech, 1908, Riis MSS, LC; Jacob A. Riis, "Experiences of a Popular Lecturer," *World's Work,* 16 (July 1908), 10494–95.

8. Jacob A. Riis, "What Ails Our Boys?" *Craftsman,* 21 (October 1911), 3–4; Riis, lecture notes, Harlan, Iowa, 1907, and Springfield, Mass., 1912, Riis MSS, LC.

9. T. C. T. Crain to McClellan, 20 February 1905, McClellan MSS, New York Archives; Jacob A. Riis, "America's Civic Awakening," *Charities and the Commons,* 19 (15 February 1909), 1598; Riis to Mrs. Thomas, 6 April 1904, Riis MSS, NYPL; Riis, *Battle with the Slum,* p. 149.

10. Frank L. Mott, *A History of American Magazines, 1885–1905* (Cambridge, Mass., 1957), pp. 741–45; Clarke A. Chambers, *Paul U. Kellogg and the Survey: Voices for Social Welfare and Social Justice* (Minneapolis, 1971), pp. 12–32; Riis, lecture notes, St. Louis, 23 January 1908, Riis MSS, LC; Bremner, *From the Depths,* pp. 154–56.

11. Davis, *Spearheads for Reform,* pp. 172–73; Riis, lecture notes, 23 January 1908, Riis MSS, LC; Jacob A. Riis, "One Thing the Sage Foundation Can Do for New York," *Charities and the Commons,* 18 (13 April 1907), 77–78.

12. Riis to Steffens, 8 August 1906, Steffens MSS, Columbia; Riis to Robbins, 14 March 1908 and 3 October 1911, Riis MSS, LC. Professional reformers and social workers claimed that their secular view of poverty rid the deserving poor of the onus of guilt or shame. But Nathan I. Huggins, in *Protestants against Poverty: Boston's Charities, 1870–1900* (Westport, Conn. 1971), p. 199, wrote that relief and welfare programs have persistently connected poverty to character defects. "In time, the language was to change, pauper and unworthy poor would no longer be explicit accusations," Huggins wrote. "But the case worker's eligibility criteria implied these concepts nonetheless. . . . Morals, without ultimate, personal obligation became moralism and sentiment, regardless of harsh or antiseptic tone."

13. Jacob to Mary Riis, 18 January 1910, Riis MSS, LC; Riis to DeForest, 7 March 1910; Veiller to Riis, 8 March 1910, Riis MSS, NYPL.

14. Riis to DeForest, 7 March 1910, Riis MSS, LC; Veiller to Riis, 8 March 1910; DeForest to Riis, 5 April 1910, Riis MSS, NYPL.

15. Jacob A. Riis, pamphlet, Riis MSS, LC; Allen, "Reminiscences," COHP, p. 406.

16. Riis, undated notes, Riis MSS, LC; Jacob to Mary Riis, 21 November and 2 December 1911, Riis MSS, LC. See also Jacob A. Riis, "The Best of All Christmas Plans," *World's Work*, 15 (December 1907), 9623.

17. Jacob to Mary Riis, 21 November 1911, Riis MSS, LC; "Chips from the Maelstrom," *Outlook*, 93 (2 October 1909), 275.

18. Riis, undated notes, Riis MSS, LC; Riis *Children of the Tenements*, p. 363.

19. Riis, lecture notes, from speeches in Milwaukee (1911), Chautauqua (1908), and Chicago (1910), Riis MSS, LC; see also Jacob A. Riis, "The Plight of St. Louis," *Charities and the Commons*, 20 (9 May 1908), 275.

20. Riis, "Humanly Speaking," lecture notes, April 1909, Riis MSS, LC; Higham, *Strangers in the Land*, pp. 239–41; Edward G. Hartmann, *The Movement to Americanize the Immigrant* (New York, 1948), pp. 47, 59.

21. See Jacob A. Riis, "The Ghost of the Heath," *Outlook*, 95 (23 July 1910), 636–44; Jacob A. Riis, "Cooperation in Denmark," *Craftsman*, 23 (March 1913), 609–11; Jacob A. Riis, "A Word About Niels Finsen," *McClure's*, 20 (February 1903), 360–61; Jacob A. Riis, *Hero-Tales of the Far-North* (New York, 1910).

22. Riis to Roger William (Billy) Riis, 5 December 1909, and 24 January 1910; Riis to Katherine Owre, 8 March 1913, Riis MSS, L.C.

23. Mowry, *Era of Theodore Roosevelt*, pp. 269–73; Riis to Roosevelt, 10 November 1910, Roosevelt MSS, LC.

24. Robert H. Wiebe, "The House of Morgan and the Executive, 1905–1913," *American Historical Review*, 65 (October 1959), 55–60; Jacob to Mary Riis, 13 and 14 November and 2 December 1911, Riis MSS, LC.

25. Riis to J. W. Rhoades, 1 May 1912, Roosevelt MSS, Harvard; George E. Mowry, *Theodore Roosevelt and the Progressive Movement* (New York, 1946), pp. 253–54.

26. Riis to Ben Lindsey, 28 January 1906, 6 November 1908, and 6 June 1912, Lindsey MSS, LC; Riis to Roosevelt, 27 June 1912, Roosevelt MSS, LC; Riis to Katherine Owre, 19 July 1912; Riis to Reinsholm, 7 September 1912, Riis MSS, LC.

27. Davis, *Spearheads for Reform*, pp. 197–98; Harbaugh, *Theodore Roosevelt*, pp. 415–16.

28. Walter I. Trattner, *Homer Folks: Pioneer in Social Welfare* (New York, 1968), pp. 101–2; William Allen White, *Autobiography of William Allen White* (New York, 1946), pp. 487–88; Commager, *Documents*, II, pp. 253–55.

29. Harbaugh, *Theodore Roosevelt*, pp. 416–18; Trattner, "Election of 1912," 68–70; Jane Addams, "My Experiences as a Progressive Delegate," *McClure's*, 40 (November 1912), 14; Riis to Katherine Owre, 25 January 1911, Riis MSS, LC.

30. Riis, lecture notes, 1 October 1912, Riis MSS, LC; Springfield, Mass., *Daily Republican*, 2 October 1912; Chicago *Tribune*, 25 October 1912.

31. Jacob to Mary Riis, 12 November 1912, Riis MSS, LC; Davis, *Spearheads for Reform*, pp. 206–7; John Riis to Pinchot, 30 November 1913, Pinchot MSS, LC.

32. Jacob A. Riis, "The Nation-Wide Battle against the Slum," *Survey*, 29 (21 December 1912), 349–51; Jacob A. Riis, "The Battle with the Slum," *Century*, 87 (November 1913), 49–51.

33. Harbaugh, *Theodore Roosevelt*, p. 431; *New York Times*, 14 January 1914; Jacob to John Riis, 17 December 1910, Riis MSS, LC; New York *World*, 21 February 1911; Riis to W. B. Howland, 5 June 1912, Roosevelt MSS, LC.

34. *New York Times*, 28 May 1913.

Chapter 12

1. Jacob A. Riis, "How We Found Our Farm," *World's Work*, 23 (February 1912), 475–79; Riis to Emma Reinsholm, 28 June 1911, Riis MSS, LC; Jacob A. Riis, "Our Happy Valley," *Craftsman*, 25 (November 1913), 145; Ware, *Jacob Riis*, p. 277.

2. Riis to Mr. and Mrs. Oscar Owre, 19 December 1912; Riis to Reinsholm, 5 March 1913; Ida A. McAfee, scrapbook, Riis MSS, LC; Owre, *Epilogue*, pp. 292–93; *New York Times*, 1 January and 19 December 1913.

3. Riis to Reinsholm, 4 March and 19 April 1910 and 5 March 1913, Riis MSS, LC; Ware, *Jacob Riis*, p. 242.

4. Riis to Reinsholm, 20 June 1911, and 1 April and 7 September 1912, Riis MSS, LC.

5. Riis, lecture notes, Riis MSS, LC.

6. Jacob A. Riis, "Making a Way Out of the Slum," *American Review of Reviews*, 22 (December 1900), 690–96; Boris D. Bogen, *Jewish Philanthropy* (New York, 1917), pp. 56–71.

7. Jacob A. Riis, "Sentiment as an Asset," *Sunset* (December 1909); Riis lecture notes, Doylestown, Pa., 1911, Riis MSS, LC.

8. Riis to Reinsholm, 20 June 1913, Riis MSS, LC; Riis, "John Bancroft Devins," 1062.

9. Riis to Reinsholm, 7 September 1912 and 14 December 1913; Jacob to Mary Riis, November [undated, probably 17] 1913, Riis MSS, LC.

10. K. H. Damren to Riis, 13 January 1913, Riis MSS, NYPL; Riis to Reinsholm, 28 January 1913; Roosevelt to Mary Riis, 12 September 1913, Riis MSS, LC.

11. Jacob to Mary Riis, 14 January 1914; Riis to Kate, 12 February 1914, Riis MSS, LC.

12. *New York Times*, 14 January 1914.

13. Owre, *Epilogue*, pp. 335–36.

14. Kingsbury to Bailev B. Burrett, 12 June 1914, Kingsbury MSS, LC; Ware, *Jacob Riis*, p. 288. Most condolence letters are in the Riis MSS, NYPL.

15. Paul U. Kellogg, "A Seer," *Survey*, 33 (12 December 1914), 299.

16. Henry F. May, "The Rebellion of the Intellectuals, 1912–1917," in Wilson (ed.), *Reform, Crisis, and Confusion*, pp. 39–50; Daniel Levine, *Jane Addams and the Liberal Tradition* (Madison, 1971), p. xvii.

17. Quoted in Burton, *Comrades in Service*, p. 23.

BIBLIOGRAPHY

Books

Aaron, Daniel, *Men of Good Hope*. New York, 1951.

Addams, Jane. *Twenty Years at Hull-House*. New York, 1910.

Altgeld, John Peter. *Live Questions*. Chicago, 1890.

Atkins, Gordon. *Health, Housing, and Poverty in New York City, 1865–1898*. Ann Arbor, Michigan, 1947.

Barnard, Harry. *Eagle Forgotten: The Life of John Peter Altgeld*. New York, 1938.

Beer, Thomas. *The Mauve Decade*. New York, 1926.

Bernstein, Barton J., ed. *Towards a New Past: Dissenting Essays in American History*. New York, 1968.

Bliss, William D. P., ed. *The Encyclopedia of Social Reform*. New York, 1897.

Blum, John Morton. *The Republican Roosevelt*. New York, 1967.

Blumberg, Dorothy Rose. *Florence Kelley: the Making of a Social Pioneer*. New York, 1966.

Bogen, Boris D. *Jewish Philanthropy*. New York, 1917.

Braeman, John, Robert H. Bremner, and Everett Walters, eds. *Change and Continuity in Twentieth-Century America*. New York, 1966.

Bremner, Robert H. *American Philanthropy*. Chicago, 1960.

_____. *From the Depths: The Discovery of Poverty in the United States*. New York, 1967.

Brooks, Van Wyck. *The Confident Years: 1885–1915*. London, 1953.

Burton, Margaret E. *Comrades in Service*. New York, 1915.

Callow, Alexander B., Jr. *The Tweed Ring*. New York, 1966.

Campbell, Helen S., Thomas W. Knox, and Thomas Byrnes. *Darkness and Daylight in New York*. Hartford, 1897.

Chalmers, David M. *The Social and Political Ideas of the Muckrakers*. New York, 1964.

Chambers, Clarke A. *Paul U. Kellogg and the Survey: Voices for Social Welfare and Social Justice*. Minneapolis, 1971.

Charity Organization Society of New York. Fifth Annual Report. New York, 1887.

Charnwood, Lord. *Theodore Roosevelt*. London, 1923.

Chessman, G. Wallace. *Governor Theodore Roosevelt*. Cambridge, Massachusetts, 1965.

Clarke, Joseph I. C. *My Life and Memories*. New York, 1925.

Cohen, Sol. *Progressives and Urban School Reform: The Public Education Association of New York City, 1895–1954*. New York, 1964.

Commager, Henry Steele, ed. *Documents of American History*. 2 vols. New York, 1949.

Cordasco, Francesco, ed. *Jacob Riis Revisited*. Garden City, New York, 1968.

Danstrup, John. *A History of Denmark*. Copenhagen, 1949.

Davis, Allen F. *Spearheads for Reform: The Social Settlements and the Progressive Movement, 1890–1914*. New York, 1967.

DeForest, Robert W., and Lawrence Veiller, eds. *The Tenement House Problem*. 2 vols. New York, 1903.

Devine, Edward T. *When Social Work Was Young*. New York, 1939.

Dos Passos, John. *Nineteen Nineteen*. Boston, Sentry ed., 1963.

Duffus, Robert L. *Lillian Wald: Neighbor and Crusader*. New York, 1938.

Ellis, Edward R. *The Epic of New York City*. New York, 1966.

Emery, Edwin. *The Press and America*. Englewood Cliffs, New Jersey, 1962.

Faulkner, Harold U. *Politics, Reform and Expansion: 1890–1900*. New York, 1963.

Feder, Leah H. *Unemployment Relief in Periods of Depression*. New York, 1936.

Felt, Jeremy P. *Hostages of Fortune: Child Labor Reform in New York State*. Syracuse, New York, 1965.

Filler, Louis. *Crusaders for American Liberalism*. Yellow Springs, Ohio, 1961.

Ford, James. *Slums and Housing with Special Reference to New York City.* Cambridge, Massachusetts, 1936.

Garraty, John A. *The New Commonwealth, 1877–1890.* New York, 1968.

George, Henry. *Progress and Poverty.* New York, 1879.

Glaab, Charles N., ed. *The American City: A Documentary History.* Homewood, Illinois, 1963.

Glaab, Charles N., and A. Theodore Brown. *A History of Urban America.* New York, 1967.

Goldman, Eric. *Rendezvous with Destiny.* New York, 1952.

Gosnell, Harold F. *Boss Platt and his New York Machine.* Chicago, 1924.

Gould, E. R. L. *The Housing of the Working People.* Washington, 1895.

Green, Constance M. *Washington: Capital City, 1879–1950.* Princeton, New Jersey, 1963.

Hackett, Alice Payne. *70 Years of Best Sellers, 1895–1965.* New York, 1967.

Haller, John S., Jr. *Outcasts from Evolution: Scientific Attitudes of Racial Inferiority, 1859–1900.* Urbana, Illinois, 1971.

Handlin, Oscar. *The Uprooted.* Boston. 1951.

Harbaugh, William H. *The Life and Times of Theodore Roosevelt.* New York, 1963.

Hartmann, Edward G. *The Movement to Americanize the Immigrant.* New York, 1948.

Hawes, Joseph M. *Children in Urban Society: Juvenile Delinquency in Nineteenth-Century America.* New York, 1971.

Henderson, C. R. *Social Settlements.* New York, 1899.

Higham, John. *Strangers in the Land: Patterns of American Nativism, 1860–1925.* New York, 1968.

Hofstadter, Richard. *The American Political Tradition.* New York, 1948.

Holl, Jack M. *Juvenile Reform in the Progressive Era: William R. George and the Junior Republic Movement.* Ithaca, New York, 1971.

Huggins, Nathan I. *Protestants against Poverty: Boston's Charities, 1870–1900.* Westport, Connecticut, 1971.

Hurwitz, Howard L. *Theodore Roosevelt and Labor in New York State, 1880–1900.* New York, 1943.

Husband, Joseph. *Americans by Adoption.* Boston, 1920.

Irvine, Alexander. *From the Bottom Up.* New York, 1910.

Johnson, Robert U. *Remembered Yesterdays.* Boston, 1923.

Jones, Maldwyn, A. *American Immigration*. Chicago, 1960.

Keefer, Truman F. *Ernest Poole*. New York, 1966.

Klein, Woody. *Let In the Sun*. New York, 1964.

Larsen, Charles E. *The Good Fight: The Life and Times of Ben B. Lindsey*. Chicago, 1972.

Lasch, Christopher, ed. *The Social Thought of Jane Addams*. Indianapolis, 1965.

Lee, Joseph. *Constructive and Preventive Philanthropy*. New York, 1902.

Levine, Daniel. *Jane Addams and the Liberal Tradition*. Madison, 1971.

Loomis, Samuel L. *Modern Cities and Their Religious Problems*. New York, 1887.

Lubove, Roy. *The Professional Altruist: The Emergence of Social Work as a Profession*. Cambridge, Massachusetts, 1965.

—————. *The Progressives and the Slums: Tenement House Reform in New York City, 1890–1917*. Pittsburgh, 1962.

—————. *The Urban Community: Housing and Planning in the Progressive Era*. Englewood Cliffs, New Jersey, 1967.

McJimsey, George T. *Genteel Partisan: Manton Marble, 1834–1917*. Ames, Iowa, 1971.

Mandelbaum, Seymour J. *Boss Tweed's New York*. New York, 1965.

Mann, Arthur. *Yankee Reformers in the Urban Age*. Cambridge, Massachusetts, 1954.

Manniche, Peter. *Denmark: A Social Laboratory*. London, 1939.

May, Henry F. *The End of American Innocence*. Chicago, 1964.

Meier, August, and Elliott M. Rudwick. *From Plantation to Ghetto*. New York, 1966.

Monod, Sylvere. *Dickens the Novelist*. Norman, Oklahoma, 1968.

Morison, Elting E., and John M. Blum, eds. *The Letters of Theodore Roosevelt*. 8 vols. Cambridge, Massachusetts, 1951–54.

Mott, Frank L. *A History of American Magazines, 1885–1905*. Cambridge, Massachusetts, 1957.

Mowry, George E. *The Era of Theodore Roosevelt and the Birth of Modern America, 1900–1912*. New York, 1958.

—————. *Theodore Roosevelt and the Progressive Movement*. New York, 1946.

Muirhead, James F. *America the Land of Contrasts*. New York, 1898.

Nash, Roderick, ed. *The Call of the Wild: 1900–1916*. New York, 1970.

Nellemann, Aksel H. *Schools and Education in Denmark*. Translated by John B. Powell. Copenhagen, 1964.

Neumann, Henry. *Spokesmen for Ethical Religion*. Boston, 1951.

Nevins, Allan. *Abram S. Hewitt, with Some Account of Peter Cooper*. New York, 1935.

New York Association for Improving the Condition of the Poor. *Annual Report, 1893–94*. New York, 1894.

Noble, David M. *The Paradox of Progressive Thought*. Minneapolis, 1958.

——————. *The Progressive Mind, 1890–1917*. Chicago, 1970.

Nugent, Walter T. K. *Modern America*. Boston, 1973.

O'Brien, Frank M. *The Story of the Sun*. New York, 1918.

Owre, J. Riis, ed. *The Making of an American by Jacob A. Riis*. New York, 1970.

Parkhurst, Charles H. *My Forty Years in New York*. New York, 1923.

——————. *Our Fight with Tammany*. New York, 1895.

Patton, Clifford W. *The Battle for Municipal Reform: Mobilization and Attack, 1875–1900*. Washington, 1940.

Peterson, Lorin W. *The Day of the Mugwump*. New York, 1961.

Powderly, Terence V. *The Path I Trod*. New York, 1940.

Pringle, Henry F. *Theodore Roosevelt: A Biography*. New York, 1931.

Rainwater, Clarence E. *The Play Movement in the United States*. Chicago, 1922.

Richardson, James F. *The New York Police: Colonial Times to 1901*. New York, 1970.

Riis, Jacob A. *The Battle with the Slum*. New York, 1902.

——————. *Children of the Tenements*. New York, 1903.

——————. *Hero-Tales of the Far-North*. New York, 1910.

——————. *How the Other Half Lives*. New York, Hill and Wang ed., 1957.

——————. *Is There a Santa Claus?* New York, 1904.

——————. *The Making of an American*. New York, 1904.

——————. *Nibsy's Christmas*. New York, 1893.

——————. *The Old Town*. New York, 1909.

——————. *Out of Mulberry Street: Stories of Tenement Life in New York City*. New York, 1898.

——————. *The Peril and Preservation of the Home*. Philadelphia, 1903.

——————. *Theodore Roosevelt the Citizen*. Washington, 1904.

Riis, John. *Ranger Trails*. Richmond, Virginia, 1937.

Schlesinger, Arthur M. *The Rise of the City, 1878–1898.* New York, 1933.

Schneider, David M., and Albert Deutsch. *The History of Public Welfare in New York State, 1867–1940.* Montclair, New Jersey, 1967.

Schoener, Allon, ed. *The Lower East Side: Portal to American Life (1870–1924).* New York, 1967.

Seton, Ernest Thompson. *Boy Scouts of America: A Handbook of Woodcraft, Scouting and Life-Craft.* New York, 1910.

Simkhovitch, Mary K. *Neighborhood: My Story of Greenwich House.* New York, 1938.

Steffens, Lincoln. *The Autobiography of Lincoln Steffens.* 2 vols. New York, 1931.

Still, Bayrd. *Mirror for Gotham: New York as Seen by Contemporaries from Dutch Days to the Present.* New York, 1956.

Stoddard, Lothrop. *Master of Manhattan: The Life of Richard Croker.* New York, 1931.

Tansill, Charles C. *The Purchase of the Danish West Indies.* Baltimore, 1932.

Tishler, Hace Sorel. *Self-Reliance and Social Security, 1870–1917.* Port Washington, New York, 1971.

Trattner, Walter I. *Homer Folks: Pioneer in Social Welfare.* New York, 1968.

Veblen, Thorstein. *Theory of the Leisure Class.* New York, Mentor ed., 1959.

Wade, Louise C. *Graham Taylor: Pioneer for Social Justice, 1851–1938.* Chicago, 1964.

Wald, Lillian D. *The House on Henry Street.* New York, 1915.

Ware, E. Louise. *Jacob A. Riis: Police Reporter, Reformer, Useful Citizen.* New York, 1939.

Warner, Sam Bass, Jr., ed. *How the Other Half Lives by Jacob A. Riis.* Cambridge, Massachusetts, 1970.

Watson, Frank D. *The Charity Organization Movement in the United States.* New York, 1922.

Weber, Adna F. *Labor Legislation in New York.* Albany, 1904.

Weinstein, Gregory. *The Ardent Eighties and After: Reminiscences of a Busy Life.* New York, 1947.

Weisberger, Bernard A. *The American Newspaperman.* Chicago, 1961.

Westergaard, Waldermar C. *Denmark and Slesvig, 1848–1864.* London, 1946.

White, William Allen. *Autobiography of William Allen White.* New York, 1946.

Wiebe, Robert H. *The Search for Order: 1877–1920.* New York, 1967.

Wilson, R. Jackson, ed. *Reform, Crisis, and Confusion, 1900–1929.* New York, 1970.

Woods, Robert A., and Albert J. Kennedy. *The Settlement Horizon.* New York, 1922.

Yellowitz, Irwin. *Labor and the Progressive Movement in New York State, 1897–1916.* Ithaca, New York, 1965.

Ziff, Larzer. *The American 1890s: Life and Times of a Lost Generation.* New York, 1966.

Articles

Abbott, Lyman. "A Republic in a Republic." *Outlook,* 138 (15 February 1908).

Addams, Jane. "My Experiences as a Progressive Delegate." *McClure's,* 40 (November 1912).

_____. "The Subtle Problems of Charity." *Atlantic Monthly,* 83 (February 1899).

Creelman, James. "Joseph Pulitzer—Master Journalist." *Pearson's* 21 (March 1909).

Davis, Allen F. " 'Theodore Roosevelt—Social Worker', A Note." *Mid-America,* 48 (January 1966).

Dewey, John. "The School as a Social Center." *National Education Association Journal of Proceedings* (1902).

Gilder, Joseph B. "The Making of Jacob A. Riis." *Critic,* 46 (January 1902).

Gladden, Washington. "The Junior Republic at Freeville." *Outlook,* 104 (31 October 1896).

Hapgood, Hutchins. "Jacob A. Riis's *The Making of an American.*" *Bookman,* 14 (January 1902).

"How the Other Half Lives." *Critic,* 17 (27 December 1890).

Humphreys, Mary Gay. "The Smallest Republic in the World." *McClure's,* 9 (July 1897).

Huntington, J. O. S. "Tenement-House Morality." *Forum,* 3 (July 1887).

Kellogg, Paul U. "A Seer." *Survey,* 33 (12 December 1914).

_____. "What Jacob A. Riis and a Thousand Boys Are Up To." *Charities and the Commons,* 17 (27 October 1906).

Lodge, Henry Cabot. "Restriction of Immigration." *North American Review,* 152 (January 1891).

Lowell, Josephine S. "The Economic and Moral Effects of Public

Out-Door Relief," National Conference of Charities and Correction, *Proceedings* (1890).

Lubove, Roy. "Lawrence Veiller and the New York State Tenement House Commission of 1900." *Mississippi Valley Historical Review,* 47 (March 1961).

McGee, James I. "Teddy and the New York Police." *Central,* 12 (12 November 1919).

"The Movement for Neighborhood Social Halls." *The Commons,* 9 (May 1904).

Muccigrosso, Robert. "The City Reform Club: A Study in Late Nineteenth-Century Reform." *New York History,* 109 (July 1968).

"Paragraphs in Philanthropy: Housing Reform in Washington," *Charities,* 12 (9 January 1904).

Parkman, Mary R. "A Modern Viking: Jacob Riis." *St. Nicholas,* 44 (January 1917).

Pauling, James K. "Public Schools as a Center of Community Life." *Educational Review,* 15 (February 1898).

Rezneck, Samuel. "Unemployment, Unrest and Relief in the United States during the Depression of 1893–1897." *Journal of Political Economy,* 61 (August 1953).

Riis, Jacob A. "America's Civic Awakening." *Charities and the Commons,* 19 (15 February 1908).

—————. "The Battle with the Slum." *Atlantic Monthly,* 83 (May 1899).

—————. "The Battle with the Slum." *Century,* 87 (November 1913).

—————. "The Best of All Christmas Plans." *World's Work,* 15 (December 1907).

—————. "The Boy Scouts." *Outlook,* 105 (25 October 1913).

—————. "Boys' Fun in the Old Town." *Outlook,* 83 (2 June 1906).

—————. "The Case of the House of Refuge." *Charities,* 11 (4 July 1903).

—————. "The Children's Plea." *Outlook,* 82 (31 March 1906).

—————. "Chips from the Maelstrom." *Outlook,* 93 (2 October 1909).

—————. "Christmas in Denmark." *The Churchman,* 15 (21 December 1907).

—————. "A Christmas Reminder." *Forum,* 16 (January 1894).

_____."The Christmas Stamp." *Outlook*, 86 (6 July 1907).

_____. "The Clearing of Mulberry Bend." *American Review of Reviews*, 12 (August 1895).

_____. "Cooperation in Denmark." *Craftsman*, 23 (March 1913).

_____. "Experiences of a Popular Lecturer." *World's Work*, 16 (July 1908).

_____. "Feast Days in Little Italy." *Century*, 57 (August 1899).

_____. "Fighting the Gang with Athletics." *Collier's*, 46 (11 February 1911).

_____. "The Gambling Mania." *Century*, 73 (April 1907).

_____. "The Ghost of the Heath." *Outlook*, 95 (23 July 1910).

_____. "A Gift of Health." *Outlook*, 83 (21 July 1906).

_____. "Heading Off the Slums in the West." *Charities and the Commons*, 19 (7 March 1908).

_____. "The Heart of New York." *Independent*, 76 (4 December 1913).

_____. "How Helena Became a Clean City." *Charities and the Commons*, 19 (28 March 1908).

_____. "How We Found Our Farm." *World's Work*, 23 (February 1912).

_____. "In the Gateway of Nations." *Century*, 65 (March 1903).

_____. "The Island Playgrounds of the Future." *Charities*, 11 (5 September 1903).

_____. "The Jacob Riis Neighborhood Settlement." *Outlook*, 92 (29 May 1909).

_____. "John Bancroft Devins." *Survey*, 27 (21 October 1911).

_____. "A Kindly Journey." *Outlook*, 96 (31 December 1910).

_____. "The Last of the Mulberry-Street Barons." *Century*, 58 (May 1899).

_____. "Letting in the Light." *Atlantic Monthly*, 84 (October 1899).

_____. "Making a Way Out of the Slum." *American Review of Reviews*, 22 (December 1900).

_____. "The Making of Thieves in New York." *Century*, 49 (November 1894).

_____. "The Man Who Is an Immigrant." *Survey*, 25 (18 February 1911).

—————. "Midwinter in New York." *Century,* 59 (February 1900).

—————. "A Modern St. George." *Scribner's,* 50 (October 1911).

—————. "My Boyhood's Black Friend." *Outlook,* 85 (19 January 1907).

—————. "The Nation-wide Battle against the Slum." *Survey,* 29 (21 December 1912).

—————. "New York's Wayfarers' Lodge." *Outlook,* 48 (2 December 1893).

—————. "Niels Juel's Chair." *Outlook,* 100 (10 February 1912).

—————. "One Thing the Sage Foundation Can Do for New York." *Charities and the Commons,* 18 (13 April 1907).

—————. "One Way Out." *Century,* 51 (December 1895).

—————. "Our Beautiful Summer." *Outlook,* 80 (6 May 1905).

—————. "Our Happy Valley." *Craftsman,* 25 (November–December 1913).

—————. "Paolo's Awakening." *Atlantic Monthly,* 76 (November 1896).

—————. "The Passing of Cat Alley." *Century,* 57 (December 1898).

—————. "The People's Institute of New York." *Century,* 79 (April 1910).

—————. "Playgrounds in Washington and Elsewhere." *Charities and the Commons,* 20 (18 April 1908).

—————. "The Plight of St. Louis." *Charities and the Commons,* 20 (9 May 1908).

—————. "Preaching and Practice." *Charities and the Commons,* 21 (2 January 1909).

—————. "Religion by Human Touch." *World's Work,* 1 (March 1901).

—————. "The Special Needs of the Poor in New York." *Forum,* 14 (December 1892).

—————. "The Story of Sea Breeze." *Outlook,* 107 (9 May 1914).

—————. "Tammany the People's Enemy." *Outlook,* 69 (26 October 1901).

—————. "The Tenement-House Problem." *Harper's Weekly,* 39 (12 January 1895).

—————. "The Tenement the Real Problem of Civilization." *Forum,* 19 (March 1895).

————————. "An Unnecessary Story." *Century,* 62 (May 1901).

————————. "What Ails Our Boys?" *Craftsman,* 21 (October 1911).

————————. "What Settlements Stand For." *Outlook,* 89 (9 May 1908).

————————. "Will It Last?" *Outlook,* 64 (21 April 1900).

————————. "A Word about Niels Finsen." *McClure's,* 20 (February 1903).

Robinson, Wilhelmena S. "Changing the African-American Image through History." *Negro History Bulletin,* 33 (February 1970).

Shapiro, Herbert. "Lincoln Steffens: The Muckraker Revisited." *American Journal of Economics and Sociology,* 31 (October 1972).

Skolnik, Richard. "Civic Group Progressivism in New York City." *New York History,* 51 (July 1970).

Steffens, Lincoln. "Jacob A. Riis, Reporter, Reformer, American Citizen." *McClure's,* 21 (August 1903).

Stein, Henry H. "Theodore Roosevelt and the Press: Lincoln Steffens." *Mid-America,* 54 (April 1972).

Swett, Steven C. "The Test of a Reformer: A Study of Seth Low, New York City Mayor, 1902–1903." *New York Historical Society Quarterly,* 44 (January 1960).

"A Ten Years' War." *Literary Digest,* 20 (14 April 1900).

Thelen, David P. "Social Tensions and the Origins of Progressivism." *Journal of American History,* 56 (September 1969).

Tolman, William H. "A Half Century of Improved Housing Effort." *Yale Review,* 5 (February 1897).

Trattner, Walter I. "Theodore Roosevelt, Social Workers, and the Election of 1912: A Note." *Mid-America,* 50 (January 1968).

Vecoli, Rudolph J. "*Contadini* in Chicago: A Critique of *The Uprooted.*" *Journal of American History,* 51 (December 1964).

Voss, Carl Hermann. "The Lion and the Lamb—An Evaluation of the Life and Work of Stephen S. Wise." *American Jewish Archives,* 21 (April 1969).

Whisnant, David E. "Selling the Gospel News, or: The Strange Career of Jimmy Brown the Newsboy." *Journal of Social History,* 5 (Spring, 1972).

Whitbread, Jane. "What's a Leg to a Newsboy?" *Christian Century,* 54 (6 January 1937).

Wiebe, Robert H. "The House of Morgan and the Eexecutive,

1905–1913." *American Historical Review,* 65 (October 1959).

Winnington, Laura. "Sea Air for Tuberculosis." *Outlook,* 80 (8 July 1905).

Newspapers

Boston *Globe,* 1891.

Chicago *Times-Herald,* 1898.

Chicago *Tribune,* 1900, 1912.

Detroit *Free Press,* 1912.

New York *Evening Journal,* 1901.

New York *Evening Post,* 1896, 1897.

New York *Evening Sun,* 1891–1898.

New York *Herald,* 1894, 1897, 1901.

New York *Mail and Express,* 1885, 1890, 1895.

New York *Mercury,* 1884–1886.

New York *Morning Journal,* 1883, 1888.

New York *Sun,* 1885, 1888, 1891, 1896–1905.

New York Times, 1874, 1895, 1896, 1900–1906, 1913, 1914.

New York *Tribune,* 1870, 1884, 1886, 1888, 1892–1897, 1901, 1903, 1910.

New York *World,* 1883, 1895–1899, 1903–1906, 1911.

Springfield (Massachusetts) *Daily Republican,* 1912.

Washington *Post,* 1891, 1903.

Manuscript Collections

American Jewish Archives, Cincinnati, Ohio. Felix M. Warburg Papers.

Columbia Oral History Project, Columbia Uinversity, New York, N.Y.
    William Harvey Allen.
    Homer Folks.
    Louis H. Pink.
    Lawrence Veiller.

Columbia University, New York, N.Y.
    Willard Bartlett Papers.
    Seth Low Papers.

Edwin R. A. Seligman Papers.
Lincoln Steffens Papers.
Lillian D. Wald Papers.
Cornell University, Ithaca, New York. William R. George and George Junior Republic Papers.
Ethical Culture Society Archives, New York, N.Y. Felix Adler Papers.
Harvard University Library, Cambridge, Massachusetts.
    Endicott Peabody Papers.
    Bliss Perry Papers.
    Theodore Roosevelt Papers.
Library of Congress, Washington, D.C. Manuscript Division.
    John Adams Kingsbury Papers.
    Benjamin B. Lindsey Papers.
    George B. McClellan Papers.
    Gifford Pinchot Papers.
    Jacob A. Riis Papers.
    Theodore Roosevelt Papers.
Municipal Archives and Records Center, New York, N.Y.
    Early Mayors' Papers.
    Seth Low Papers.
    George B. McClellan Papers.
    Robert A. Van Wyck Papers.
National Archives, Washington, D.C. Numerical File 1906–1910.
    Department of State.
New York Public Library, New York, N.Y.
    Bryant-Godwin Collection.
    Andrew Carnegie Collection.
    Century Collection.
    Richard Watson Gilder Papers.
    Jacob A. Riis Miscellaneous File.
    Jacob A. Riis Papers.
    Albert Shaw Papers.
    Lillian D. Wald Papers.
    Everett P. Wheeler Papers.
New York State Chamber of Commerce Archives, New York, N.Y.
    Lexow Committee File.
Russell Sage Library, City College of New York, N.Y. Jacob A. Riis Papers.
Southern Historical Collection, University of North Carolina, Chapel Hill, N.C. Silas McBee Papers.
Swarthmore Peace Collection, Swarthmore, Pa.
    Jane Addams Papers.
    Anna Garlin Spencer Papers.

INDEX